Bakersfield Guitars

Bakersfield Guitars

THE ILLUSTRATED HISTORY

WILLIE G. MOSELEY

GUILFORD, CONNECTICUT

In memory of
J. R. Cobb, a legendary songsmith
and
Jimmy Johnson, a consummate professional technician:

Practitioners of integrity, and friends

An imprint of Globe Pequot, the trade division of
The Rowman & Littlefield Publishing Group, Inc.
4501 Forbes Blvd., Ste. 200
Lanham, MD 20706
BackbeatBooks.com

Distributed by NATIONAL BOOK NETWORK

Copyright © 2021 by Willie G. Moseley and Bob Shade

CREATIVE COMMONS LICENSES
Images on pages 22 and 75 are licensed under the Creative Commons Attribution CC0 1.0 Universal (CC0-10) Public Domain Dedication. [https://creativecommons.org/publicdomain/zero/1.0/legalcode]
Image on page 209 is licensed under the Creative Commons Attribution 2.0 Generic license (CC BY 2.0). [https://creativecommons.org/licenses/by/2.0/legalcode]
Image on page 210 is licensed under the Creative Commons Attribution-ShareAlike 4.0 International license (CC BY-SA 4.0). [https://creativecommons.org/licenses/by-sa/4.0/legalcode]

All rights reserved. No part of this book may be reproduced in any form or by any electronic or mechanical means, including information storage and retrieval systems, without written permission from the publisher, except by a reviewer who may quote passages in a review.

British Library Cataloguing in Publication Information available

Library of Congress Cataloging-in-Publication Data

Names: Moseley, Willie G., author.
Title: Bakersfield guitars : the illustrated history / Willie Moseley.
Description: Lanham : Backbeat, 2021. | Includes bibliographical references.
Identifiers: LCCN 2021018762 (print) | LCCN 2021018763 (ebook) | ISBN 9781493060627 (cloth) |
  ISBN 9781493060634 (epub)
Subjects: LCSH: Electric guitar—Construction—California—Bakersfield—History—20th century. | 1935-1992. | Hall, Joe. |
  Gruggett, Bill.
Classification: LCC ML1015.G9 M679 2021 (print) | LCC ML1015.G9 (ebook) | DDC 787.87/1979488--dc23
LC record available at https://lccn.loc.gov/2021018762
LC ebook record available at https://lccn.loc.gov/2021018763

∞™ The paper used in this publication meets the minimum requirements of American National Standard for Information Sciences—Permanence of Paper for Printed Library Materials, ANSI/NISO Z39.48-1992

Contents

Foreword *by Marshall Crenshaw*   vii

Acknowledgments   ix

Lexicon   xi

Introduction   xiii

PART 1: MOSRITE

1. Early Days in the LA Area   3
2. Early Bakersfield Guitars and the Standel-Assisted Birth of an Icon   11
3. The Advent of the Ventures   19
4. Glory Days   25
5. Diversification, Including Soundholes (None, One, or Two)   39
6. Beyond Stringed Instruments   47
7. The Gospel According to Semie   51
8. Storm Clouds over P Street   55
9. Rarities, One-Offs, and Experimental Instruments   59
10. Surname Instruments and the 1970s   65
11. The Gospel Goes Onward   77
12. Further Migration   79
13. Gospels in the Blue Ridge Mountains   85
14. Jonas Ridge Rarities   89
15. Finale in the Arkansas River Valley   95

PART 2: HALLMARK

16. Starting Solo with Sterling Instruments   103
17. The Standel Interlude   107
18. The Encor Initiative   109
19. The Swept-Wing Takes Flight   113
20. The Epcor Project   121
21. "Rebirth" in Maryland   125
22. The Gospel According to Bob   153

PART 3: GRUGGETT

23	Native Californian	157
24	Mosrite (Part 1) and Hallmark	159
25	The (Short-lived) Saga of the Stradette	161
26	Custom Luthiery, Mosrite (Part 2), Back to Custom Luthiery	165

PART 4: ANCILLARY BRANDS

27	Acoustic	175
28	Dobro	179
29	GM Custom	185
30	Melobar	191
31	Osborne	197
32	Standel: The Mysterious "Third" Manufacturer	203

Coda	209
Bibliography and References	217

Foreword

Marshall Crenshaw.
Gayle Miller

I still remember one Christmas Day a few years ago when my brother John and I tried to make a list of "The Ten Greatest Rock Albums of All-Time." We came up with:

1. *Bo Diddley's 16 All-Time Greatest Hits*
2. *Fun House* by the Stooges
3. *(The) Ventures in Space*

But then we gave up because we couldn't think of any albums that were as good as those three. We were drunk at the time....

Anyway, 1964's *(The) Ventures in Space*, one of the most innovative rock albums of its time (and of all time), is and will remain a big favorite of mine. It's the first album by the Ventures where they used Mosrite guitars, and the edgy, aggressive sound of those instruments were and are a perfect match for the bold, futuristic sounds that the guys laid down (on three-track tape).

Soon after that album came out, Mosrite guitars were in music stores all over the country. Fashion changes constantly in the world of electric guitars, but for a few minutes in the early to mid-1960s, Mosrite guitars made everything else seem passé. It seemed like whoever designed these things just threw out the old rulebook and wrote their own.

I managed to buy one in 1966 with my paper-route money—a Mark V (I couldn't afford a Mark I). It would turn out to be the first of many Mosrites that I've owned and have been inspired by over the years. I still remember their original ad slogan, "The Guitars with Built-In Soul"—what's not to love about that?

I would say at this point that the look and sound of Mosrites are quintessential Americana, that their appeal has stood the test of time, and that a book about the guitars is way overdue. I'm glad that Willie G. Moseley has taken up the challenge, and even more glad that he decided to go several steps further and chronicle the *whole big picture* of the Bakersfield guitar-building milieu of the "guitar boom" years of the 1960s and beyond. Semie Moseley, Andy Moseley, Joe Hall, Bill Gruggett, Ed Sanner, and others, were in each other's orbit, are part of one another's story. Mosrite is the dominant story, but you can read all about *all* of it right here in these pages.

Going through the list in my mind, whether it's Joe Maphis, Sugarfoot Bonner of the Ohio Players, Johnny Ramone, Larry Collins, or the guy that plays lead guitar on "Psychotic Reaction" by the Count Five (John "Mouse" Michalski), Toulouse Engelhardt, Ricky Wilson of The B-52s, Eric Brann and Lee Dorman of Iron Butterfly, Fred Smith of The MC5, Bob Bogle, Nokie Edwards, Don Wilson, country virtuoso Phil Baugh, Terry Terauchi, Buck Trent, Dave Alexander, and on and on, I can't think of a single Mosrite player whose work I don't enjoy, a whole lot.

Anyway, I've already read this book; I hope you'll love it as much as I do!

—Marshall Crenshaw

Acknowledgments

This one took me a bit further, distance-wise, and took a bit longer, time-wise.

I'm not getting any younger, either. The up-and-down flight itinerary from Birmingham to Dallas–Fort Worth to Phoenix to Bakersfield and back made me feel like a jet-lagged kangaroo.

Moreover, I apparently have a case of basophobia that's increasing in intensity, which means that I will *never, ever* drive on California State Highway 178 from Bakersfield to Lake Isabella again (even though the scenery was spectacular). If for some reason I was compelled to make another sojourn to visit with Ed Sanner in that mountain community, I'd have to swing around the long way, through Tehachapi, via Highway 14.

Those episodes noted, the cooperation of everyone who participated in the research for a history book about guitars made in Bakersfield and the surrounding area made such travels worth the effort.

Once again, the initial and primary individual to thank is my life partner, Gail. For decades, the Missus has been fully aware of my incessant urge to develop and nurture writing projects, and her ongoing tolerance of my proclivities is perpetually appreciated.

It was gratifying whenever one interviewee or instrument owner referred me to someone else who had some recollections or instruments or photos or memorabilia that might be appropriate for consideration of inclusion with this project. Such a word-of-mouth, "domino" phenomenon has happened with previous books as well, and it's always an encouraging experience.

So my sincere appreciation and thanks go out to the following sources: The Bob Shade collection, Larry Collins and his collection, the Scotty Allen collection, the Marc Lipco collection, the Artie Niesen collection, the Adam Tober collection, the Carter Granat collection, Marshall Crenshaw, Heritage Auctions, Skinner Inc., Michael G. Stewart, Steve "The Surfin' Librarian" Soest, the Bill Gruggett estate, Jim Shaw at Buck Owens Productions, the Buck Owens Private Foundation, Tommy Shaw, Joseph Deas, Ed Sanner, Ed King (RIP), George Bunnell, John Morton, John Selby Smith, Ted Smith, Hallmark Guitars, Aaron Piscopo, the Kern County Museum, Jim Phillips, Eugene Moles, Bob Spalding, Jack Clutter at the Country Music Hall of Fame and Museum, Steve Brown at vintaxe.com, Robert Price, Wayne Jarrett, Jeff Carlisi, Stan Ellis, Tony Brown, Jorma Kaukonen, Angie Pentz, Tim Bogert (RIP), Del Halterman, Fred Newell, Mike Gutierrez, Gordy Lupo, Chuck Seaton, Dusty Wheeler, Davie Allan, Tony Bacon, Jackson Smith, Steve Mayer, Pierre Laflamme, Jay Rosen, Sibila Savage, Bob Haggard, Jim Page, Leni Sinclair, Roger Fritz, Ralph Scaffidi, Jr., Susan Scaffidi, Peter Scaffidi, Bryce Martin, John Majdalani, Daniel Escauiza, and Fiona Taylor.

Thanks once again to Colonel Glenn Mackey, US Air Force, Retired, for his now-standard presubmission perusal of the text.

Here's a tip of the headstock to Rie Fujita and Warren Moseley for translation of Japanese resource material.

And of course, here's the usual "read-between-the-lines" salute to the Messrs. Spilman for perpetually encouraging my writing aspirations.

When the 1960s "guitar boom" erupted, the closest I got to owning a Mosrite instrument in those times was a gold-leaf Semie Moseley business card, displaying the round semi-starburst Mosrite logo. I do not recall where and how I acquired it back then, and of course, I wish I still had it

And as detailed herein, the Ventures and Mosrite guitars were indeed the first "band–brand" association that many teenage Baby Boomers—particularly those of us who played in garage bands—would recall. However, the Ventures' brief, half-decade association with Mosrite ended in an unfortunate dissolution, and the band and the guitar company were never able to reconcile.

ix

The history of Bakersfield guitars may cite Semie Moseley as the keystone figure in its chronology, but there were other builders—some of whom are still unknown—who participated in a unique era of American guitar building in a unique locale.

I hope you enjoy reading their stories and viewing their instruments, as well as examining a few of the very cool modern guitars and basses that have been inspired by the original Bakersfield brands and designs.

—W. G. M.

Lexicon

ARCH-TOP: Somewhat self-explanatory; some hollow or semihollow instruments have a curved or contoured top that is sometimes carved. The term is usually associated with guitars rather than basses, and isn't necessarily used when discussing solidbody instruments, although "carved top" *is* used regarding solidbody instruments (see separate definition).

BINDING: Material that is usually made from flexible plastic; "binds" edges of wood together, but sometimes its use is strictly cosmetic.

BOLT-ON: Refers to a type of attachment of a neck to a body (as found on most Bakersfield-made instruments)

BOUT: Upper and lower portions of a standard-shape guitar or bass body, separated by an indentation or "waist." The two sections have a connotation that implies viewing an instrument that is on display vertically—"upper bout" refers to the part of the body nearer to the neck joint, while "lower bout" refers to the portion nearer the end of the body, where the bridge, tailpiece, and controls on electric instruments are usually found.

BRIDGE: Metal, wood, or plastic part on the top of an instrument where strings "transmit" vibrations for sonic reproduction. A bridge usually has small grooves in it to accommodate each string. Many bridges have adjustable "saddles" for individual strings, to allow intonation and fine tuning. Most bridges on electric guitars and basses also have threaded bolts on either side to facilitate adjustment of string height.

CARVED TOP: This term usually describes a contoured top found on many guitars and basses, including solidbodies. The carved top may be part of the same wood as the body, or a different wood may be attached. Semie Moseley's "German carve" on Mosrites and other instruments is a definitive and distinctive example of a carved top.

"CASE CANDY": Items found in the pocket of a guitar case, including straps, strings, picks, song lists, cords, warranty cards, and instruction manuals.

CONTOUR: Beveling on solidbody instruments to enhance comfort. Such contouring often consists of a "belly cut" on the back, and a "forearm bevel" on the top—and both of those terms are self-explanatory. As noted earlier, "contouring" can also refer to a carved top on an instrument body.

CUTAWAY: Portion of instrument near the neck–body joint that appears to have been "cut out" to allow access to higher register of the neck. Such shaping creates a "horn" on the body silhouette. Instruments may be single-cutaway (the Mosrite Brass Rail is a rare example for that brand), symmetrical double-cutaway (such as Mosrite's Celebrity series), or offset double-cutaway (most solidbody Bakersfield guitars and basses).

FLAT-TOP: Another self-explanatory term. This is the classic configuration of an acoustic guitar.

"FLOOR-SWEEP": a term used to describe instruments that were made with leftover parts, just to use up such items. While such guitars and basses might be rare, there can be potential controversy over how collectable they might be, since most of them were pieced together in a somewhat hodgepodge manner.

FRET: A metal strip on a fretboard. Each space between frets serves the same sonic function as a piano key by changing the pitch of a string by one note. The metal strips that delineate each space are usually made of "fret wire," an alloy.

FRET MARKERS: Also known as "position markers." Decorative dots, blocks, or other inlay on the fretboard playing surface or side of the neck for visual reference.

FRETBOARD: Also known as a "fingerboard." The top surface of a guitar or bass neck where notes are selected and played. Rosewood and ebony are among the most popular fretboard woods laminated to the top of a neck. A maple fretboard is often part of a maple neck itself instead of being a laminated part.

HARDTAIL: A guitar that does not have a vibrato. Such an instrument usually has a tailpiece (or combination bridge and tailpiece) installed on the top.

HEADSTOCK: Top end of instrument where the tuning keys and brand name are (usually) found.

JACK: Receptacle for guitar cord on an electric instrument.

LUTHIER: An individual builder who hand-makes stringed musical instruments, usually in a small shop.

NAMM: Acronym for "National Association of Music Merchandisers," an organization of retail music businesses. New instruments and other musical wares usually debut at "NAMM shows," which are currently held twice a year. Originally, NAMM shows were held in Chicago, Illinois; as of this writing they are presented in Nashville, Tennessee, and Anaheim, California.

"NEW OLD STOCK": Guitar collectors' term for instruments or parts that have languished in storage or layaway for years without being sold or used. The abbreviation for such items, "NOS," is also cited in vintage guitar parlance.

NUT: Small grooved part for string spacing and height, located between headstock and fingerboard, usually made of bone, plastic, metal, or, in more recent times, space-age composite material.

PICKGUARD: Somewhat self-defined item, usually made of plastic or metal, that shields a guitar or bass body from pick damage (if the player happens to use a pick); also known as a "scratchplate."

PICKUP: Microphone-like device consisting of magnet or magnets and wiring that "picks up" string vibrations. "Single-coil" pickups have a self-explanatory designation, while "humbucking" pickups have two coils, wired in opposition to each other to cancel out annoying electrical noise.

POTENTIOMETERS: "Pots" aren't visible, but are critical to the function of an electric guitar or bass—they're the electronic controls underneath a volume or tone knob.

RADIUS: Arc or curvature of fretboard from one side to the other. Measured in inches (from which the radius is figured)—the smaller the number, the more pronounced the arc.

SCALE: Distance from nut to bridge. Scales found on most electric guitars are either 24.75 inches or 25.5 inches, both of which are considered industry standards. The guitar scale on classic Mosrite guitars was 24.5 inches. Bass scales are 30 inches or 30.5 inches (short), 32 inches (medium), or 34 inches (standard).

SET-NECK: Refers to the glued-in neck style found on some guitars or basses.

STRING TREE: Hardware attached to headstock to stabilize strings between nut and tuning keys.

TAILPIECE: Anchor point for "ball end" of string. Independent tailpieces are "stop"-type (attached to the top of the instrument) or somewhat trapeze-shaped, attached to the bottom rim of a guitar body.

THINLINE: A hollow or semihollow guitar or bass configuration with a body that has a shorter depth (usually around two inches) than most acoustic stringed instrument bodies, as exemplified by the Mosrite Celebrity series.

TOGGLE SWITCH: Turns individual pickups off and on. The most common configuration is found on a two-pickup instrument, with a three-position toggle switch that works either pickup individually or both at the same time. Toggle switches are also used to control other functions of a guitar or bass.

TRUSS ROD (and TRUSS ROD COVER): Most modern guitars and basses have a metal truss rod inside the neck to alleviate string tension (which, if not controlled, could cause the neck to warp). The truss rod is usually adjustable, and is accessed (depending on the brand and model) via a plate located on the headstock (just behind the nut–headstock juncture) or on the butt end of the neck.

VIBRATO: A device with an "arm" that is part of the tailpiece on some models. It is manipulated by a player's hand to change the pitch of a note or a chord on stringed instruments.

ZERO FRET: An extra piece of fret wire positioned where the neck joins the headstock; utilized to facilitate better-sounding chords. Some luthiers will note that if a zero fret is found on a fretboard, the part that is normally referred to as a "nut" should be referred to as a "string guide."

Introduction

Bakersfield, California, has a unique location and a unique history. It's situated in the southern portion of the San Joaquin Valley, a huge, diverse agricultural area in central California. Books and periodical articles chronicling the area's history usually cite transplanted laborers, primarily from Oklahoma, Arkansas, and Texas, who migrated to the area during what was known as the Dust Bowl era of the middle to late 1930s.

World War II also generated voluminous migration to the Golden State, as jobs became available in aircraft factories, shipyards, and munitions plants.

And dust is also a factor in Bakersfield itself.

One resident explained that smog and dust drift downstate in a southeast direction from California's Bay Area, and the pollutants are trapped by two mountain ranges to the south and east of Bakersfield. It's often difficult to see the nearby mountains through the haze.

"We generate plenty of our own dust," a local journalist added. "The lack of rain makes it much worse. Fires don't help, either."

In addition to agriculture, Bakersfield also developed around local oil fields. There's even an adjacent area known as Oildale, where some of the rigs are still in operation, their incessant up-and-down probing visible from a nearby freeway.

Many country music fans are aware of a genre known as the "Bakersfield Sound," and numerous histories and biographies have documented its rightful place in the pantheon of American music. While it was influenced by other musical styles during its evolution, the Bakersfield Sound is usually described as a gritty type of country music with drums for dancing, anchored by the twang of a Fender Telecaster electric guitar. Its fans tend to be stereotyped, sometimes unfairly, as farm laborers and oil workers.

The origins of the Bakersfield Sound date back to the middle of the twentieth century. Performers remembered with reverence include multi-instrumentalist, band leader, disc jockey, and stock car racer Bill Woods (who nurtured the early careers of Buck Owens, Merle Haggard, and others); Cousin Herb Henson (and his "Trading Post" television show); Jimmy Thomason (who hosted more than one TV show); Billy Mize; Ferlin Husky; Red Simpson; and underappreciated guitarists like Gene Moles.

Legendary venues included the Blackboard Café, the Lucky Spot, the Pumpkin Center Barn Dance, and Trout's, among others.

One historian opined that the music that developed in Bakersfield was ancillary to an overall lifestyle and environment.

"I'm not sure that the 'Bakersfield Sound' is a sound at all," said veteran newsman and author Robert Price. "My perspective is that it was a time and a place, not so much of a 'sound.'"

The twin pillars of the Bakersfield Sound were and are, of course, Owens and Haggard.

At one point, Owens had actually recorded some pop/rock songs under the moniker of Corky Jones before settling into a legendary career with his band, the Buckaroos.

And while the upbeat, twangy guitar-with-drums description of the Bakersfield Sound might usually be applicable to much of Owens's material, many of Haggard's songs were contemplative about the harsh working life in that area, as exemplified by a succinct, quasiautobiographical 1971 song titled "Tulare Dust." That town is located about sixty-five miles north of Bakersfield via Freeway 99. Haggard's backing band was known as the Strangers.

Musical differences aside, the "classic" lineups of the Buckaroos and the Strangers featured phenomenal lead guitarists—Don Rich's Telecaster riffs and high-harmony vocals were key components of the Buckaroos' presentation, and Haggard had been a fan of his future lead guitarist, Roy Nichols, for many years before the Strangers were founded.

Indeed, Lynyrd Skynyrd lead vocalist Ronnie Van Zandt tipped his hat to Nichols by acknowledging the rapid-fire guitar licks on that band's 1977 cover of Haggard's "Honky Tonk Night Time Man"—"Sounds like Roy!" Van Zandt chortled. The riffs were being played by the band's new guitarist, Steve Gaines, who had been raised in Oklahoma. Van Zandt and Gaines were among the decedents when Skynyrd's chartered aircraft crashed in October of that year.

Businessman Marc Lipco, whose family used to own a music store in downtown Bakersfield, is among those music buffs who feel that other legendary musicians from the area still haven't gotten their due on a wider scale.

"I don't want to say this in a derogatory way, but the 'Bakersfield Sound' was more than Buck and a Telecaster," said Lipco. "There was Gene Moles and other people who were instrumental in local music but otherwise were absolutely unknown, nationally. Don Rich was an important part of the story, but there were a lot of guys out there who weren't 'A-list'; they were 'B-list' and 'C-list,' in the trenches."

The agrarian area of California that includes Bakersfield and Tulare also has an interesting significance to guitar collectors. Many of the guitar brands made in the southern part of the Golden State's agricultural belt seem to have been on an "information periphery" regarding classic American-made instruments, possibly because many of those brands were (originally) flashes in the pan.

In the 1960s, some guitar players may have been aware that Mosrites were made in Bakersfield, but it was likely that they originally became familiar with Mosrite guitars because of that brand's association with an iconic instrumental band known as the Ventures.

Historical information about the ultimately migratory Mosrite company, as well as brands that were briefly built in Bakersfield such as Hallmark, Gruggett, Standel, and others, has always been somewhat nebulous and elusive. Like trying to view the dust-enshrouded mountains nearby, ascertaining the history of Bakersfield guitar builders and brands is sometimes difficult. There were and are plenty of guitar-oriented legends and rumors hovering around Kern County.

And if Bill Woods was the primary progenitor of the Bakersfield Sound, his peer in the history of Bakersfield-built guitars was a tall, Oklahoma-born gospel singer with a big grin named Semie Moseley.

Part 1
Mosrite

Ca. 1954 Mosrite solidbody guitar, cited by Andy Moseley as the first guitar Semie Moseley made.
Willie G. Moseley

1
Early Days in the LA Area

Irene and John Moseley were stereotypical Okies.

Like an untold number of agrarian families in Oklahoma and other states, the Moseleys were forced to move from the Great Plains area of the central United States because of the effects of the devastating Dust Bowl phenomenon in the 1930s. They would migrate westward in late 1940, settling in Bakersfield, California, the following year.

Andy Moseley had been born to Irene and John on February 24, 1933, and his younger brother, Semie, came along on June 13, 1935. The Moseleys had an interest in gospel music, and the boys began to play guitar at an early age. In a 2012 video interview that was part of the National Association of Music Merchandisers (NAMM) "Oral History" series, Andy recalled that his brother was a much better player than he was.

Semie also developed an interest in repairing and renovating instruments, and continually honed his woodworking skills.

Both boys dropped out of school in their early teens. They would go on the road as musical support for traveling evangelists, and were stranded in the Midwest when their migratory mission work abruptly collapsed. They were forced to work their way back to California by doing manual labor, including picking cotton

Semie eventually relocated to the Los Angeles area, and began seeking work at guitar-building shops. In a letter of authentication dated April 16, 2007, Andy detailed his brother's initial footsteps into the guitar business:

> The first real off-the-wall repair Semie did was to cut and customize the head of his wife's guitar. About that time, I moved my family from Bakersfield, California, to Santa Ana, California, where I had been offered a music teaching position and Semie and his wife were evangelizing in the area, so they were staying with us.
>
> Then Semie went to the Rickenbacker guitar company and sold himself to be familiar with building guitars. He was hired at no pay for 2 weeks then became a full-time employee.

Semie himself remembered applying unsuccessfully for employment at the Fender and Magnatone guitar companies before he was hired by Rickenbacker company official Paul Barth for a wage of one dollar an hour. The young would-be builder recalled being mentored by German émigré Roger Rossmeisl, whose "German carve" contouring on guitar bodies would later be emulated by Moseley. Andy's letter continues:

> About a year went by as Semie got a place for his family and continued to do his evangelizing. We worked as a team sometimes. It was during this time we became good friends with Rev. Ray Boatwright. Semie then decided he would build himself a guitar because his Epiphone did not play to his satisfaction. He bought a slab of Mahogany wood from the factory and was working after hours on Mosrite #1 with his bosses' approval. However the owners found out and they fired him. He brought the guitar in rough shaped [sic] to my house where we used a file to shape the neck.
>
> Then Ray Boatwright took Semie to Sears and co-signed for Semie a band saw, tabletop drill press, air compressor and spray gun, belt sander and other small tools. Semie moved them all to Ray Boatwright's one-car garage and that is where Mosrite #1 was finished in early 1954.

Andy Moseley's missive was written as authentication of the primitive burgundy-finished solidbody guitar shown here.

The guitar's parts, as well as unique facets of its construction, were detailed in Andy's letter:

> Semie made all the parts by hand except the keys, radio knobs, screws, and string hold down. The very large pickup was hand wound. The string guide was made by the use of an extra fret and he used the zero fret for the first time. The bridge was made from a solid bar of aluminum. The bridge adjustment nuts were fashioned from solid brass. The

logo, "Mosrite," was hand lettered by Semie for the first time. ["Mosrite" was a combination of Semie's surname and Boatwright's surname.]

This guitar was played by Semie until he finished his first triple neck guitar. He then sold Mosrite # one [sic] to a man in Los Angeles. When it reappeared for sale in 1979 Semie bought it to go in his museum he was planning. He moved it, took care of it but his dream was never to be. He gave it to me when he knew he was dieing [sic] of multiple myeloma in 1992. I have kept it safe.

The guitar displays some primeval aesthetics that would be seen on future Mosrite instruments, including an allusion to an "M" on the headstock silhouette, tiny fret markers, and angled pickup polepieces. As is obvious, the pickup was mounted under the pickguard. The angled alignment of polepieces directly below strings would also be seen later on Mosrites and other instruments made by other Bakersfield builders.

The aluminum plate on which the volume and tone controls were mounted was reportedly just a piece of scrap metal that was crudely shaped to fit on the instrument.

In a 1981 interview, Semie would recount that he also developed other projects during his time at Rickenbacker, including a volume pedal and split/stereo guitar pickups. He also recalled Boatwright taking him under his (financial) wing, and remembered doing repair work for a year and a half before he began building his own guitars.

In the middle of the decade, Semie would move his shop to the San Fernando Valley area.

Andy's allusion to Semie's "first triple neck guitar" is appropriate, since that unique instrument's dramatic look is what originally called the attention of many pro musicians to Moseley's guitar-building prowess.

Moseley's creation had an octave guitar in the upper position, a standard guitar with a crude vibrato in the middle, and a mandolin in the lower position. The six-tuners-on-one-side headstock silhouettes of the octave guitar and standard guitar alluded to Bigsby guitars as well as the Fender Stratocaster, but the tuning-key sides of the Mosrite six-on-a-side headstocks were slightly curved. Its original pickups were made by the Carvin company, which was also located in southern California.

The triple-neck instrument was heavy and cumbersome, but was obviously versatile and eye-catching.

And two noted Los Angeles–area players were soon owners of doubleneck instruments crafted by Semie.

Moseley with his first triple-neck instrument.
Courtesy of the Andy Moseley Estate

Dubbed "The King of the Strings," lightning-fast guitarist Joe Maphis was a longtime regular on California's *Town Hall Party* radio and television shows. As the television show's popularity increased, other musicians were added to its roster, including Lorrie and Larry Collins, also known as the Collins Kids. A big sister–kid brother act that came onboard in 1954, the Collins Kids were viewer favorites. Their family was also originally from Oklahoma. Inspired by Hank Williams as well as by blues and gospel music, Larry had already been recognized as a guitar prodigy by the time his age reached double digits.

"We auditioned on a Friday night and they put us on as regulars on Saturday night," Collins detailed in a 2013 interview.

Television audiences took to the duo's exuberant performances of up-tempo songs abetted by Larry's enthusiastic dancing as he barreled through tunes without missing a note, while his sister, Lorrie, held down the beat with a strong rhythmic style.

"I was the original poster boy for Ritalin!" Collins recalled with a laugh. "Whatever we did—even songs like 'You Are My Sunshine'—was high-energy. That's why some people branded it 'rockabilly.' For me, it was just 'Give me something to dance to!'"

Obviously, Joe Maphis was a mentor to Larry, as was Merle Travis, another dynamic guitarist who appeared on the show. When the Collins Kids first appeared on *Town Hall Party*, Larry was playing a small Gibson acoustic guitar. Then came an early 1950s Gibson ES-140 3/4, his first electric guitar.

Larry vividly recalled meeting Semie Moseley when, in 1955, the luthier brought his first tripleneck to the television studio for the musicians to peruse.

"We played with it for awhile backstage," he recounted. "Joe thought it was a little over-the-top, and its weight was a concern. Joe asked me what I thought. I agreed, but told him I thought a doubleneck would be cool."

Joe could relate to the practicality of more than one instrument neck on one body, and a couple of months after visiting the studio with his triple-neck, Semie delivered an all-maple, natural-finish instrument with a standard guitar neck and an octave guitar neck to Maphis.

The body of Joe's instrument had a slight German carve around the top and back of the body (a nod to Roger Rossmeisl), and also heralded the ornate/"gingerbread" look that other Mosrite instruments from the 1950s would exhibit—whorled elevated pickguards and armguards, intricate headstock designs, and owners' names inlaid on fretboards were often found on such one-of-a-kind creations.

While one person's "ornate" may be another person's "gaudy," Maphis used his instrument extensively, treating his doubleneck as a player's guitar instead of a do-not-touch showpiece. The guitar would undergo numerous modifications and upgrades in the ensuing months, years, and decades, including replacement necks and replacement pickups. The body would be routed out to provide weight relief soon after Maphis acquired the instrument, and the application of a sunburst finish also happened fairly quickly.

Obviously, the guitar's aesthetics were unique enough to merit its placement on numerous album covers. By sometime in 1957, it was already sporting replacement necks with different headstocks.

Joe Maphis with his doubleneck, mid-1950s.
Michael Ochs Archives / Stringer / Getty Images

Joe Maphis with his already modified doubleneck on the cover of a 1957 album, *Fire on the Strings*

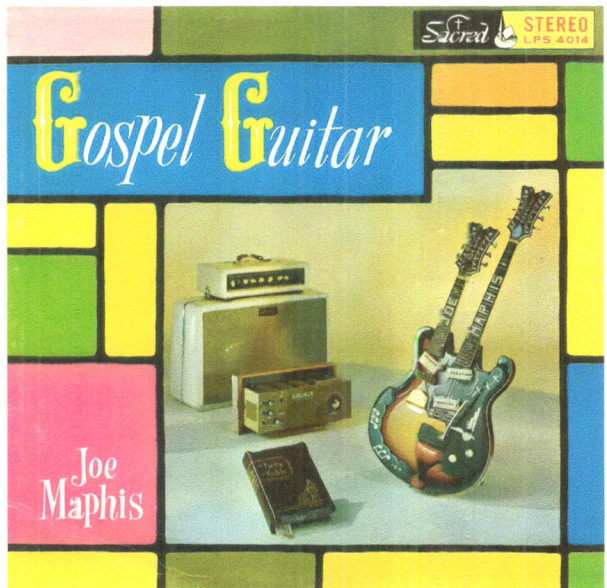

Maphis's guitar was also seen on the cover of 1961's *Gospel Guitar*. Also shown in the cover photo were a Bible, a Standel amplifier, and a primitive Ecco-Fonic echo device.

During the 1960s, Joe Maphis's guitar would become a veritable Frankenstein instrument, as it underwent further modifications:

- The necks were apparently replaced for the final time by the mid-1960s. The octave guitar neck's headstock sported a designation that read "The Original," while the standard guitar neck's headstock had a standard Mosrite logo with a medallion image.
- A standard Mosrite intonatable bridge was installed on the standard guitar, and what appears to have been a custom-built brass bridge was placed on the octave guitar.
- The black pickguard and armguard were superseded with white parts decorated with black curlicues.
- A modern vibrato system replaced the earlier, crude hand-built vibrato. The new vibrato included a custom-made large arm requested by Maphis. The ring at the end of the arm was designed to accommodate Maphis's pinky finger (and Semie liked that style of vibrato arm as a player himself).

The funnel-shaped, violin-style wooden tailpiece on the standard guitar portion of Joe's doubleneck was apparently installed for purely decorative reasons.

Some kind of work was done on the Maphis guitar around 1970, as the standard guitar headstock acquired a "Moseley of California" brand name and a block-M logo, which Semie had been compelled to use for some two and a half years (see chapter 10, "Surname Instruments and the 1970s").

Semie's relationship with *Town Hall Party* cast members took another important turn a month after Maphis received his instrument, according to Larry Collins.

"On live television, Joe and Semie presented me with my own doubleneck," the veteran guitarist recalled. "They let me rock out with it for an hour or so, and before I was done, all the acts scheduled for that time were with me onstage."

Not surprisingly, Larry's guitar featured his inlaid first and last names—one on each neck—just like Joe Maphis's instrument. It was also no surprise that the body was smaller, compared to Joe's guitar.

"The guitar was beautiful, and played great. It will always be my treasure," Collins said. "It's been around the world several times and appeared on countless shows, as well as tours with Johnny Cash, and of course *Town Hall Party*. Its most notable appearance may have been the first live network presentation of *The Grand Ole Opry*."

Not long after the two *Town Hall Party* guitarists acquired their instruments, Semie reportedly hollowed out the interiors of both guitars for weight relief. Collins's instrument was modified first, then Maphis's instrument was hogged out yet again.

Lorrie's main guitar was an early 1950s Martin flat-top, and that instrument received a "monikered" replacement neck made by Semie, also in 1955.

"It wasn't a repair job," Lorrie explained in the same 2013 article in which Larry was interviewed. "It was customized, and played better because its new neck was thinner; the original was way too wide."

Joe and Rose Lee Maphis on the cover of a 1964 album, *Mr. and Mrs. Country Music*. Joe's guitar appears to be in its final configuration, with another set of replacement necks as well as an improved vibrato system. Rose's guitar was also built by Semie, who used an acoustic body from an outside source. Her name is in script on the pickguard.
Courtesy of the Country Music Hall of Fame® and Museum

The Joe Maphis doubleneck as displayed in the Country Muic Hall of Fame and Museum, with a "Moseley of California" logo on the standard guitar's headstock.
Courtesy of the Country Music Hall of Fame® and Museum

Larry Collins's 1955 doubleneck Mosrite guitar, highly modifed over the decades.
Photo by David Silva

From Larry Collins's personal scrapbook, this archval photo shows him with his original Mosrite doubleneck and Lorrie with her Martin guitar with a replacement Mosrite neck.
Courtesy of Larry Collins

Moseley also installed a larger, decorative pickguard on Lorrie's guitar.

The modified Martin would be Lorrie's go-to instrument for decades. She played it so hard that she wore a hole in the upper bout, but she noted in the early twenty-first century, "It stills sounds fine, even with the extra soundhole!"

By 1959, Larry's guitar had been updated with a new headstock design, and it, too, would undergo other modifications and repairs over the decades. Larry would recall that Semie made a total of five doubleneck guitars for him.

Moseley also recalled briefly doing work (post-Rickenbacker) for iconic guitar craftsman Paul Bigsby, but that relationship ended acrimoniously, as Semie was physically thrown out of Bigsby's shop.

Semie was, of course, also building single-neck instruments during the 1950s, and in 1956, Larry helped Moseley build a single-neck guitar dubbed the "Larrico." Collins remembered:

> We developed the design from a three-inch block of wood. I drew the cutaway. They wouldn't let me get anywhere close to the band saw, so Semie cut it. The headstock was one Semie had been working on for his signature design. My job was to sand, sand, and sand some more!
>
> I chose the pickguard material from a pile of plastic, and Semie had me sign a piece of cardboard that was then cut as a template for the pickguard. He then matched the signature with the "Larry" inlay. The black-and-burgundy sunburst color was my choice. Semie gets credit for naming the guitar.

One unique instrument made by Semie in the same era was a two-pickup mandolin created for renowned clothier Nuta Kotlyarenko, whose professional

Larrico guitar, 1956.
Photo by David Silva

Early Days in the LA Area

name was Nudie Cohn. For decades, professional musicians in more than one genre would custom-order extravagant, gaudy, rhinestone-decorated suits from Nudie's Rodeo Tailors in North Hollywood.

Another 1950s Mosrite tripleneck exemplifies the numerous modifications, repairs, and upgrades such instruments underwent over the decades. A Semie Moseley–signed label in its control cavity notes that it was made in 1957. Like the original Joe Maphis and Larry Collins doublenecks, it was later modified, most likely in the 1960s, with a then-modern Mosrite vibrato, as well as replacement pickguard, arm guard, and accoutrements. It, too, was originally a natural finish but was refinished in sunburst. The instrument originally had a name on the standard guitar fretboard but the moniker was later covered with black lacquer.

Larry Collins retired his 1955 doubleneck instrument in the mid-1960s, when he acquired another Semie-made doubleneck. The new guitar was named "Betsy," and Larry used it when the Collins Kids toured Vietnam and played the Las Vegas–Reno–Lake Tahoe club circuit.

1957 tripleneck. Note that the brand name on the standard guitar headstock is hyphenated, as found on some other Mosrite instruments in the 1950s.
Courtesy of Michael G. Stewart

"Betsy," a doubleneck made in 1964.
Photo by David Silva

This ca. 1959 two-pickup solidbody is patterned after the guitar that Andy Moseley pronounced to be "Mosrite #1." It, too, has concealed pickups, and also features a primitive vibrato unit.
Willie G. Moseley

Semie's marriage failed in the late 1950s, and he returned to Bakersfield. Moving into his mother's residence, he began building instruments in her garage. Some of his late-1950s instruments may have been started in the San Fernando Valley and completed in Bakersfield. Quickly outgrowing the garage, he moved into a tractor barn on Panama Lane owned by local musician Jelly Sanders. Around the time of his relocation, he had begun "diversifying," creating less-ornate guitars as well as electric basses.

One of Semie's earliest basses had a single-cutaway body that referenced a Fender Telecaster guitar, but the body also had a German carve. It was short scale (30 inches) and the 20-fret neck was 1.5 inches wide at the nut. The body sported a dark sunburst finish.

Its serial number, #3000, indicates that it may be the first of its type; many early Mosrite models had serial numbers in quasinumerical order, beginning or ending with "00" or "000" as the first or last two or three digits.

Another early bass was a left-handed instrument that looked more like a Fender Precision Bass, which had been introduced in 1951 and had undergone several cosmetic and electronic changes before settling into its "classic" configuration in 1957.

Early Mosrite bass, serial #3000.
Willie G. Moseley

Left-handed bass, ca. 1960.
Willie G. Moseley

The body of Semie's southpaw bass still had a German carve, as well as multiple body binding. The pickguard was multilayered. One of its most unique features was the fretboard "inlay," which consisted of strips of stainless steel hammered into the rosewood.

Overall, the silhouette of the left-handed bass is more modern-looking than earlier Mosrite instruments. It may have been influential in the concept and design of the series that would ultimately become Mosrite's most famous instruments.

Ca. 1960 "scroll" guitar owned and later modified by Joe Hall.
Willie G. Moseley

2
Early Bakersfield Guitars and the Standel-Assisted Birth of an Icon

Semie began working on several unusual and similar instruments around the time he returned to Bakersfield. Not quite as flashy as some of Moseley's earlier work, they featured a scrolled look, and were hollowed out (chambered) on the inside during their construction (whereas the doublenecks owned by Joe Maphis and Larry Collins had been hogged out as a postconstruction modification). While hollow from the outset, the new guitars did not have soundholes. A metal back was attached after the wood was removed from what would be the interior of the instrument body.

Two of the "scroll" guitars went to Rose Lee and Joe Maphis. Mrs. Maphis recalled receiving the instruments from Semie in about 1961. Another was purchased by Mosrite associate Joe Hall, who later added his own pickups and vibrato arm.

Hall was one of Mosrite's earliest Bakersfield workers, and in a 2004 interview, recalled how he got to know the company founder:

> About 1959, Semie Moseley moved to Bakersfield. A friend of mine, Carl Moore, told me I should check out the guitars he was building. I met Semie and was so impressed with his work that I bought one of his guitars. I gave him my almost-new Gibson [guitar] and four hundred dollars. [NOTE: In this recollection, Hall was most likely referring to the "scroll" guitar seen here, as the chronologies of Hall's order and the guitar's construction align.]
>
> At the time, I was performing and doing a lot of recording sessions for Global Records. I needed my guitar and was losing money without it. I started going to Semie's shop every day in hopes I could speed him up. Semie gave me a few small jobs to do, which freed him to work on my guitar.
>
> As time went by, he taught me all he had learned about guitar building, which was the only compensation I received from our association. And I think I got the better part of the deal! How often do you get the chance to work one-on-one with a master of the craft?

Moseley also allowed Hall to work on some of his own guitar projects within the Mosrite facility. Another similar guitar crafted during the same time frame was a "Mosrite Special" built for D. C. Herbert. Semie signed the instrument inside, and dated his signature on July 8, 1960.

Semie's brother Andy moved to Nashville in late 1959, attempting to get Music City players interested in Mosrite guitars.

Around 1961, early Mosrite guitars attracted the attention of the Standel company of Temple City, California. Their powerful guitar amplifiers had been giving the Fender company a run for their money for about a decade, and were highly regarded by such players as Hank Thompson, Joe Maphis, Merle Travis,

Mosrite Special, 1960.
Courtesy of Carter Granat

Larry Collins, and others. So it wasn't surprising that Standel founder Bob Crooks was interested in expanding his company's line by offering Standel-branded guitars.

Semie's initial collaboration with the amplifier company was to build basic instruments that had a "Standel" sticker on their headstocks instead of a "Mosrite" moniker. Joe Hall was involved in the construction of the original Standel-by-Mosrite instruments.

"Bob Crooks was approached by Semie," Hall remembered, "and he agreed to accept ten units for the NAMM trade show. After these were finished and delivered, Bob was not at all pleased with the overall quality of our work. These were good guitars; they just didn't quite look or feel the same as a Mosrite."

A Standel catalog citing the company's 1962 line proffered a single-cutaway, two-pickup twelve-string "Riviera" model guitar with a "Trombly Convertible Bridge" (named after guitarist Lou Trombly, who endorsed Standel amplifiers). The device could mute half of the strings to evoke a conventional six-string guitar sound. The Riviera was offered in "a high luster gun metal grey finish."

A single-pickup "thin body model" was known as the "Stardust." Its silhouette was similar to that of earlier Mosrite solidbodies, including the instrument Andy Moseley pronounced to be "Mosrite #1." The Stardust had a short, 23-inch scale and was finished in a "Standel red color for attractive contrast with the chrome plated parts," according to the catalog text. Given its smaller size, short scale, and low price, it may have been intended to be marketed as a student model.

The "Thunderbird" bass was essentially a clone of an early Mosrite single-cutaway bass.

Another curiosity about the 1962 Standel catalog is that a standard six-string two-pickup guitar like the one seen here (serial #105) was not illustrated. Accordingly, this instrument compels a closer look, as it is a representative of the earliest Standel-branded instruments to be built in Bakersfield.

The thin, one-piece maple neck has a rosewood fretboard with twenty-one frets and tiny fret markers. The neck is a set-in type, and the legendary small, flat fret wire that distinguished many Mosrite guitars is in place on this instrument, as is a zero fret. The scale is 24.75 inches. The body, finished in a crème-to-brown sunburst, is two-piece alder. While its silhouette has an obvious Fender Telecaster influence, its sides are more rounded. Hardware includes Kluson tuners, as well as a unique bridge and tailpiece. The bridge is aluminum, and appears to be hand-carved. The high-relief pickguard is also intriguing—it's clear

"Riviera" 12-string guitar, as seen in 1962 Standel catalog.
Courtesy of Steve Brown/vintaxe.com

"Stardust" six-string guitar, as seen in 1962 Standel catalog.
Courtesy of Steve Brown/vintaxe.com

"Thunderbird" bass, as seen in 1962 Standel catalog.
Courtesy of Steve Brown/vintaxe.com

Plexiglas, and is shaded from underneath in a charcoal sunburst. It's elevated (0.125 inch) above the surface of the body on four posts.

The controls include a three-way toggle switch—the tip of which is a brass ball—on the treble cutaway, and master volume and tone controls. By the time this guitar was made, Moseley had discontinued the use of Carvin pickups and had begun winding his own for his instruments; these pickups are early Mosrite-made units.

Semie recalled doing some consulting work in the early 1960s for Guild, a New York City–area guitar company that had gone into business in 1952. He advised Guild about their finishing process, and worked on a vibrato system. The bridge/vibrato units had unique flip-up mutes, and a "harp"-shaped section with a Guild script logo, as well as "Vibramute" on the bottom portion of the anchor plate.

Guild owner Al Dronge turned down the Moseley-made vibratos, complaining that they were too crude. Not wanting the vibratos to go to waste, Semie then ground out the Guild logo from the "harp"-shaped section and painted that area black. He would use the units, still with "Vibramute" on the base, on other guitars he was developing.

Ca. 1962 Standel-by-Mosrite.
Courtesy of Jim Page

The early history and legend of the guitar model that would become Mosrite's keystone instrument is somewhat hazy. Bob Crooks's dissatisfaction with the initial examples of Standel-branded Mosrite instruments reportedly led to a meeting with Semie, at which the Standel founder informed the Mosrite founder that he wanted a guitar line that was as close as possible to Fender stringed instruments. Not surprisingly, Crooks was insistent that the guitars bearing the Standel name should be as high-quality as Standel amplifiers.

Moseley returned to his Bakersfield shop, and began working with Joe Hall on an alternate solidbody guitar style that would evolve into its own unique and easily recognized silhouette.

Unlike brands such as Fender, the new body's lower, treble cutaway extended further outward than the upper, bass cutaway horn. The aesthetics of the Mosrite body, which was perceived as upside down and also had body edge binding, immediately commanded attention simply because it looked different.

The treble pickup's polepieces had a straight alignment with the strings. The bass pickup was angled so polepieces would still be located directly under each string, as had been the case with earlier Moseley-made instruments.

The fretboard inlay consisted of tiny dots—two on the appropriate frets of the first octave, three on the twelfth octave fret, and one on the higher register. This pattern would ultimately be seen on almost all production Mosrite models, although the dots would become larger in later years.

Sharp-eyed guitar enthusiasts may have wondered about the round black plate that wrapped around the base of the (erstwhile Guild) Vibramute. It isn't particularly unsightly, but it isn't strictly cosmetic, either—the guitar's set-neck construction meant that the angle of the neck to the body could not be adjusted, and if Moseley's Vibramute was placed directly on the body surface, the strings' alignment over the fretboard was far too high. Semie was compelled to hollow out a cavity approximately 0.375 inches deep in which to drop the mechanism so the strings would be at a normal low position. The new cavity would be covered with a piece of black plastic.

Semie would quickly make such adjustments in the basic manufacturing of the body to align the Vibramute properly, but the earliest Mosrite guitars with the soon-to-be-iconic body style would sport a black item around their Vibramutes that has come to be known as the "mistake plate" in vintage guitar parlance.

The initial examples of the new guitar that were apparently intended for the Standel company reportedly had plainer-looking headstocks that were straight across the top edge, compared to the "notched M" style later seen on production Mosrites. The generic silhouette on the would-be Standels' headstocks intimates that the instruments were prototypes, with a final decision not having been made on the aesthetics of that part of the guitars.

Preliminary presumptions aside, however, one anecdote indicates that the straight top edge may have happened thanks to a misunderstanding. Rick Hammond was a young (and apparently noncompensated) apprentice at Mosrite in the early 1960s. Decades later, he would recall his involvement with the headstocks of primeval Mosrite/Standel guitars to luthier and collector Bob Shade. Hammond remembered that he had been instructed to cut the top edge of the headstock on the prototypes by Semie, who then left for the day without providing any further cosmetic details. So Hammond played it safe—or so he thought—by cutting a plain, straight top edge on the headstock.

A plain headstock on any Standel prototype would turn out to be a moot point. For whatever (business) reasons, the new-look Standel instruments never attracted serious attention in the marketplace. For that matter, to what extent they were actually marketed is unknown since so few were made. Estimates range from a mere handful to Semie's recollections in one interview that twenty were made; in another interview he placed the number at twenty-five.

Semie recalled that following the failure of the Standel initiative, Mosrite then built another dozen instruments with their own brand name on the headstocks, which now had an M-shaped top edge. Those instruments also had bound bodies. Moseley averred that the first of those instruments was acquired by guitarist Gene Moles, a respected Bakersfield player.

FAST-FORWARD: Almost sixty years later, veteran California guitar repair icon and musician Steve Soest recalled purchasing a black, Mosrite-style guitar in September 1990 that was apparently an early would-be Standel model, as it conformed to the specifications of such "prototypes"—future-classic Mosrite body, plain headstock, erstwhile Guild Vibramute with a plain black "harp" section, and a "mistake plate."

"I'd never seen another one like that," Soest said. "I got it in a store in Santa Barbara. The salesman thought it had been a homemade project—'Somebody thought they were gonna build a Mosrite'—and he kind of laughed about it, and sold it to me for ninety bucks."

After he purchased the instrument, Soest managed to take a photo of Semie Moseley with the guitar. The Mosrite founder examined the instrument in a hotel lobby during a NAMM show in Anaheim, California.

"Semie told me it was one of the earliest examples of what was to become the Joe Maphis model," Soest remembered, "which morphed into the Ventures Model. But since the headstock shape was different from the production models, he surmised it might have been a sample for Standel.

Semie is shown in 1991 with an early-1960s instrument (then owned by Steve Soest) that was probably intended to be a Standel-by-Mosrite guitar. The outline of the "mistake" plate can be seen beside the vibrato.
Courtesy of Steve Soest

"I kept it for years," Soest said of the guitar, "and then it went to a buyer in Japan." Soest also wrote an article about the instrument for a Japanese guitar magazine.

Moles, another Oklahoma transplant, had been on the Bakersfield musical scene for over a decade, having come to local notice in the middle of the century with bands like Johnny Barnett and the Happy-Go-Lucky Boys, as well as Tex Butler's band.

Beginning in the early 1950s, Moles played on Jimmy Thomason's Bakersfield television show on KERO-TV, and also performed on the "Cousin Herb's Trading Post" show on the same channel. He would ultimately forge an ongoing career as a studio musician in Bakersfield and at Capitol Records in Los Angeles, to which he commuted on a frequent basis. Moles played on "Sing a Sad Song," Merle Haggard's first hit recording.

Moles befriended Semie and Andy Moseley, and admired their guitars' thin necks and flat frets.

Moles's sunburst-finished instrument has a set-in neck. The body is bound, but what appears to be binding around the headstock is actually a white paint.

Moles's instrument had what would become standard Mosrite parts and appointments, including a zero fret, tiny fret markers, and an angled neck pickup. It also had an early and perhaps experimental type of vibrato system that doesn't appear to be Guild-based.

The truss rod could be adjusted at the neck juncture; however, the strings had to be loosened (or removed) and the neck/bass pickup also had to be removed for access. The instrument also has a "mistake plate" around its vibrato.

Gene's guitar has an original side jack, but a top jack on the pickguard is also seen. Andy's letter of authentication cited that modification and others: "Gene broke the wood nut and replaced

TANGENT: Andy Moseley composed an authentication letter for Moles's early instrument, as well. It asserted that Moles bought the guitar from Mosrite in 1962.

Gene Moles's primeval Mosrite guitar. Note the stubby vibrato arm.
Willie G. Moseley

This early-1960s snapshot shows Moles (left) with another early Mosrite solidbody (note the knob placement and the wide headstock). It was taken at the Lucky Spot nightclub.
Courtesy of Bryce Martin and Eugene Moles

Early Bakersfield Guitars and the Standel-Assisted Birth of an Icon   15

it with a metal one. He had Semie make a finger rest with his name in it. . . . Gene had a jack added to the pickguard for playing through 2 amps."

Andy's note implies that the two jacks were wired to where each pickup could be played through a separate amplifier.

Soon after the production of the post-Standel, plain-branded new solidbody guitars that reportedly included Gene Moles's guitar, Semie designated his new guitar design as a Joe Maphis signature model. While the new moniker was an asset, the instrument was basically the same as its no-model-name predecessor. It was around this time that Mosrite made adjustments to the body to accommodate the vibrato system—some early-1960s Joe Maphis models had "mistake plates" and some didn't.

Mosrite also introduced a production model Joe Maphis doubleneck instrument, with an octave guitar on top and a standard guitar on the bottom. An advertisement for the signature model showed a single-neck standard guitar and a doubleneck instrument, both of which appeared to be sporting wooden pickup covers, which were experimental or special-order items. Both instruments also had "mistake plates" but did not have white trim of faux binding on their headstocks.

Some Joe Maphis models from this era had headstocks with an offset silhouette; the left-facing side was shorter but the top edge still retained the "M notch." This look was subsequently seen on almost all standard-production Mosrite instruments.

In 1963, Mosrite would experience a sea change regarding its business fortunes. Early that year, Gene Moles was the instigator of a fateful meeting between Semie Moseley and guitarist Nokie Edwards.

Andy Moseley's authentication letter for Gene Moles's early guitar includes a succinct summary: "This guitar is the father of Mosrites [sic] relationship with The Ventures and THE VENTURES MODEL. There is only one and this is it. If you want a piece of Mosrite history and The Ventures history all in one this is it. One of a kind."

Instruments seen in an early Mosrite Joe Maphis model ad.
Courtesy of Steve Brown/vintaxe.com

Guitarist Eugene Moles Jr., Gene's son, had started playing guitar at age five, and had the same point of view about his father's iconic instrument. "It soon became a prototype for the Ventures Model," he said of his father's early Mosrite. "My dad and Nokie Edwards were good buddies."

Left: Early-1960s Mosrite Joe Maphis model with erstwhile-Guild Vibramute. This instrument was crafted after Semie adjusted the installation depth of the vibrato; i.e., there is no "mistake plate."
Courtesy of Creative Photography

Right: Closeup of the early-1960s Joe Maphis model headstock, with a new, asymmetrical silhouette.
Courtesy of Creative Photography

Andy Moseley (left) and an associate work on Joe Maphis solidbody guitars in the Mosrite shop. The modified "harp" area of the bridge/Vibramute is seen on the guitar Andy is holding.
Courtesy of the Andy Moseley Estate

Early Bakersfield Guitars and the Standel-Assisted Birth of an Icon

Ventures Model with side jack and Vibramute, serial number 0037.
Willie G. Moseley

Ventures Model with side jack and Vibramute, serial number 0049.
Courtesy of Michael G. Stewart

3
The Advent of the Ventures

Gene Moles had moved to Tacoma, Washington, in 1960 to work a gig with steel player Dusty Rhodes's band at the Britannia Tavern. While there, he befriended fellow guitarist Nokie Edwards of the Ventures, whose cover version of guitarist Johnny Smith's "Walk, Don't Run" was a smash hit that year.

Nokie had decided that the pace of the Ventures' touring schedule was too hectic, and had stepped back from the road—temporarily, as it turned out—to perform and record in his local area, and to try new musical ideas.

It wasn't surprising that Moles's and Edwards's mutual respect resulted in songwriting collaborations and recording, and they released several songs under the band name of the Marksmen. Nokie would recommit to the Ventures, and Moles would move back to Bakersfield, but the two guitarists stayed in touch. At one point, Nokie had mentioned that he wasn't comfortable with the chunky neck on his Fender Telecaster guitar, and was wondering who might be able to trim it down for faster playing.

Moles ultimately introduced Nokie to Semie Moseley, pronouncing the young Bakersfield luthier to be a capable repairman who could modify the Telecaster's neck. Around the time of the introduction, Nokie had examined Gene's Mosrite guitar, and he encountered a similar instrument when he visited Semie's shop.

Moles recalled to Steve Soest that the visit happened during colder-than-usual weather in Bakersfield, and that Semie's shop was set up in a barn. Semie was burning trash in a barrel for heat.

Nokie himself recounted that after trying out one of Semie's guitars, he bought the instrument for $300 and showed it to the other members of the Ventures. Edwards began to use the guitar in recording sessions and performances. For the record, Semie would recall that the guitar that was in his shop had been originally crafted as one of the would-be Standel guitars, and that he sold it to Edwards for $200.

At the time, the membership of the Ventures consisted of the "classic" lineup of the band—Don Wilson (guitar), Bob Bogle (bass), Nokie Edwards (guitar), and Mel Taylor (drums). The collaboration between Mosrite and the Ventures began with a simple business arrangement, where Nokie would be paid a commission on any guitar order the company received as a referral from his use of the instrument. He would leave the guitar propped up onstage during a break, and numerous audience members would gravitate to the edge of the stage to see what he was playing. The display tactic sold a lot of guitars, according to Edwards.

The rest of the Ventures soon became interested in Mosrite instruments. Boosted by the success of a gold album, *The Ventures Play 'Telstar' and 'The Lonely Bull'* (released in January 1963), the Ventures opted to endorse and invest in Mosrite. An office in Los Angeles was established for worldwide distribution of the brand. Mosrite Distributing Company was located on North Highland Avenue in the Hollywood area, next door to the headquarters of the Ventures International Fan Club. The obvious frontline products of the distribution company would be the Mosrite Ventures Model guitar and bass.

With both the Ventures and Mosrite logos affixed to their headstocks, Ventures Model guitars and basses would debut in 1963 as instruments that were based on the Mosrite Joe Maphis model, with a set neck, a side jack, and a bound body. The guitar's scale was 24.5 inches and the matching one-pickup bass had a scale of 30.25 inches.

From the outset, Ventures Model instruments would feature the smaller, offset headstock profile that was also seen on some earlier Joe Maphis models. The headstock still retained an M-notch profile along its top edge.

Both of the 1963 guitars seen here have additional validation as early instruments, as their string guides/nuts are made of wood. They also have sand-cast tailpieces polished out to make them look like die-cast items.

The Ventures first appeared with Mosrite guitars on the back cover of *(The) Ventures in Space*, released in late January 1964. A citation intoned: "Guitars courtesy of Mosrite Dist. Co.," and the neighboring addresses for the Mosrite Distributing Company and the Ventures International Fan Club were also displayed.

Ventures Model serial #0049, rear view.
Courtesy of Michael G. Stewart

Ventures Model bass, 1963.
Willie G. Moseley

The popular music scene underwent a seismic shift less than a month after *(The) Ventures in Space* debuted, when the Beatles appeared on "The Ed Sullivan Show" in mid-February. The performance, abetted by shrieking teenage females in the audience, was a hormonal epiphany for an untold number of adolescent American males—here was a way to meet girls besides being a jock! You could play in a band!

Other English bands became popular in America almost immediately, and the musical phenomenon quickly became known as the British Invasion. It's no wonder that more than one music poll has cited the Ed Sullivan broadcast as the most significant event in rock music history.

All of a sudden, electric guitar sales in the United States exploded with the force of a nuclear blast. American manufacturers that focused on no-frills and student instruments were unable to keep up with the demand, which would result in a massive influx of imported instruments. Such a business phenomenon would lead to the extinction of the American-made guitar industry's "budget" category within several years.

And the Ventures and Mosrite would be the first "band–brand" association that most aspiring teen-age guitarists would encounter. Sure, other bands played Fenders, Gibsons, or Gretsches, but here was a band of pro musicians that had been around *before* the British Invasion (and even before the surf music phenomenon),

1964 ad for the Mosrite Ventures Model guitar.
Courtesy of Steve Brown/vintaxe.com

and their name and the guitar's brand name were on the headstock of each instrument. The rapid success of the Mosrite Ventures Model instruments compelled Semie to open a bona fide factory at 1500 P Street in downtown Bakersfield.

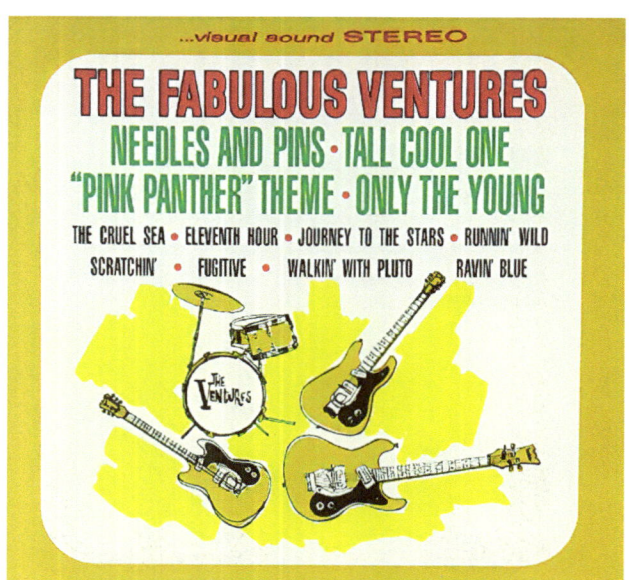

The Ventures' next album, *The Fabulous Ventures*, released in July 1964, had drawings of Mosrite guitars on the front cover. The back cover had a large photo of the Ventures Model guitar, the same contact information for the fan club and Mosrite Distributing, and a statement that intoned: "The Ventures use only the Mōsrite guitar."

The Mosrite Ventures Model guitar and bass underwent several alterations not long after their introduction. The body binding was discontinued and the neck switched to a bolt-on style. Not surprisingly, the uniquely shaped plate through which the four neck bolts were attached would become known as the "peanut plate."

Mosrite Ventures Model instruments sported other distinctive hardware, including toggle switch caps, strap buttons, and UFO-shaped control knobs. The frontline guitar would later have "Mark I" added to its model name, and the bass would have "Mark X" added.

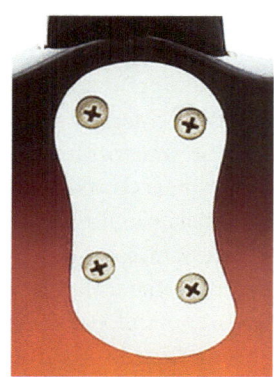

Neck attachment "peanut plate."
Willie G. Moseley

The Ventures with their namesake instruments: Left to right, Bob Bogle, Nokie Edwards, Mel Taylor, Don Wilson.
Public Domain / Wikimedia Commons

The placement of both the Mosrite logo and the Ventures logo on the same headstock looked crowded to some observers, so in mid-1964, a transition to a smaller Ventures logo began.

The Vibramute on the guitar would be refined, and its muting mechanism would be eliminated.

October 1964 saw the Ventures releasing *Walk Don't Run, Vol. 2*. The album was intriguing for more than one reason. The album's more-or-less title track was "Walk, Don't Run, '64," a remake of the band's 1960 monster hit. The song's two-hit-versions-of-the-same-tune-recorded-by-the-same-band status would later become a trivia question on popular music personality Casey Kasem's syndicated radio show.

The front cover of *Walk, Don't Run, Vol. 2* showed Don Wilson's wife, Nancy Bacon, posing in front of the members of the band (who were in a pile behind her, sporting Mosrite instruments with discontinued large Ventures logos on their headstocks).

Mosrite's fortunes continued to mushroom, and Gene Moles was hired in 1964 to work at the factory, in the final inspection section of quality control. Semie had actually been seeking Moles's input regarding guitar innovations before Moles went to work at Mosrite, and Gene had tired of the commute between Bakersfield and the Capitol Records studio in Los Angeles.

Ventures Model Mark I, Pearl White with rare large white logo on natural-finish headstock, 1964. The Ventures toured Japan that year with a matching set of instruments in this color scheme.
Courtesy of Koji Shimada

Ventures Model Mark I, Sunburst with Vibramute.
Courtesy of Heritage Auctions

"I was working in clubs as a musician at night, and worked part-time for Semie during the morning hours," Moles told Steve Soest in 1990. "After production stepped up in 1964, I quit working the clubs, and worked for Semie at the P Street factory full-time. I was doing final inspection and setup."

Moles's duties at Mosrite in the final inspection sector also included making sure the truss rod could be adjusted correctly and ascertaining that the strings would tune properly. He also supervised the building of a small Mosrite guitar for his son, Eugene.

Around the same time, however, business relations between at least one member of the Ventures and Mosrite began to sour. Bob Bogle would sell his portion of Mosrite Distributing to the other three members, but would continue to play Mosrite basses.

The Advent of the Ventures 23

Original-style Ventures II.
Courtesy of Heritage Auctions

4
Glory Days

The years 1965 and 1966 were exciting for Mosrite. As 1965 rolled around, the company had over one hundred employees in the P Street factory.

Because of the 1960s guitar boom and Mosrite's association with the Ventures, it came as no surprise that the company outgrew its facility once again. However, Semie and his associates didn't move too far, migrating from 1500 P Street to 1424 P Street. Around the same time, Mosrite also acquired the Dobro resonator instrument company of Gardena, California, (see chapter 28, "Dobro") and began to gear up to manufacture amplifiers and effects pedals.

And the Ventures Model lineup would also expand beyond a guitar and a bass. One of the more interesting chronologies was that of the Ventures II, later known as the Mark V. Andy Moseley had been thinking that Mosrite should have a budget instrument for student players, to compete with models such as Fender's Musicmaster and Duo-Sonic, as well as Gibson's Melody Maker. In early 1965, he supervised—of his own volition—the design and construction of a fewer-frills model called the Ventures II. Original production examples had a narrower headstock, a slab-like body (no German carve), smaller pickups, and a vibrato that was a different "center-point" mechanism compared with the Vibramute vibrato.

Semie apparently hadn't been informed of his older brother's plans, and quickly put the kibosh on Andy's initiative when he found out about it, declaring that such instruments were too plain—or words to that effect—to merit the Mosrite moniker.

Andy would ultimately get an okay to make a simpler Mosrite model that still had a full-size headstock and a German carve on the top. The pickups were the same size as standard Mosrite pickups but did not have exposed polepieces. The new model would be touted in catalogs as being "smaller and lighter," and it listed for about $100 less than the Mark I. The new model briefly retained the Ventures II designation but would later become known as the Ventures Mark V. However,, while it did attempt to fill a perceived "budget" niche for Mosrite instruments, the revised Ventures II/Mark V cost as much to produce as the Mark I model.

As for leftover flat bodies that were supposed to have been used on original Ventures II guitars, some were used, along with other leftover parts, to make single-pickup guitars that were not catalogued (see chapter 9, "Rarities, One-Offs, and

Ventures II with wide headstock.
Courtesy of Heritage Auctions

25

Mark I Sunburst with Moseley vibrato.
Courtesy of Heritage Auctions

Ventures Mark I Metallic Blue with Moseley vibrato.
Courtesy of Heritage Auctions

Experimental Instruments"). Other flat bodies ended up on unique Mosrite-made steel guitars in 1967 (see chapter 30, "Melobar").

Flat-bodied Mosrite Ventures IIs were rare birds, but in the mid-1970s, one New York guitarist would call attention to that obscure model in a loud, frenetic manner (see chapter 10, "Surname Instruments and the 1970s").

The Ventures Model lineup continued to undergo changes, cosmetically and construction-wise. The name on the base plate of the vibrato was ultimately changed from "Vibramute" to "Moseley," in mid-1965.

Truss rod adjustment would ultimately end up on Ventures Model headstocks under a plate that looked like a planaria (flatworm) head. To others, the plate looked like a spade symbol from a deck of playing cards.

Obviously, many young guitar players took lessons and, in a shrewd move, the Ventures recorded and marketed a series of instructional albums for both guitar and bass. Don Wilson recalled that the tutorial LPs actually charted in 1965.

In 1966, a twelve-string Ventures Model joined the lineup. Perhaps not surprisingly, it was called the Mark XII, and was a rare example of a twelve-string electric guitar that was available with a vibrato as an option.

The sunburst finishes on most mid-1960s Mosrite instruments were quite vibrant. Soon after the Ventures Models were introduced, the company reportedly began using a type of cream mixed in with the base lacquer coat, which gave the body a type of opaque undercoating. Because of this treatment, the sunburst colors on the bodies really stood out.

Custom-order finishes were also available during Mosrite's preeminent decade. Sparkle and glitter finishes were among the most difficult to accomplish, according to Andy Moseley. The flake size on such finishes varied.

In those times, the Ventures usually performed wearing matching outfits, and Wilson, Bogle, and Edwards would usually play matching instruments (red or pearl white). One favorite part of a typical Ventures concert was Mel Taylor's drumstick tattoo on Bogle's bass during "Caravan." It was often compared to another primeval electric bass solo by John Entwistle of the Who on that band's hit single, "My Generation"—but Entwistle performed his solo by himself. Of his interplay with Taylor, Bogle said:

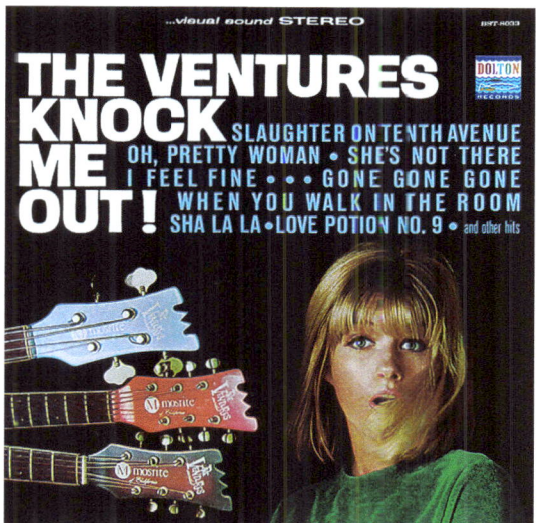

The Ventures *Knock Me Out!* (Released February 1965; note the large headstock logos. These headstocks match instruments being held by the band on the cover of *Walk Don't Run, Vol. 2*, released in October 1964.)

The Ventures' *Christmas Album* (released November 1965; note the small headstock logos)

> I'd move around to his side during his drum solo and he'd keep the beat going on the hi-hat while playing his sticks on the E string of the bass. I'd move my hand up and down the neck at the same time. In fact, we'd break a lot of E strings doing that.
>
> Once when we were on tour, I went into a music store and asked an employee if they sold bass strings *individually*. He said that they did, but when I said "I want to get about a half dozen E strings," he asked why, and I responded "Well, I break them all the time." He couldn't believe it! I had to explain that it was due to the drummer playing on my bass.

A definitive example of the Taylor-Bogle collaboration on "Caravan" is heard on the Ventures' *On Stage*, from 1965.

Ventures Mark X bass, Sky Blue.
Photo by Jim Page / Courtesy of Bob Shade

Ventures Mark X bass, Candy Apple Red.
Courtesy of Heritage Auctions

Ventures Mark V—Sunburst, truss rod cover on headstock.
Courtesy of Heritage Auctions

Ventures Mark V—blue, truss rod cover on headstock.
Courtesy of Heritage Auctions

Ventures Mark I—Candy Apple Red, truss rod cover on headstock.
Courtesy of Heritage Auctions

In 1966, the Ventures Model Mark X bass, having been seen as a one-pickup model in a brochure dated the same year, switched to a two-pickup configuration. Its control layout was similar to Ventures Model guitars.

The bass also acquired unique tuners that Mosrite produced in-house. They were supposed to reference the M-notch silhouette on the top edge of Mosrite headstocks, and were made from die-cast pot metal. Accordingly, they weren't particularly stable, since cheap metal was used. They would ultimately be dubbed as "duckfoot" tuners among guitar collectors.

A design for similar-shaped tuners for guitars didn't advance beyond the experimental stage. The M-notch tabs on the would-be prototypes were made of black vinyl. Two-pickup basses would also be available in custom sparkle finishes.

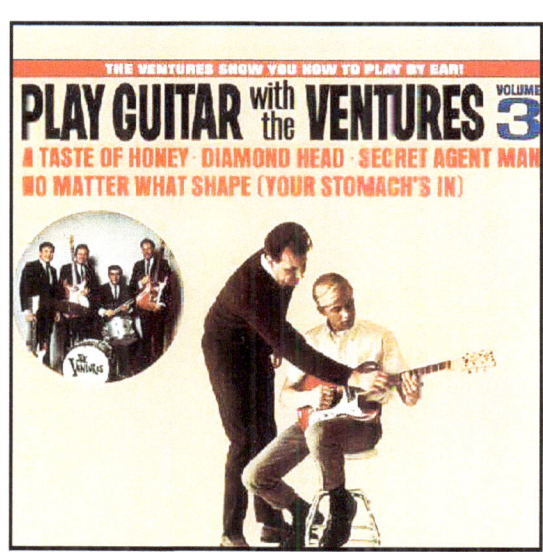
One of several *Play Guitar with the Ventures* albums.

Glory Days 29

Ventures Mark XII, Sunburst.
Willie G. Moseley

Since both a (now-smaller) Ventures logo and a Mosrite logo were still being printed on a Ventures Model headstock, such labeling was somewhat hard to see. Around the time the Mark X bass evolved into a two-pickup model, Mosrite made a series of instruments in pearl white for the Ventures that had a large Mosrite medallion logo and the brand name displayed on the tortoiseshell pickguard.

The uniquely branded instruments apparently weren't limited to two guitars and a bass for the Ventures, however. Mexican musician Mike Laure would be seen with a similar guitar on the cover of more than one of his albums.

The Ventures' godlike status in Japan meant that many of the guitarists in that nation also sought to own and play Mosrite instruments. One of the most famous and enduring Mosrite guitar legends in Japan was Takeshi "Terry" Terauchi, who fronted bands such as the Blue Jeans and the Bunnys.

Obviously, Mosrites would make inroads into America's primarily instrumental surf music craze, since many of that genre's players idolized the Ventures. One surf band, the Avantis, featured two brothers of Native American–Mexican heritage named Pat and Lolly Vasquez. A jacket for a 45-rpm single displayed a mysterious publicity photo that shows members holding what looked like *very* early classic-configuration Mosrites. The one headstock that was visible appeared to have a straight top edge, and there was only a Mosrite logo on it (no Ventures logo). Moreover, two of the three bodies were bound.

The Vasquez siblings ended up as close associates of the Ventures. Following their transition to a vocal-centric group known as the Vegas Brothers, Pat and Lolly appeared on the February 10, 1965, episode of the iconic teen music show *Shindig!* The Ventures were guests on the same show, and loaned Pat and Lolly their Mosrite guitars to use.

In the 1970s, the Vasquez/Vegas brothers would found a band called Redbone that emphasized the members' Native American heritage. That aggregation recorded several hits, including "Come and Get Your Love" and "The Witch Queen of New Orleans."

One unusual aggregation that relied on Mosrites was the public incarnation of the T-Bones. In late 1965, a unique cover version of an instrumental called "No Matter What Shape (Your Stomach's In)" hit the national charts. It was a surprise hit mainly because it happened to be the theme from an Alka-Seltzer television commercial, of all things.

Sparkleburst Mark I with Vibramute, painted by Semie and exhibited at the 1965 NAMM show.
Courtesy of Michael G. Stewart

Sparkle blue Mark X, one pickup.
Willie G. Moseley

Fine-flake red sparkle Mark I with Moseley vibrato.
Willie G. Moseley

Two-pickup Mark X, Sunburst.
Courtesy of Heritage Auctions

Metallic red Mark X bass, two-pickup.
Willie G. Moseley

"No Matter What Shape" had actually been recorded by a group of regular and semianonymous Los Angeles studio musicians, including guitarist Tommy Tedesco and drummer Hal Blaine. "The T-Bones" was simply a moniker of convenience, created to accompany such veteran players' recordings.

Ultimately, a band of younger musicians went on the road as the T-Bones. They were capable players, but none of them had participated in the recording of the hit single they were purveying in concert. Sporting matching outfits and matching Mosrite instruments, the band appeared on television programs such as *Shindig!*, *Where the Action Is*, and even England's *Ready Steady, Go!*

The "touring version" of the T-Bones would eventually record its own album. At one point the lineup included Danny Hamilton, Joe Frank Carollo, and Tommy Reynolds. A few years later, those three musicians would form a successful vocal-oriented band called Hamilton, Joe Frank, and Reynolds.

An unfathomable number of teenage bands—composed almost exclusively of males—would germinate during the "guitar boom" of the mid-1960s, fulfilling the inspiration of the Beatles on "The Ed Sullivan Show." History would chronicle that many of the adolescent "garage bands"—so named because that's where many of them rehearsed—didn't last too long.

That said, even minimally talented players became aware of Mosrite instruments as cool and unique alternatives to Fenders, Gibsons, or more-affordable budget brands. The thin necks and flat frets on Mosrites felt terrific to many players who were just getting started. However, Ventures Model guitars and basses were usually out of most youngsters' price range.

Accordingly, if a guitarist or bassist played a Mosrite, he usually commanded an instant boost in respect from his peers, regardless of said player's talent. Some 1960s garage band veterans would go on to bigger and better gigs. Tommy Shaw of Montgomery, Alabama, had started playing guitar at a very young age, and was aware of the Ventures–Mosrite connection. Shaw remembered:

> Everybody knew "Walk Don't Run" and "Wipeout." I always loved the shape of the Mosrite guitars and studied every little detail. I'd gone from my little nylon string acoustic to a Silvertone single pickup with an amp and speaker built into the case; from there to a Kent solid body electric with a separate Gibson combo amp. There would be a couple more tradeups before I finally got the used Ventures Mosrite I played in my first real band, the Vagabonds.
>
> It was a dream come true; my pride and joy. I was thirteen, and it was my first pro-level guitar. So cool, so elegant. I would walk around the house with it strapped across my shoulder

Mark X bass with large Mosrite logo on pickguard.
Courtesy of Bill Ingalls Jr.

checking myself out in the mirror. I was a teenager and I was in a band and this was my axe! Its thin-profile neck and low frets made it very easy to play.

Shaw would also record for the first time with the Vagabonds, playing his Mosrite on a 45-rpm single of "Poison Ivy" backed with "Comin' Home."

The Alabama youngster became a professional musician after graduating from high school, and would hit the big time in the mid-1970s when he joined a Chicago rock band called Styx. He considers his Mosrite guitar to be "the one that got away."

Like Tommy Shaw, singer-songwriter Marshall Crenshaw developed an interest in Mosrite at a very young age in a Detroit suburb. He recalled:

I saw the *Ventures in Space* album at a friend's house when the album was new. I looked on the back cover and got a real shock. That album cover instantly created a buzz about Mosrite/Ventures guitars, with *me* for sure. I have been into

Takeshi "Terry" Terauchi displays a Ventures Model Mark I on the cover of a 1966 album by his band, the Blue Jeans.

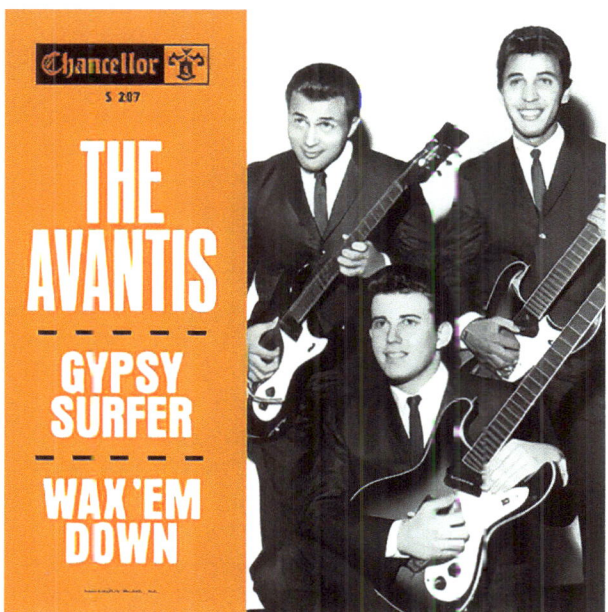

The Avantis—note the (pre-Ventures) Mosrite guitars.

Glory Days 35

guitars since forever; I started sending away for catalogs when I was still in grade school. There were certain players, like Bo Diddley, Johnny and The Hurricanes, and the Ventures, who would almost always be holding instruments on their album covers, which I'd stare at. For my money, *Ventures in Space* is one of the all-time great rock albums, and a real forward step for the band, sonically and musically.

They were definitely the first rock band that had their own brand of guitars—the only band that had the clout to make something happen with a guitar brand in 1963 or 1964, because to a lot of kids back then, they were *synonymous* with guitars. I bought myself a Mark V in 1966—the first guitar that I ever bought with my own money.

Aspiring guitarist Jeff Carlisi of Jacksonville, Florida, also took an interest in Mosrites during the 1960s, albeit for primarily visual reasons. He remembered:

I first saw a Mosrite guitar on the cover of the Ventures' 1965 live album and I was intrigued by it. It didn't look like anything I'd seen before—Gibsons or Fenders or the Harmonys and what have you in the Sears catalog were more familiar. I wasn't moved to the point where I said, "Wow, I've got to have one," but it was interesting, since it was what Nokie and the other guys played.

Carlisi studied the Ventures Model's aesthetics closely, but didn't necessarily think the Ventures Model looked like a flipped-over Fender (a common perception among players). Moreover, he wasn't impressed by what he considered to be a zigzag look on the top edge of the headstock.

"I don't think I got as far as comparing the asymmetry of it [to a Fender]," he said, "and I just couldn't 'wrap my arms' around the headstock design."

What is intriguing about Carlisi's perspective as a teenager is that such attention to form and detail was perhaps a harbinger of his college major, architecture.

"It could've been," he said of such perhaps-subliminal influence. "Maybe it was starting to seep in there, because at that point in time I was starting to sketch and draw. Mostly, it was automobile design—I was really into slot cars back then— but that led me to architecture, as well. But I haven't forgotten how different Mosrites looked."

Carlisi would earn an architecture degree from the Georgia Institute of Technology, but instead of brandishing a T-square and venturing into the world of building design, he became the founding lead guitarist for the platinum-selling Southern rock band 38 Special.

McKinney, Texas, in the Dallas–Fort Worth metropolitan area, begat the Excels, who played Mosrite instruments and garnered a regional hit called "Let's Dance." They would cross paths with the Ventures during their brief existence.

Bakersfield native Chuck Seaton was also an aspiring teenage guitarist in the 1960s, and had noticed Mosrite guitars being played on local television shows.

I was around twelve years old when I first played a Mosrite," he remembered. "My best friend Nicky Bryant lived a few houses down the street; his older brother Billy played lead guitar and happened to be good friends with some of the Ventures. Billy played a Mosrite and would show us stuff he had learned. That was around 1966. I got to play his Mosrite, but had no idea they were made here.

The Ventures and Mosrite guitars would also inspire future luthiers. Roger Fritz, who would later create the Roy Buchanan and Fritz Brothers lines, had been listening to the band since the original version of "Walk, Don't Run" in 1960. He, too, recalled the band–brand association:

The first time I saw that they had their own brand of guitar was *(The) Ventures in Space*. (The guitars) were definitely spacey-looking and I could hear the difference from Fenders immediately—especially on Nokie's guitar.

I was listening to *Walk Don't Run '64* and their *Surfin'* album when I finally found a store that carried Mosrite instruments. This really opened my eyes to Semie's distinct artistry—the German carve and contours on the top, along with the Vibramute. All of the parts were so different and beautiful; they seemed to be three-dimensional. Then I got to play one, and it was like butter. The pickups had a unique tonal warmth and clarity, with a snappy organic sound unlike any other guitar, before or since.

In the mid-1960s, Semie turned down offers from Sears, Roebuck as well as Liberty Records (the Ventures' label) to buy the Mosrite company.

As for dating Mosrite instruments, serial numbers were embossed into the fretboard near the neck–body joint, but the numbers didn't follow any stringent or complicated code system. Moreover, there doesn't appear to have been any factory "paper trail" of registered serial numbers that cite the model and color of the guitar or bass on which the numbers appeared. The company would usually continue its policy of starting a new model's serial numbers with a letter or number, then "0000" for the first example. However, sometimes such "zero" serial numbers would be applied to the first example of more than one production run of a particular model, so redundant numbers were embossed.

Neck pocket date: November 4, 1965.
Courtesy of Olivia's Vintage

Many bodies and bolt-on necks were stamped with dates, so determining the year model is often feasible for many Mosrites made in the 1960s. The neck pocket date and neck butt neck date shown here are on a Ventures Model Mark I finished in Candy Apple Red. The instrument would most likely have been assembled soon after the later date, so this guitar would be cited as an early 1966 example. Some dates have been found stamped on the top surfaces of bodies (under pickguards) or on the undersides of pickguards.

Ironically, many Bakersfield musicians, particularly the purveyors of the stereotypical Bakersfield Sound, didn't cotton to Mosrite instruments. For many guitarists, the feel of the neck and frets didn't allow for a firm grip or string bending. Mosrite's highly wound, single-coil pickups were hot, but such high gain would sometimes cause the guitar to become "microphonic," emitting annoying feedback.

Neck butt date: January 4, 1966.
Courtesy of Olivia's Vintage

There was also the "twang" factor—Mosrite guitars couldn't emulate the sound of a Fender Telecaster. That brand and model eventually won over players like Chuck Seaton, but he still admired Mosrites.

"Roy Nichols played a Tele," Seaton recalled. "I always thought it fit him better, and I've always preferred the Telecaster because it was a better fit for my own style. I loved the way Mosrites looked, and the Ventures made them sound great, but I thought the neck was too thin for me; I like a wider neck with more finger space. But I've always felt both types of guitars fit the Bakersfield Sound."

And in addition to Gene Moles, some Bakersfield-area musicians did indeed line up behind the local guitar brand. Mosrite players included Ronnie Sessions, Al Brumley Jr., and Daryl Stogner (bassist for his father Dave's band).

1964 Joe Maphis doubleneck, Candy Apple Red.
Courtesy of Olivia's Vintage

5
Diversification, Including Soundholes (None, One, or Two)

Given the massive appeal of Mosrite's Ventures Model instruments, the original Joe Maphis six-string solidbody guitar had been discontinued, since the Ventures Model was practically the same instrument, with improvements. The Joe Maphis doubleneck continued to be made. Some headstocks weren't labeled with Maphis's name.

A newly designed series of single-neck Joe Maphis instruments was marketed in 1965. The models had bolt-on necks and bodies that were larger than Mosrite solidbody instruments. The new bodies were hollowed out inside and had no soundholes, but would be described as a semiacoustic style.

"Our first thin hollow body guitar with arched top and magnificent double cutaway shape meets the most exacting demands of the professional, with complete flexibility for the spirited player," the text on the introductory flyer trumpeted. The new configuration came in two variants of six-string guitars. Both featured a "music grade" solid spruce top and walnut body.

The Joe Maphis model I (with a lower-case "m" in its name) had cutaway horns that referenced Mosrite solidbody instruments. Its walnut base was routed out inside to cut down on weight and allow for the installation of electronics. Accordingly, it had top binding only. The model I was the standard Maphis guitar seen in advertisements.

The aforementioned flyer showed Maphis models with bullet-shaped truss rod covers on their headstocks. However, some early new-configuration Maphis models still had necks that had to be adjusted by removing the neck pickup (no truss rod cover on the headstock). "Planaria-head" truss rod covers were later seen on the headstocks of new-style Maphis models.

The rarer and shorter-lived Joe Maphis model II featured elaborately scrolled cutaway horns. Its walnut body was routed all the way through (i.e., it was basically a type of frame). The instrument had a flat walnut back and side rims, as well as front and rear body binding. Tapping on different portions of the back evokes different sounds that indicate there are hollow sections inside.

A short-scale Joe Maphis bass with twenty frets and a scale of 30.25 inches was proffered, as was a twelve-string guitar. Vibratos were standard on six-string guitars and optional on the twelve-string model.

Joe Maphis model I, back.
Courtesy of Heritage Auctions

Joe Maphis model I, bullet truss rod cover.
Courtesy of Heritage Auctions

Joe Maphis model II, truss rod adjusts at neck–body juncture.
Willie G. Moseley

Joe Maphis bass.
Courtesy of Bill Ingalls Jr.

Joe Maphis twelve-string.
Willie G. Moseley

Joe Maphis model II flat back.
Willie G. Moseley

Some examples in the new spruce-walnut configuration of Joe Maphis models didn't have his name on the headstock, either.

Among the artists who would play Maphis models were gospel icons Wendy Bagwell and the Sunliters.

And as perhaps the antithesis of a venerable gospel group, the Count Five was a longhaired, one-hit-wonder band from San Jose, California, whose guitarist, John "Mouse" Michalski, utilized a Maphis model I in performances of their legendary smash, "Psychotic Reaction," which peaked at number five on the *Billboard* hits chart in the summer of 1966.

Around the time the new Maphis series debuted, the doubleneck settled into a standard twelve-string-over-six-string configuration.

One rock musician associated with the Maphis twelve/six doubleneck was guitarist Davie Allan, who, along with his band, the Arrows, specialized in distortion-centric instrumentals that served as soundtrack music for movies released by American International Pictures. One of their more notable tunes was "Blues Theme," from a 1966 movie called *The Wild Angels*, starring Peter Fonda in a pre–*Easy Rider* biker role. The film was directed by Roger Corman.

Joe Maphis doubleneck, sunburst, bullet truss rod covers.
Courtesy of Olivia's Vintage

Joe Maphis doubleneck, Pearl White, planaria-head truss rod covers. Note the differences in the color of the two rosewood fretboards. The six-string headstock has a "Joe Maphis model" designation while the twelve-string headstock does not.
Courtesy of Olivia's Vintage

Joe Maphis doubleneck, Candy Apple Red. There's no Maphis designation on the twelve-string headstock of this example, either.
Willie G. Moseley

Diversification, Including Soundholes (None, One, or Two) 41

Some music fans considered Davie Allan and the Arrows to have been a surf band that got into soundtracks, but that presumption was erroneous, according to the guitarist. "I have never thought it was correct," Allan said of the band's stereotype. "Even during the 'surf era,' most of my recordings had Indian titles, because of 'Apache '65,' our first hit." Perhaps not surprisingly, Allan had become aware of Mosrite because of the Ventures (and the Ventures covered "Apache '65").

The Mosrite endorsement deal for Davie Allan and the Arrows came along in 1967. A publicity photo of the band that also appeared on record covers showed the members sporting we-mean-business countenances and an all-Mosrite stringed instrument lineup, including a Ventures Model bass and a Celebrity CE-I in addition to Allan's doubleneck.

"We were given the doubleneck, a bass, and two six-string guitars," Allan remembered. As for his use of the doubleneck, the guitarist recalled, "It looked so unique and I figured I could have a blast with it and show it off. The highlight was using the doubleneck onstage, and having the fans 'Oooh' and 'Ahhh.'"

Allan didn't use the twelve-string neck all that much, but recalled playing it on a passage of a song called "Cycle-Delic." He also noted that he experienced back problems because of the weight of the instrument.

By 1967, the Joe Maphis model II guitar was gone, and the "Mark" designations had also been applied to the Maphis series (six-string guitar = Mark I, bass = Mark X, twelve-string guitar = Mark XII, doubleneck = Mark XVIII). The entire series would be discontinued in 1968.

Another mid-1960s series was the Combo, which had a body silhouette and a bound top that was similar to the new Joe Maphis lineup, except its body was basswood.

Its body style would also be described as "offset semiacoustic," and exuberant catalog prose would note: "This new concept in design and sound answers the dreams of the finest musicians who have the desire for a combination of the sound of the acoustic and solidbody guitars."

The Combo's differences from the Joe Maphis model I included a standard single f-hole and a flat back with rear binding. The f-hole also had the appearance of being bound, but the "binding" was actually a white molded unit that was plugged into the raw, unbound hole. Some Combo examples were seen with no "binding" in the f-hole.

Once again, a vibrato was standard on the six-string model and optional on the twelve-string. The Combo six-string's bridge and vibrato, which were installed on a single plate, would evolve into being installed as separate items.

Mosrite's Celebrity series was composed of hollowbody instruments in a somewhat traditional configuration. The Celebrity's laminated maple, "archtop symmetric" body had Venetian (rounded) cutaway horns, much like a Gibson ES-335 or a Guild Starfire of the same era, and most examples had the faux, plug-in f-hole binding as found on the Combo series. What's more, the pickups on Celebrity instruments lined up evenly; the neck pickup was not angled.

Former Mosrite employee Ed Sanner recalled that the company bought Celebrity tops, backs, and rims from a furniture manufacturer in the Carolinas, and that such items were "already formed. All we had to do was assemble them."

A few very early, experimental Celebrity models were set-neck instruments with mahogany necks. Their volume and tone controls were installed from underneath the top. However, the series quickly shifted to a bolt-on style with a maple neck.

Top left: CO Mark I, no f-hole binding, Sunburst, earlier variant with full vibrato/bridge assembly.
Courtesy of Heritage Auctions

Top right: CO Mark I, Transparent Cherry Red, separate vibrato and bridge.
Courtesy of Olivia's Vintage

Bottom left: CO Mark X bass, Cherryburst.
Courtesy of Heritage Auctions

Bottom center: CO Mark XII, Sunburst, no f-hole binding.
Courtesy of Heritage Auctions

Bottom right: CO Mark XII Sunburst.
Courtesy of Heritage Auctions

The bolt-on Celebrities would evolve through neck attachment styles that were two-bolt, three-bolt, and four-bolt, in that order. Reportedly, only about ten of the two-bolt models were made.

Ultimately, three different styles of Celebrity instruments would become available in six-string guitar, bass, and twelve-string guitar models, as documented in a 1967 catalog promoting the upcoming 1968 Mosrite line. All three styles featured a blob-shaped pickguard, as well as a top-mounted control plate shaped like a painter's palette.

Since the Celebrity body had an arched top, the standard plate on which the bridge and vibrato were installed was unusable. The bridge and vibrato were mounted onto the top of Celebrity bodies as two separate units.

Shown on a separate catalog page, the top-of-the-line CE-I model had a body depth of 2.75 inches, neck binding, multiple body binding front and rear, a wider early Mosrite-style headstock profile, "deluxe chrome" tuners, and standard pickups with polepieces. As was the case on other Mosrites, a vibrato was standard on the six-string guitar and optional on the twelve-string. Glen Campbell used a Celebrity CE-I in studio recordings.

Ca. 1965 early Celebrity set-neck guitar, front and back.
Willie G. Moseley

Early two-bolt Celebrity, front and back. Note that the through-the-top controls have been installed in a slightly different configuration compared to the early set-neck Celebrity.
Courtesy of Heritage Auctions

CE-1, as seen in Mosrite's 1967 catalog featuring the 1968 line.
Courtesy of Steve Brown/vintaxe.com

CE-II instruments were essentially the same as the CE-I, except for a thinline body depth of 1.875 inches and a smaller offset headstock silhouette.

CE-III models were no-frills, budget-style instruments with the same body depth as CE-IIs. The neck was unbound, and the body edges had single-layer binding. Tuners had white plastic buttons, and pickups did not have polepieces. The CE-III six-string had a perhaps-expected aberration—a vibrato was optional on the model instead of standard. A trapeze-shaped tailpiece would be used on a nonvibrato example.

Moreover, the CE-III Mark X bass was the only production bass in the entire Mosrite line with a guitar-like 24.5-inch scale.

Mosrite would manufacture acoustic instruments, but, like Fender, was saddled with the stereotype of being a company that made electric solidbody guitars. The acoustics made in Bakersfield were somewhat of a supplemental or ancillary line. "We bought a Martin guitar," Ed Sanner recalled. "I had to get a band saw and cut it in two to see what was inside of it."

Left: CE-II guitar, Sunburst.
Courtesy of Heritage Auctions

Right: CE-II bass, Sunburst.
Courtesy of Heritage Auctions

Left: CE-III, Sunburst, standard tailpiece.
Courtesy of Heritage Auctions

Right: CE-III twelve-string Transparent Cherry Red.
Courtesy of Heritage Auctions

CE-III bass—guitar scale. Sunburst.
Courtesy of the Chicago Music Exchange

Diversification, Including Soundholes (None, One, or Two) 45

ACOUSTIC FLAT-TOP GUITARS

Courtesy of Steve Brown/vintaxe.com

Courtesy of Steve Brown/vintaxe.com

The first acoustic Mosrite guitar was the Serenade, a somewhat-petite instrument that had a spruce top and maple back and rims. It was offered in natural, transparent sunburst or a transparent cherry red finish for a list price of $198. The Serenade looked clean but wasn't sonically impressive. Sanner opined that the model was "too small to have a good sound."

An early brochure page advertising the Serenade featured a Ventures logo on the catalog page opposite the photo of the model, even though the Serenade didn't have anything to do with the band. However, the top of the page noted the Mōsrite Distributing Company, which was indeed owned by the Ventures at the time.

Later Mosrite acoustic models included the Balladere I and Balladere II.

The Balladere I was inspired by the Serenade, as its body depth was only 3.25 inches. While it still had a spruce top like the Serenade, its back and sides were made of mahogany.

A larger, "dreadnought"-size instrument, the Balladere II had a spruce top and rosewood back and sides. Its body depth was five inches. Research indicates that this model apparently never advanced beyond the prototype stage.

A late 1967 catalog page promoting the Balladeres was intriguing for more than one visual reason. For one thing, the images of the guitars were printed backward. An initial glance might have made observers think they were left-handed instruments, but the Mosrite logos on the headstocks were reversed.

Moreover, a close inspection of the spruce tops revealed that their graining had a mirror-image look from the center line. Such a technique with laminated woods is called "bookmatching" and is also found in the furniture manufacturing industry, on items such as dining room tables and occasional tables.

6
Beyond Stringed Instruments

As its success in the marketplace boomed, Mosrite would, perhaps not unexpectedly, get into the accessory market for electric guitars. Such items included picks, strings, cords, microphones, and guitar straps.

The company also distributed bumper stickers to publicize their wares, and offered "Authorized Dealer" window signs for their accounts.

Another interesting expansion of Semie's operations, Mosrite Records, opened for business in the mid-1960s. A jacket for one Mosrite Records 45 rpm record proclaimed Bakersfield to be the "Country Music Capital of the West."

The Mosrite Records roster included Joe and Rose Lee Maphis, local singers and guitarists Ronnie Sessions and Al Brumley Jr., as well as Tommy Duncan, former vocalist for Bob Wills and His Texas Playboys. Among Sessions's recordings on the Mosrite label was a 1966 single titled "Big O," a tribute to Buck Owens.

However, Mosrite Records' primary historical legacy is that the label marketed the first recordings by a teenage singer and multiinstrumentalist from Oceanside, California, named Barbara Mandrell. Her father, Irby, owned a music store and was an authorized Mosrite dealer.

Willie G. Moseley

Gene Moles recorded at least one single for Mosrite Records and played guitar on many of the recordings that were marketed by the company. He'd been offered an instrumental album deal with Capitol Records, but had turned it down because he liked Semie. However, Moles never recorded his own album on the Bakersfield-based label.

Not surprisingly, Semie himself would record gospel songs for Mosrite Records. Andy Moseley would become so imbued with the recording business that he would remain in that field for decades.

It almost goes without saying that Mosrite, coordinating with the Ventures, would attempt to get into the amplifier business. The initial research and development had been done by Howard Dumble and Ed Sanner. The latter employee was delighted to get into the electronics facet of the musical instrument manufacturing business.

A California native, Sanner had exhibited a talent for electronics work at a very young age, and recalled meeting Semie in the mid-1950s "when he was making the doublenecks for Joe Maphis and Larry Collins. He was out in the San Fernando

Gene Moles's publicity photo for Mosrite Records.
Courtesy of Eugene Moles

Valley, and we were introduced by [El Monte luthier] Dick Allen. Dick wanted to show Semie the pickguard he'd put on my guitar. The first pickguard he made was patterned after Semie's design, and [Allen] was proud of it."

After completing military service with the Air Force, Sanner was trying to find a decent job in the electronics field in the greater Los Angeles area, and was playing guitar in clubs at night. He recalled:

> I was working in El Monte and ran into some musicians from Bakersfield; they said that Mosrite was looking for a guy to build amps for them. I drove up to Bakersfield and talked with Semie and Andy. I hadn't seen Semie since Dick Allen introduced me to him, but for some reason he remembered me.
>
> I started at the 1424 P Street factory; [Mosrite] had moved out of the 1500 P Street factory because it wasn't big enough. I was working under Bill Gruggett, wet-sanding guitars. It seemed like forever, but it was only for a couple of weeks. Then they moved me up to Assembly, putting necks on bodies.

Ed Sanner, playing bass, backs up Semie at Mosrite's 1966 company Christmas party.
Courtesy of the Andy Moseley Estate

Sanner then spent some time in the Dobro division of Mosrite soon after the company acquired the resonator line, and was later put in charge of pickup assembly, which is where he was working when he was assigned an additional task of developing amplifiers.

Mosrite's move into the amplifier field seemed like an appropriate direction for growth, and it was the reverse of what Standel's tack had been at the beginning of the 1960s—Standel was an amplifier company that wanted to get into the guitar business, while Mosrite was a guitar manufacturer that wanted to get into the amplifier business.

"The Ventures wanted an amplifier; Semie wanted an amplifier," Sanner said. "I wanted to go with solid state, but it was very new at the time. I was working on those designs, but I knew tubes because I'd learned about those in high school. I came up with some prototypes."

Not surprisingly, Gene Moles would field-test some of the experimental designs. Sanner detailed:

> Gene needed a lot of treble for his picking and a lot of transistor amps didn't have that. My thoughts about amplifiers as a musician—not a great one, but I *did* work—included an admiration of Bob Crooks' ideas with Stancel amplifiers—compact, easy to carry, and powerful. [Mosrite representatives] took some of my prototypes to some stores in Hollywood, but the response was "It's got tubes and it's too small." This was before transistors got a bad name.

Sanner's amplifier research would continue.

Interestingly, Mosrite's most iconic nonstringed item (and perhaps Sanner's crowning achievement) would be the FUZZrite, a distortion device designed by Sanner that would become an item prized by guitar collectors for its legendary sound. At the time of Sanner's initial research and development, Gibson's popular Maestro fuzztone had a perceived monopoly on the American market. For many players, amateur and professional, a signature song and first (sonic) encounter with a fuzztone had been the Rolling Stones' "(I Can't Get No) Satisfaction."

Sanner recalled his work on the innovative FUZZrite with an obvious sense of pride:

> Leo LeBlanc was a friend who played steel guitar with a Maestro fuzztone. He got a lot of good effects out of his steel guitar—not just distortion, but also simulating a violin with sustain. He didn't like two or three things about it, including how the notes on the high strings would decay quickly. He told me, "Since you work for Semie, why don't you try to come up with something?" This happened when I was trying to build amps part-time and was still working on the production line.

(LeBlanc had also recorded for Mosrite Records.)

> I looked at the Gibson Maestro and saw that it had three germanium transistors. I put two transistors together, did some experimenting, adjusted the bias to where it would distort fairly "clean," and came up with a different design. I built it to have a lot more sustain, and a lot of treble because the high strings are weak. The Maestro is more mellow; not as bright.
>
> I gave it to Leo to try, and I gave one to Gene Moles. Everybody was raving about them. We made 250 on the first run, with germanium transistors, but they were noisy and had what you'd call "that transistor sound"; no overtones. I had been using silicon transistors in my amplifier designs, which was kind of a new thing. I wondered how those would do in a fuzz tone, so I made some with a streamlined design. It improved the sustain, and the silicon transistors were all the same; they sounded consistent so I knew this was the way to go.

It was also Sanner's idea to call the new device the FUZZrite. The device's two control knobs were the same derby hat-shaped items as found on Mosrite guitars of that era. On the FUZZrite, the knobs controlled depth and volume. The depth circuit actually worked between two levels of distortion.

"I had two transistors in there," Sanner explained, "and that control varied between overdriving with one stage or two."

Pro musicians were immediately impressed by the new Mosrite gizmo. Davie Allan had been using a Gibson Maestro device on his fuzz-drenched recordings with the Arrows, but quickly switched to a FUZZrite. "What had gotten me into distortion was Marty Robbins's 'Don't Worry' and 'Zip-A-Dee Doo-Dah' by Bob B. Soxx and the Blue Jeans," Allan recounted. "And I was using the same fuzz box as heard on 'Satisfaction,' a Gibson Maestro. I borrowed a FUZZrite and used it on a few of the *Wild Angels* tracks, including 'Blues Theme.' The FUZZrite was nastier, and had a ton more sustain."

As for a favorite track he recorded using a FUZZrite, Allan remembered, "The one that sticks out—and I wish I had written it—was 'Devil's Angels.'"

FUZZrite.
Courtesy of Heritage Auctions

Iron Butterfly, a band founded in San Diego, would figure into the FUZZrite's success in a huge way. Their debut album, *Heavy*, had been recorded in the summer of 1967 and was released in January 1968. The introduction of the final track, an instrumental titled "Iron Butterfly Theme," kicked off with a FUZZrite-driven, reverb-soaked power chord from guitarist Danny Weis that crashed into a listener's ears like a sonic tsunami, immediately validating the song as a masterpiece of psychedelic rock. The lead guitar passages by Weis on "Iron Butterfly Theme" were also engorged with thick-yet-bright distortion, offering a richer sound than a Gibson Maestro fuzztone. Weis and bassist Jerry Penrod were shown with Mosrite instruments in the cover artwork, which appeared to have been inspired by the classic Percy Bysshe Shelley poem "Ozymandias."

By the time the band's sophomore album was released in June, Weis and Penrod had been replaced by Eric Brann and Lee Dorman, respectively. However, *In-A-Gadda-Da-Vida* would call attention to the Mosrite FUZZrite in an even bigger manner, as the album hit number four on the *Billboard* record chart. Like their predecessors, Brann and Dorman were seen with Mosrite instruments on the front cover, which was a concert image, complete with a psychedelic colored oil light show behind the band.

In-A-Gadda-Da-Vida's title track was a side-long, "everybody-gets-a-solo" presentation that was stereotypical for the times, and the FUZZrite's sonic capabilities were also heard on the song's memorable anchor riff. The album would eventually be certified as hitting the quadruple-platinum mark in sales.

Jimi Hendrix was reported to have used a FUZZrite on "Spanish Castle Magic" on his *Electric Ladyland* album, released in 1968. A FUZZrite even figured into one artist's legendary *electric bass* solos during that musical era. Tim Bogert, bassist for progressive rock pioneers the Vanilla

Fudge, had been looking for ways to expand the sonic capabilities of his instrument. His quest had included trying out primeval electronic devices operated by footswitches.

"I finally got a great old Mosrite fuzz that worked just fine with the equipment I had back then," Bogert recalled in a 1993 interview. "That fuzztone was heard on record; it's the one that's on the introduction and my bass solo on 'Break Song,' the side-long live cut on the *Near The Beginning* album."

Debuting in early 1969, *Near the Beginning* was the fourth album by the Fudge, and "Break Song" was another stereotypical side-long effort replete with individual solo segments. It was recorded live at the Shrine Auditorium in Los Angeles.

The song, which clocked in at 23:27, was introduced by Carmine Appice's pounding drums and a howling, FUZZrite-boosted bass string bend by Bogert. When Bogert's solo segment came along, he plunked some interesting multistring riffs, then noodled around with some jazz-like muted picking before kicking in the FUZZrite, whereupon the solo exploded in a firestorm of distortion. Bogert's innovative bends exploited the cacophony in an adroit manner, and over fifty years after it was recorded, it's still a landmark performance.

The FUZZrite was a huge success for Mosrite. "We made a thousand FUZZrites a month," said Sanner. "Manny's (Music) in New York was buying one hundred or more a month on their own."

7
The Gospel According to Semie

In spite of Mosrite's success as a secular guitar brand, Semie yearned to stay active within the gospel music field as a singer, player, and songwriter. Reportedly, he occasionally gave away guitars he'd crafted to churches, gospel musicians, and preachers.

So it wasn't particularly a revelation when Moseley ultimately decided to market a tangential line branded as Gospel instruments, which were slightly different variants of more than one Mosrite model. The new brand was featured in the same 1967 Mosrite catalog that hyped the company's 1968 line. The Gospel guitar that was shown was a six-string model that looked a lot like Mosrite's Celebrity CE-1.

In addition to multiple binding on a bookmatched top and single-bound f-holes, the Gospel variant had step-up features that included "an unusually outstanding natural finish with a golden brown tinted headpiece," according to the catalog. While a Mosrite Celebrity model had master volume and tone controls (two knobs), the Gospel guitar had separate volume and tone controls for each pickup (four knobs).

A Gospel twelve-string guitar and short-scale bass were also listed on the same catalog page (but not shown).

The early Gospel-branded guitar on display here has cosmetics, electronics, and a body style that are even more like a Mosrite CE-I, with plainer binding, and master volume and tone knobs. The instrument is finished in metallic blue, which has turned a teal color because of yellowing. It's been proclaimed to be an early Gospel prototype and, while it does have an apparently low serial number (#GA009), it appears that the only differences between it and a Mosrite CE-1 Mark 1 are an alternate headstock silhouette (top edge) and decal, as well as Japanese tuners.

Among the potential explanations for such an instrument is that it may have been crafted before the specifications of the Gospel variant were finalized, or perhaps it was built to use up parts in the Bakersfield factory.

Gospel brand instruments that conformed to catalog specifications did indeed end up with more than one gospel band. A guitar and bass appeared on the front cover of Happy Goodman Family's 1968 album *Portrait of Excitement*. The cover of an LP by the Gospel III with Alvis Barnett showed the bass player with a Gospel Mark X Model 601 bass (the two electric guitars on the front cover were Mosrite solidbody instruments).

Gospel Mark I Model 600 guitar, as seen in Mosrite's catalog for the 1968 line.
Courtesy of Steve Brown/vintaxe.com

Gospel-branded CE-1 Mark 1, blue finish.
Willie G. Moseley

Gospel guitar, owned and played by Kurt Cobain, front and rear view.
Courtesy of Heritage Auctions

Mosrite also put out a few Gospel-branded solidbody guitars in the late 1960s. Such instruments were based on the company's Mark V instrument, and may have also been marketed to use up parts. Differences between the Gospel model and its Mosrite sibling included Japanese tuners on the Gospel model as well as no "peanut"-shaped neck plate.

And one late 1960s Gospel solidbody is an iconic instrument that was played by Nirvana's Kurt Cobain (1967–1994). Shown on page 53, it's strung left-handed (Cobain was a southpaw), and is missing its truss rod cover and vibrato arm.

Cobain's Gospel guitar would fetch a phenomenal amount at auction on more than one occasion. "It first sold for $117,000 in 2004, then re-auctioned in 2006," said veteran memorabilia auction specialist and appraiser Mike Gutierrez. "Keep in mind that the sale price of $131,450 was based strictly on celebrity value."

The inherent "specialty" vibe surrounding Gospel-branded instruments meant that many, if not most of them, had unique and often one-of-a-kind attributes. Accordingly, such guitars and basses were rarer than similar Mosrite models. The same made-in-the-same-facility scenario regarding Mosrites and Gospels would be ongoing in future decades.

1967 Gospel solidbody.
Courtesy of Michael G. Stewart

Rear of headstock showing Japanese tuners.
Courtesy of Michael G. Stewart

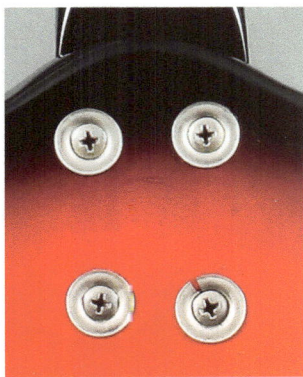

Neck–body joint showing bolts and ferrules.
Courtesy of Michael G. Stewart

8
Storm Clouds over P Street

During a business relationship of approximately half a decade, the Ventures had become increasingly alienated in their dealings with Mosrite (and with Semie in particular). By 1967, the bloom was off the rose to the point that the band would part ways with the Bakersfield guitar company in that annum. Band members would continue to use certain Mosrite guitars and basses (without the Ventures logo on the headstocks) but also relied on other brands and models of instruments (primarily Fenders).

In the nostalgia section of many fans' minds, however, the Ventures would be always be playing Mosrites. Bob Bogle acknowledged the permanent band-brand fixation in 1997, noting, "A lot of details about the Mosrite years are a bit vague, because we only used those for about five years. . . . [T]hat brand will probably follow us around for the rest of our lives. That happened during a very dynamic part of our career, and we can't seem to shake off the connection."

Around the time the Ventures and Mosrite split, however, the band signed up with an amplifier manufacturer in Minnesota. The amplifier brand name was Award, but the Ventures compensated Semie with a one-time payment to allow the Mosrite name to be placed on the amplifier as well (as was the Ventures logo).

Ed Sanner had been scrambling to develop amplifiers in Bakersfield, and Mosrite began manufacturing its own solid-state line shortly after the Minnesota line debuted. Some Mosrite amplifiers had FUZZrite distortion circuits built into them.

Alleged quality issues and distribution problems sank the Ventures-Award collaboration in fairly short order.

At one point, Semie traveled to Puerto Rico to examine the possibility of opening a factory. The concept was not unlike the maquiladoras that would evolve in future years along the US–Mexico border. Parts were to be manufactured in Puerto Rico, and would be assembled in the United States. The idea never came to fruition, and Semie recalled that soon after his sojourn in the Caribbean, his company got into financial trouble.

As for the Mosrite guitar line, the frontline solidbody series became known as the Mark series following the split with the Ventures. The lineup had the same I, V, X, and XII model numbering system.

Gene Moles traded in his early solidbody guitar for a new Mark I instrument. Andy Moseley would end up with the earlier guitar, which would become known as the historically important "Moles Mosrite."

One of the post-Ventures Mosrite solidbody guitars that was most often seen was a sunburst Mark XII in the hands of Glen Campbell. It was displayed on the front cover of his 1967 album *Gentle On My Mind* and in publicity photos as well.

Another sunburst Mark XII would later show up onstage in the hands of Ian Hunter, singer for British hard rock band Mott the Hoople. Following the dissolution of the

This label inside a Balladere I guitar made for Tom Smothers avers that the Mosrite company was trying to distribute their products direct from the factory to retailers.
Courtesy of Bob Shade

Ventures' Mosrite Distributing Company in Hollywood, Semie and his associates tried to distribute the line themselves as Mosrite Sales, but inexperience soon extinguished that effort.

A subsequent 1968 distribution deal with the Thomas Organ company, which also distributed Vox instruments, quickly failed, sending Mosrite into an even more perilous tailspin.

In spite of Mosrite's growing travails, the brand was still a factor in the guitar marketplace, particularly in the rock and gospel genres. Two notable Mosrite instruments were seen and heard in the late 1960s as part of the fabled "Detroit rock and roll" phenomenon. Of all the popular and diverse genres that germinated, blossomed, and flourished—if only briefly—during the late 1960s and early 1970s, the sound being generated in the Michigan cities of Detroit and Ann Arbor was arguably the loudest. The scene included bands such as the Stooges, the Amboy Dukes (featuring guitarist Ted Nugent), the Rationals, and SRC, among others.

And the standard bearer for the "Detroit sound" was a quintet of would-be revolutionaries known as the MC5, consisting of Wayne Kramer (guitar), Fred "Sonic" Smith (guitar), Rob Tyner (vocals), Michael Davis (bass), and Dennis "Machine Gun" Thompson (drums). Originally known as the Motor City Five, the band hooked up with radical activist John Sinclair and his White Panther Party, which espoused a credo that advocated "rock and roll, dope, and ****ing in the streets," according to its manifesto. The MC5 would be the only rock band to perform at the infamous 1968 protests during the Democratic Party's political convention in Chicago.

And in an audacious and apparently unprecedented move, the MC5's debut album, *Kick Out the Jams* (Elektra), was recorded live at the Grande Ballroom in Detroit on October 30 and 31 of the same annum ("the Zenta New Year," according to the liner notes). Released in February 1969, the album is arguably the most brutal live performance ever marketed. The album credits cited Fred "Sonic" Smith as playing a Mosrite guitar, and an image of him with a Pearl White Ventures Model Mark I solidbody was part of the album's front cover collage.

Smith was also seen playing at least one other Mosrite guitar during the heyday of the MC5. The type of music the band generated was the polar opposite of the Ventures' melodic excursions—howling feedback, abetted at times by a guitar vibrato arm, was an integral part of the Five's signature sound, so in this particular sonic scenario, any microphonic tendency of Mosrite's hot single-coil pickups was put to appropriate use.

Another frontline band in the same genre was the Stooges, from Ann Arbor. While their visual and musical focal point was a manic singer named Iggy, founding bass player Dave Alexander pounded out the low end portion of the Stooges' raucous music on a single-pickup metallic blue Ventures Model Mark X bass.

Mosrite's financial problems continued to increase, and government revenue officials got involved. Several company higher-ups began to see the handwriting on the wall regarding the company's diminishing chances for survival. "Kenny Gilstrap was the plant manager, and was the first to kind of alert the rest of the people," said Ed Sanner. "In the last couple of months, the bookkeeper would hand us our checks, and would tell us to cash them right then, because there wasn't enough money to cover the payroll."

Sanner recalled that he and several other Mosrite management employees resigned from Mosrite in the first week of December, giving the company a four-week notice. They would go to work for another local company called Rosac (see chapter 30, "Melobar"). The end of Mosrite's golden age came on Valentine's Day of 1969, when employees reportedly arrived at the factory to find the doors padlocked.

"I thought that the only maker of guitars in California that came up to the quality of Fender instruments was Semie Moseley's Mosrite company," longtime Fender employee and musician Bill Carson said in his 1998 autobiography. "But they weren't a competitor when it came to volume [of instruments produced], and they didn't offer any budget instruments. And while Semie Moseley was a pretty good builder, I don't think he was much of a businessman."

"Mosrite didn't move with the times to get the players what they wanted," Eugene Moles opined. However, despite closure of the P Street factory, the saga of Mosrite instruments (and more innovations from Semie Moseley) would be ongoing in Bakersfield and elsewhere.

"Flame" guitar prototype, front and detail view (refinished candy blue).
Courtesy of Michael G. Stewart

9
Rarities, One-Offs, and Experimental Instruments

Any time a guitar is handcrafted to the custom-ordered specifications of a player or collector, said instrument is indeed a rare—but not necessarily "collectible"—bird. Moreover, prototype guitars, by their very definition, are often one-of-a-kind instruments, but more than one prototype or experimental instrument may be created until the builder gets it right—or maybe the builder gives up.

On the other hand, some larger manufacturers have been known to use up leftover bodies, necks, and other items in the creation of what have sometimes been sarcastically but accurately dubbed as "floor sweep" guitars. While such instruments may also be "rare," to what extent they, too, are "collectible" has been an ongoing debate for decades.

During the golden age of Mosrite, the company built its share of prototypes, custom-made guitars, and instruments that were assembled to deplete inventories of surplus parts. Among the earliest unique Mosrites were two instruments—one prototype, one custom-made—that came to be known as the "flame" guitars.

Rick Hammond, who had earlier worked on the headstocks of Semie's would-be Standel prototypes, reportedly approached the Mosrite founder regarding the design of a solidbody guitar that Hammond thought would be a great instrument for rock musicians (or perhaps even the Ventures)—the instrument had a body silhouette that resembled flames. Semie wasn't enthusiastic about the design, but he crafted a one-pickup, set-neck prototype with Hammond assisting. The guitar also had handmade aluminum hardware, and it sported a Cherryburst finish.

Hammond set about pitching the model to noted players in California, including surf guitarist Dave Myers, who had been in a band called the Surf-Tones. That aggregation was noted for an iconic surf instrumental called "Church Key," and had changed its name to the Disciples.

Myers ordered a Mosrite "flame" guitar with two pickups and four knobs. It appears that those were the only two guitars made in that configuration. Myers would later superimpose an image of his guitar on his band's business card.

Both instruments had unusual fretboards with dot markers that were larger than normal for Mosrite. The single-pickup prototype had a twenty-four fret, double-octave neck; Myers's guitar had a standard twenty-two frets. The headstock had a six-on-a-side configuration, with the individual tuning keys attached in a slightly curved pattern, as seen on some of the earliest instruments that were handcrafted by Semie in the 1950s. The prototype had a side jack that was standard for the times, while the Myers two-pickup guitar had a top-mounted jack.

Dave Myers and the Disciples business card.
Courtesy of Bob Shade

The one-pickup prototype was eventually acquired by luthier and collector Bob Shade, who noted that it was "all original but not in great condition. One of the 'flames' had a chunk out of it, and the guitar needed a lot of TLC."

Shade's close examination of the guitar revealed another fretboard incongruity. "If you look closely," he said, "you can see the end of the fingerboard was added on; it's a different shade of rosewood. I am not clear if it was an afterthought or if Semie did not have a piece of rosewood that long, but it is as original as it gets."

Hammond recalled (to Shade) that Semie had thought the "flame" body's silhouette resembled cresting surf waves instead of fire. The prototype guitar was refinished in candy blue by Shade, who noted that Myers informed him that he had had his two-pickup guitar refinished in blue, as well.

An apparently singular six-string bass was crafted in 1963. Six-string basses of that era were true "bass guitars" (strings tuned an octave below standard guitar tuning) and such instruments were being marketed by companies such as Fender (Bass VI) and Gibson (EB-6).

The Mosrite one-off had a then-standard guitar body with binding and a side jack. It was either an experimental instrument or a special order.

Doubleneck instruments, by their very design, lend themselves to all sorts of mix-and-match opportunities. In the case of Mosrite, some unauthorized doubleneck instruments have been built with "post-bankruptcy auction" bodies, necks and parts (see chapter 10), and perhaps even with parts from other companies.

One legitimate custom-made experimental Joe Maphis–style doubleneck that was made in the 1960s had a unique twelve-string octave guitar installed on top and a standard guitar on the bottom.

Another early custom-made doubleneck, built for Bob Haggard of the Bill Stewart Trio, had another unusual layout. A bass was on the lower portion, and a standard six-string guitar was the upper instrument. It had a stereo output capability, so it could be played through a guitar amplifier and a bass amplifier at the same time, according to Haggard.

As was the case with other guitar manufacturers, some leftover bodies and other parts were used to make one-pickup "floor sweep" guitars (and some of the headstocks had a wider, earlier-style silhouette).

In 1962, the Gibson guitar company debuted an electric bass with built-in fuzztone circuitry. The EB-0F was around for about three years, and preceded the marketing of the Gibson Maestro footswitch-controlled fuzztone.

So it wasn't much of a surprise that Mosrite built at least one similar instrument—albeit a guitar—around the time that the Ed Sanner–developed FUZZrite was announced. The experimental guitar had four knobs. One set controlled the guitar's standard master volume and tone potentiometers, while the other set controlled the volume and depth of the

Six-string bass, 1963.
Courtesy of Bob Shade

1960s doubleneck with twelve-string octave guitar. Note the "Custom" designation on the octave guitar's headstock.
Willie G. Moseley

Single-pickup "floor sweep" guitar.
Courtesy of Gary Dick

distortion device circuitry, which was turned on and off with a slider switch installed on the pickguard.

Other indications that this guitar wasn't a production item include a flat body, a nonstandard light blue finish, the unusual display of a white logo on a natural-finish headstock, and no Ventures logo.

Some Mosrite acoustic guitars were also seen in some rare and unusual configurations during the 1960s. In addition to being a solo artist, local singer and guitarist Al Brumley Jr. also performed in Jimmy Thomason's television band on KERO-TV. Thomason's lineup varied, and at times included Gene Moles as well as bassist Mark Shannon and longtime area drummer Jim Phillips.

Al Brumley Jr., left, sports his unique Mosrite acoustic guitar with a deeper rim, wide headstock and double pickguards, along with other band members on "The Jimmy Thomason Show." Also shown are, from left, Thomason, Jim Phillips, and Gene Moles.
Courtesy of Jim Doty/KERO-TV

Mark I–style guitar with built-in FUZZrite.
Willie G. Moseley

Rarities, One-Offs, and Experimental Instruments

Brumley's Mosrite acoustic guitar was based on a Serenade/Balladere I, but the instrument had a deeper rim than the 3.25 inches of a standard model Serenade/Balladere I. The instrument also had a wider, earlier-style headstock and double pickguards. While the headstock and pickguard differences were strictly cosmetic, one wonders what kind of sound might have been evoked from this deeper-bodied variant.

Later in the decade, two slightly customized Serenade/Balladere I–style guitars were presented to television stars Glen Campbell and Tom Smothers. The only noticeable differences were original-style symmetrical headstocks and the artists' initials inlaid on the twelfth fret of each neck. Campbell's guitar had a natural finish; Smothers's instrument was sunburst.

Among the most unique and (visually) memorable instruments from Mosrite's golden era was a series of late-1960s instruments with silhouettes that were supposed to look like surfboards. They were designed with a wood, oval-shaped frame surrounding a completely functional electric stringed instrument.

Glen Campbell displayed his natural-finish Mosrite acoustic guitar on this sheet music cover.
Courtesy of Bob Shade

The "surfboard" instruments were actually made in the Los Angeles area. Steve Soest cited the builders as John Gregory and Al Hartel. "John Gregory was the sales and technical rep for Binks spray equipment, which was used at the Bakersfield Mosrite factory," Soest averred. "Semie supplied all the [guitar] parts to him."

Gregory resided south of Los Angeles, and had reportedly boasted about his own abilities as a luthier. Semie took Gregory up on such braggadocio and challenged him to build better instruments. Moseley supplied the rep with wood and metal parts as well as electronics.

Gregory enlisted his longtime friend Al Hartel to assist in the design of a series of instruments that alluded to the surfing phenomenon. Hartel was a pattern maker for an air research company in Torrance, and also had a sideline avocation as a sculptor, which served the guitar project well.

The instruments were built in Hartel's workshop. Soest's research indicates that three guitars, three basses and two twelve-string guitars were built. They were nicknamed "Surfrites."

Each instrument's body, including the oval-shaped portion, was routed from a basswood plank. While the neck was mounted to the unique body through a standard four-bolt "peanut plate," the headstock was also fastened to the frame for extra stability. Such an additional attachment reportedly boosted the instruments' resonance. The pinstriping was done at an automobile paint shop near Hartel's residence.

At least one set of the oddities—one guitar, one bass, one twelve-string guitar—was temporarily loaned to the psychedelic rock band the Strawberry Alarm Clock of "Incense and Peppermints" fame. However, the brightly painted, pinstriped instruments didn't turn out to be "keepers."

"They were given to us at Original Sound Recording Studio," Strawberry Alarm Clock bassist George Bunnell said of the unique instruments. "I seem to remember they were in cardboard boxes, not guitar cases. The deal was for

Tom Smothers's personalized guitar, sunburst finish.
Willie G. Moseley

Al Hartel in the late 1980s with a "Surfrite" six-string guitar he built in the late 1960s. It has a salmon pink finish with Mark V/CE-III–style pickups (no polepieces). Note the perpendicular standard angle of the neck pickup.
Courtesy of Steve Soest

Left: Rear view of "Surfrite" guitar shows the headstock mounted on a support bracket.
Courtesy of Steve Soest

Center: "Surfrite" bass, candy apple green (the framing of the original late 1980s image had chopped off the headstock). Note the lack of pinstriping.
Courtesy of Steve Soest

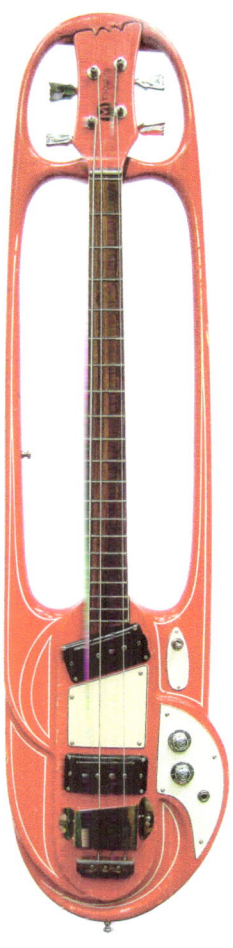

Right: This "Surfrite" bass has an orange-red finish that is somewhat similar to the guitar Hartel is holding in the archival photo. Since its headstock attachment point has a different configuration, one collector opined that it's possible this example may have been the first Surfrite made.
Courtesy of Bob Shade

Rarities, One-Offs, and Experimental Instruments

us to try them out, and if we used them in concert and on TV, we could keep them for free; otherwise we had to give them back."

At least one band member wasn't impressed with the instruments' aesthetics. "Ugly stuff," said guitarist Ed King. "We called them 'diaper pins'." The Strawberry Alarm Clock's brief "free trial period" went downhill soon after they received the three instruments, as band members also found faults regarding the practicality of playing such oddballs.

"Well, the first thing was trying to keep them in tune," Bunnell said. "I play bass, so for me, that wasn't an issue—at least, not a noticeable one. But they were definitely cumbersome. For the guitarists, it was both the tuning and the configuration." King observed that the instruments had "strange necks, and I don't think larger frets would have helped." Brunnell noted, "We jammed with them right there in the studio for a while and decided we'd give them back to Semie. I kind of wanted to keep the bass."

The erstwhile bassist for the Strawberry Alarm Clock also noted that to his knowledge, there wasn't any visual documentation of the band with the surfboard instruments. "I wish I had pictures," Bunnell lamented. "That'd be great, but all I have are memories . . . *vivid* ones." King would later go on to bigger fame in the mid-1970s with Lynyrd Skynyrd.

The Surfrites were interesting, but Mosrite ultimately declined to get into full production of the instruments, as the surf craze had pretty much crested when Hartel and Gregory crafted their eight instruments. Accordingly, while they were built with Mosrite parts, they never advanced beyond experimental status, and were never an official Mosrite product.

Left: Six-string "Surfrite" guitar. It, too, has a standard perpendicular neck pickup.
Courtesy of Tony Bacon

Center: Twelve-string "Surfrite" guitar.
Courtesy of Tony Bacon

Right: "Surfrite" bass.
Courtesy of Tony Bacon

It could be proposed that most Gospel-branded instruments created by Semie's company were rare or one-of-a-kind guitars as well. That said, they still deserve their own story as a unique ancillary brand.

10
Surname Instruments and the 1970s

The bankruptcy auction of guitars, parts, tools, fixtures, and machinery at the 1424 P Street factory took place several weeks after Mosrite closed. Numerous local and area guitar builders and musicians attended, as did amateur luthiers and woodworking hobbyists.

"I remember he got tons of bodies, necks, and Dobro resonators," Eugene Moles said of his father Gene's results at the auction. "I did not attend the auction at Mosrite," Ed Sanner recalled. "Ken Gilstrap did, and he purchased some items for Rosac."

The sale would later be considered as the genesis of an ongoing controversy regarding the legitimacy of certain so-called Mosrite instruments that were made using a body, neck, or parts that were acquired at the bankruptcy event, or perhaps even earlier. Some years later, Semie would recall that some employees had even been taking parts out of the factory when the facility was still open.

"I've seen a lot of Mosrites that were 'Frankensteins,'" Bakersfield businessman Marc Lipco said of such questionable instruments. "They were made by guys that had worked there." Such guitars or basses could have been assembled in almost anyone's backyard workshop or garage, so any assertion that they were legitimate Mosrites was dubious and controversial.

In the future, terms like "counterfeit," "forgery," and even "Parts-rite" would be utilized to describe many of the questionable instruments, and such wording would also be applied to other instruments that were actually phony from the ground up. Some of the bogus Mosrite guitars and basses in the latter category were imported.

Semie was determined to continue building instruments. He moved into a shop in Pumpkin Center, a southern suburb of Bakersfield on Freeway 99. Not only had Semie lost the physical assets of his company, but he had reportedly also lost the rights to use the Mosrite trademark and brand name. He was now compelled to build instruments labeled with his surname. Instead of the traditional "M" medallion and "Mosrite of California" appearing on the headstock, an M inside of a block alongside "Moseley of California" was seen. As might have been expected, a few variants of the logo appeared, such as a Moseley moniker alongside a traditional Mosrite "M" medallion.

As it turned out, some Moseley-branded instruments would become historically important. Soon after Mosrite shut down, Semie made overtures to Buck Owens about financing a return to guitar manufacturing. As an enticement, he presented the country music legend with at least two Moseley-branded acoustic instruments that were used by Owens on his syndicated television show, and in the first season of *Hee Haw*, the legendary music and comedy show hosted by Owens and Roy Clark.

The guitars were based on the Serenade/Balladere I model. One instrument was painted in a red, white, and blue color scheme, and the other had a light, honey sunburst finish.

Buck had decided to have a red, white, and blue endorsement model guitar created, and began preliminary discussions with more than one manufacturer. The red, white, and blue Moseley guitar was reportedly Semie's submission for Buck's consideration. However, Chicago's gigantic Harmony company got the nod for Buck's endorsement model, and the model was a huge success.

Buck is displaying one of his custom Moseley acoustic guitars in this ad for his syndicated television show.

Semie also made a completely new style of Moseley electric guitar for Buck's right-hand musical associate, Don Rich. The guitar had a Fender Telecaster–ish single-cutaway shape, but still had a pronounced German carve all the way around the top. It was hollow on the inside and had one f-hole. The headstock had a unique upside-down, beak-like appearance.

The pickups were encased in the same chrome surrounds that were seen on the Dobro D-100 thinline guitar (see chapter 28, "Dobro").

While Semie would assert in an early 1980s interview that he and Owens had briefly gone into business together, Jim Shaw, a longtime member of the Buckaroos and Operations Manager for Buck Owens Productions, recalled that such a collaboration never came to fruition. "That was made for the *Hee Haw* show in '69," Shaw said of Rich's guitar. "That was the time when [Semie] was trying to get Buck to invest."

Semie continued to pursue his gospel singing ambitions as well, and released albums on his Moseley record label, which displayed the same block-M logo as found on Moseley-branded guitar headstocks.

The "Moseley" era would also witness the Mosrite founder getting back into creating, modifying, and repairing instruments for some of his favorite musicians. The headstock on the (replacement) standard guitar neck on the original Joe Maphis doubleneck from the 1950s would end up sporting a "Moseley of California" logo, so Semie apparently worked on that iconic instrument during the "Moseley" time frame.

Around the time the Mosrite factory was closed, the company had begun developing double-coil "humbucking" pickups, and a pair of those items

One-of-a-kind Moseley-branded guitar made for Don Rich in 1969.
Willie G. Moseley

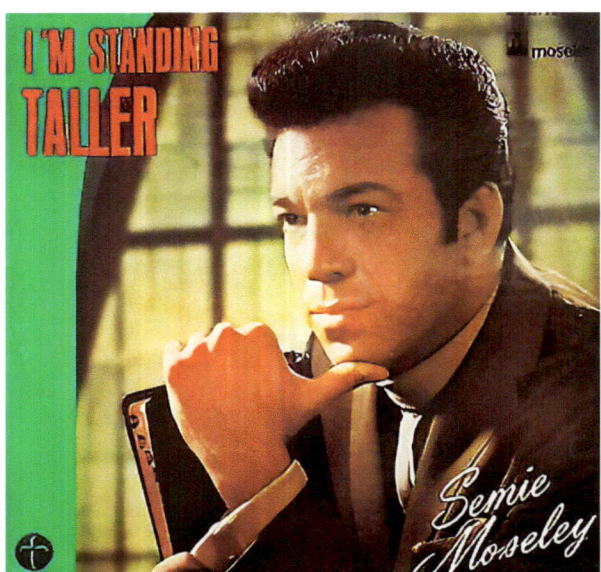

Left: Custom Moseley guitar made for Rose Lee Maphis, ca. 1970.
Willie G. Moseley

Above: Closeup of the headstock on Rose Lee Maphis's Moseley guitar.
Willie G. Moseley

would be included on a full-depth, Moseley-branded archtop Semie built for Rose Lee Maphis. The body came from another source, but Semie built his own neck for the instrument.

The treble pickup was installed directly on the top while the bass pickup and pickup controls were placed on a high-relief pickguard. A matching tortoiseshell jack plate was installed on the side.

And the Maphis family still played Mosrites. A 1971 album featuring Joe and his son Jody prominently displayed several iconic Mosrite guitars, including Joe's original doubleneck and his 1960 "scroll" guitar.

By mid-1972, Semie was using the Mosrite name and trademark again, and he had been able to get back into the factory at 1424 P Street. A not-too-spiffy brochure from that annum announced: "For 15 years, until 1969, the Mosrite guitars were manufactured in the factory owned by Semie Moseley. After 3 years Semie Moseley is once again building the original Mosrite guitar. He now introduces you to his new creations from MOSRITE of California, Inc."

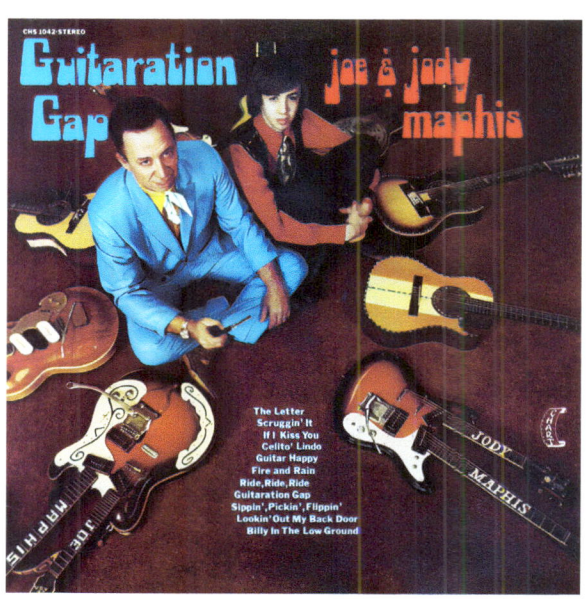

Another brochure from 1972 cited a connection to the Kustom amplifier company of Chanute, Kansas. Semie had worked up a distribution agreement with that company's president, Bud Ross, but the collaboration didn't last long.

As for instruments proffered during that annum, what had originally been the solidbody Ventures/Mark–style instruments were now known as "V" models (and interestingly, the V-I guitar had three knobs).

There were also Celebrity models; the full-depth Celebrity I had three knobs while the thinline Celebrity III had two. The controls for both models were mounted in a banana-shaped control plate (as seen on the Dobro D-100 Californian).

Several "Mobro"-branded resonator guitars and a Mobro D-100 were also advertised (the rights to the Dobro name had been acquired by OMI, a Los Angeles area-company with connections to the original Dobro

Left: Early 1970s Mosrite Celebrity model "by Semie Moseley." Note the shaded headstock and "banana" control plate.
Courtesy of John Majdalani

Center: Early 1970s Mosrite bass "by Semie Moseley."
Courtesy of Heritage Auctions

Right: Early 1970s Mosrite bass "by Semie Moseley."
Courtesy of Replay Guitar Exchange

company). Many early 1970s Moseley- and Mosrite-branded instruments had "by Semie Moseley" on the headstock, underneath the brand name.

As 1973 arrived, Mosrite introduced several new models, and signed on with another distributor, Pacific Music Supply of Los Angeles. That agreement wouldn't last long, either.

Several 1973 flyers exhibited full-color images of instruments in a outdoor setting, and had Mosrite's P Street address in Bakersfield as contact information. However, a Pacific Music Supply catalog from the same year highlighted many of the same models as being distributed by that LA company, which probably confused retailers and customers.

The fretboards on most Mosrite instruments were now being inlaid with larger dots, but the layout still followed a pattern of two dots on appropriate frets in the first octave, three dots on the twelfth-octave fret, and single dots on the higher register.

Among the 1973 refinements to previously existing Mosrites (V models and Celebrity models) were humbucking pickups with twelve polepieces, separate volume and tone controls for each pickup, and "by-pass" switches for each pickup, which ran the signal directly to an amplifier, circumventing the instrument's controls. This commendable addition allowed two different volume and tone presets for an instrument, and demonstrated that Semie was still an innovator.

Luthier Roger Fritz is the proud owner of a 1973 classic-style Mosrite solidbody. "Mine is in mint condition and plays itself," he enthused. "When you push those buttons, look out!"

Above: V-II series instruments, 1973 brochure.
Courtesy of Steve Brown/vintaxe.com

Right: Celebrity series instruments, 1973 brochure.
Courtesy of Steve Brown/vintaxe.com

There were some incongruities seen in some early 1970s Mosrite brochures. For some reason, an image of a nonvibrato Celebrity with a trapeze tailpiece and sans bypass switches was sloppily superimposed on a page for that model. In the same photo, the end of the strap on the guitar being held by the model appeared to be affixed to the pickup toggle switch on the treble cutaway. What's more, the top-of-the-line CE-I was advertised as having a body depth of over five inches.

The new models included the one-pickup 300 and two-pickup 350 guitars and basses. They had flat, single-cutaway mahogany bodies that strongly alluded to a Fender Telecaster. The necks on earlier examples were also mahogany; latter-day examples had basswood bodies and maple necks that were more typical for Mosrite.

Left: 350 guitar, natural finish.
Courtesy of Michael Wright

Right: 350 guitar, dark sunburst finish. This example appears to be a mono-only aberration as it has only one jack and a pushbutton bypass switch instead of a stereo-mono slider switch.
Courtesy of Olivia's Vintage

Surname Instruments and the 1970s

The 350 series also had separate volume and tone controls for each pickup, and stereo capability (two jacks on the pickguard/control plate). The instrument could be played monaurally via the stereo-mono slider switch near the control knobs.

And, while Mosrite's flat "speed frets" would appear on some instruments produced in the 1970s, Semie finally seemed to be getting the message that flat frets and thin necks were passé, considering the trends in contemporary music.

"The Mosrite neck is a feature that all musicians respect," proclaimed the catalog copy for the 350 guitar. "Most agreed that it could not be improved—but it has been. Still the same fast neck and low, easy action, but a wider neck and with heavier frets, set in a bound rosewood fingerboard. It is an experience and a pleasure to play this fine instrument."

Veteran Bakersfield guitar retailer Artie Niesen was working at Mosrite in the early 1970s, and recalled the company's transition to different fretwork and neck configurations. "It was a fast neck if you were sliding up and down," Niesen said of the original design, "but I think the style of music started to change, where people were bending more notes, which was difficult to do with flat frets. In the '70s, Semie realized he had to make some changes, and the new models didn't have flat frets on them; they had taller frets where you could bend notes better."

The same 1973 catalog also introduced the 500 Bluesbender, which had a somewhat-similar silhouette to the 350 series, but with different cutaways and a contoured top. Moreover, the model's neck pickup wasn't angled. The Bluesbender was touted as having a pushbutton phase switch to reverse the pickups' polarity. The model wasn't marketed in a stereo configuration.

Several resonator instruments, marketed under the Mosrite name (not "Mobro"), were also seen in a separate brochure.

1973 500 Bluesbender catalog illustration.
Courtesy of Steve Brown/vintaxe.com

Semie's ongoing gospel music efforts meant that he still traveled, particularly when his guitar enterprise was struggling. He would spend an increasing amount of time on the road, trying to make ends meet, but was always thinking about new innovations in guitar building. He briefly moved to Oklahoma in the mid-1970s, where he built a small number of plain-looking "Sooner" guitars as a one-shot deal for a music store chain. The run was supposed to have produced one hundred instruments, but Moseley recounted that only a few were made.

The Sooner had a few stereotypical Mosrite appointments, such as a metal nut and a zero fret, but other than featuring a decorative walnut strip down the center of its maple fretboard, it was a cheaply made, fairly nondescript instrument, with a bulbous headstock silhouette that seemed to be emulating the uninspiring shape of the body.

Most of the bodies were hollow with a veneer top, but at least one solidbody maple example was crafted as a prototype or experiment. The guitar had an aluminum hardtail plate that was also crafted to coordinate with the casually curved silhouette of the body. Leftover tailpieces of this type would appear on other Mosrite models later in

1973 Resonator models
Courtesy of Steve Brown/vintaxe.com

the decade. Moreover, the Sooner was yet another model that had surplus pickup housings that had originally been made for use on the Dobro D-100.

The script on the headstock decal reads, in white letters, "The Sooner by Moseley U.S.A." A small round "M" logo is also seen.

Semie soon returned to California. In 1976, he put a big push into a new idea that manifested itself in a guitar model called the Brass Rail. The primary feature of the instrument was a 0.25-inch by 0.75-inch brass rod that ran down the center of the neck. Frets were installed directly onto the brass to evoke a dramatic increase in sustain. The neck was maple, with decorative rosewood strips, on which tiny fret markers were installed. Set-neck and bolt-on versions were developed.

Collector Adam Tober estimated that the first fifteen to twenty Brass Rails, introduced during America's Bicentennial year, were the "Deluxe" variant, mostly made with leftover Bluesbender bodies. The controls for the original "Deluxe" version were complicated, according to Tober. Their layout was crowded, with six knobs, two pushbuttons, and a three-way toggle switch. There were two side jacks for stereo capability.

What appeared to be two humbucking pickups were actually four single-coil pickups that had two circuits (one active, one passive). Each coil had a push–pull volume knob (for a total of four) to turn the coil off or on. The active circuitry was powered by a nine-volt battery. The other two knobs were master volume and master tone controls.

Moreover, the three-way toggle switch functioned in an atypical manner—it was actually a circuit selector switch for active, passive, or both. The pushbuttons controlled phase on each of the two coils in the bridge position. The two jacks allowed selection of active and passive circuits in stereo, or both combined in mono.

Seeking to emphasize his company's viability, Semie screenprinted "The New Mosrite—1976" on the instruments' headstocks, and addressed the Bicentennial on a numbered metal commemorative plaque mounted on the back of the body.

Sooner guitar
Courtesy of Jay Rosen

1976 Brass Rail #007.
Courtesy of Gordy Lupo

Brass Rail #007 headstock.
Courtesy of Gordy Lupo

Brass Rail #007 commemorative plaque.
Courtesy of Gordy Lupo

Less-fancy, second-generation versions of the Brass Rail with more traditional electronics and controls were built later. Some of them had slightly different bodies (which were crafted after leftover Bluesbender bodies were used up). However, standardization was pretty much nonexistent—Brass Rail features varied, evolving from batch to batch.

The greenburst Brass Rail shown here is a clean example that has a new-for-the-times bridge plate (which would show up later on Mosrite's SM model).

More than one experimental "Aluminum Rail" instrument was made (same rod-and-bradded frets concept, different metal). One was a one-of-a-kind bass in a greenburst finish with a tortoiseshell pickguard and pickup covers. Its controls were standard, consisting of two volume and two tone knobs, a three-way pickup toggle switch, and a phase switch.

The bass has a 1976 designation on its headstock. Sharp-eyed guitar buffs will note that the neck pickup is at an opposite angle compared to other Mosrite pickup configurations.

At least one other similar bass with a standard truss rod neck has been documented; it was reportedly made around 1978.

A special Aluminum Rail acoustic guitar was built for Dolly Parton. Its chronology is somewhat similar to the Buck Owens red, white, and blue guitar—several builders were approached to build butterfly-themed instruments for Parton's syndicated television show, which ran for one season (1976–1977). Mosrite's example had a

Later Brass Rail, Greenburst finish.
Photo by Jeff Antkowiak/courtesy of Skinner Inc.

Aluminum Rail bass, 1976.
Photo by Jeff Antkowiak/courtesy of Skinner Inc.

Aluminum Rail acoustic guitar made for Dolly Parton.
Photo by Jeff Antkowiak/courtesy of Skinner Inc.

diminutive maple body with a spruce top. Its lower bout is fifteen inches wide. While the top of the instrument is flat, the back is slightly arched.

The lepidoptera influences include a headstock profile that evokes butterfly wings along its top edge (when viewed vertically) and a carved rosewood bridge crafted to resemble a butterfly in flight. The instrument had an embossed serial number, D1, and "DOLLY" was stamped on the neck block.

Unfortunately, Parton's single-season show had already ceased production when the guitar was completed. Semie reportedly sold the Aluminum Rail acoustic to one of his workers, who gave the guitar to his mother. She played it in church for some three decades.

Among the workers at Mosrite in the mid-1970s was Bill Gruggett (again), who was involved in the development of the Brass Rail concept. Gruggett would end up crafting several Brass Rail–style instruments on his own after he had departed Mosrite (again).

Eugene Moles was also a Mosrite employee in that era, having begun working for the company when he was fifteen years old. Moles recalled that he quit high school

> because I wanted to start playing locally at the clubs in Bakersfield. I also took a job with Semie; he had a small crew at the time. Semie showed me a lot, including how to wire Brass Rails.
>
> I was there for about two or three months. I had to wake up at four or five in the morning, because [Semie] started early. I was also working at a nightclub; I had to give up one of my two jobs, so I kept the nightclub job playing guitar and quit Semie.

Some leftover bodies and necks that were intended to be Brass Rails were later made as conventional instruments with standard electronics. They were marketed as the SM model.

Around this time, Semie made more than one unusual prototype guitar with a rounded body silhouette and a multilaminated top with a chevron pattern. The bridge and stop tailpiece assembly and pickguard were from the SM model, and the pickups appeared to be Brass Rail items. The model never went into production.

The example seen here was given to Larry Collins, who appeared in the 1978 film *Every Which Way But Loose*, starring Clint Eastwood, around the time the guitar was made. Collins also performed on the album's soundtrack. Collins nicknamed his guitar "Woodie."

Another patriotic effort from Semie was the creation of a few Bicentennial acoustic guitars. The headstock had the same silhouette as seen on the earlier "Sooner" guitar. The fretboard

Mid-1970s prototype. Note the "standard" layout of fretboard inlay.
Photo by David Silva

Serenade acoustic with patriotic paint scheme, owned by Andy Moseley. Note the wide headstock.
Courtesy of Bob Shade

was multilaminated, including a walnut strip that ran down the center, so it's probable that the necks were left over from Semie's brief Oklahoma residency.

Andy Moseley owned a unique Serenade model acoustic guitar with a wide headstock, and recalled that it was painted in patriotic colors sometime during the 1970s. Most likely this transformation would also have happened around the Bicentennial.

Mosrite guitars would get an in-through-the-side-door boost in publicity from the mid-1970s punk rock phenomenon, of all things.

Guitarist John Cummings (AKA Johnny Ramone) played a rare flat-bodied Mosrite Ventures II with the band from which each member took his stage surname. The New York–based Ramones were pioneers of the punk rock sound, of which Johnny's frenetic downstroke guitar style on his Mosrite was a cornerstone. The guitarist idolized Fred "Sonic" Smith of the MC5, who had also played Mosrite guitars. Cummings even appropriated Smith's hairstyle.

The chronicle regarding the Ramones guitarist's acquisition of his first Mosrite guitar recounts that Johnny visited New York City's legendary Manny's Music in early 1974, and a blue, original-style Mosrite Ventures II was the only American-made instrument he could afford.

However, Cummings quickly came to appreciate the Mosrite's light weight as well as its thin neck, which facilitated his purveyance of relentless and loud barre chords.

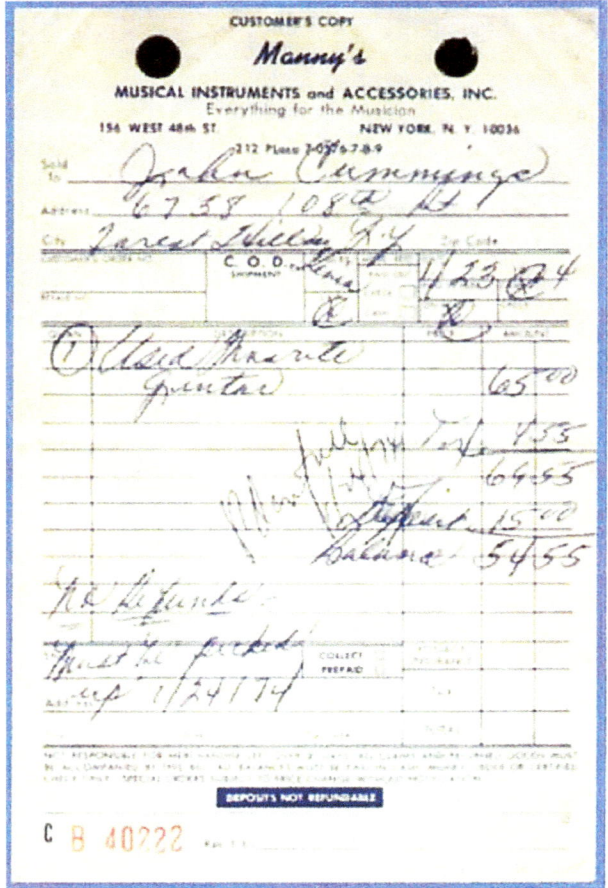

Receipt for used Mosrite guitar purchased by John Cummings at Manny's Music.
Courtesy of Bob Shade

Cummings owned several Mosrite guitars during his career, including Mark I models. He reportedly used a Mark I when recording the Ramones' first album in early 1976 at Plaza Sound Studios, located on the eighth floor of Radio City Music Hall. However, his most enduring example in the eyes of music fans was another Ventures II model that had a white finish and underwent numerous modifications.

And erstwhile MC5 guitarist Fred "Sonic" Smith himself was still gigging with Mosrites. He fronted Sonic's Rendezvous Band in the late 1970s, and married iconic rock poet/singer Patti Smith in 1980. He painted one of his Mosrites silver, according to his son Jackson.

The younger Smith recalled that his father had retained the iconic pearl white Mosrite guitar that was seen on the cover of *Kick Out the Jams*, "but nobody was allowed to touch it. I never saw it played. The silver one was in my grandpa's basement for many years. In the MC5 days, Dad played mostly rhythm. His lead work really exploded later with Rendezvous."

During the mid-1970s, guitarist and singer Leroy "Sugarfoot" Bonner of the platinum-selling funk/soul band the Ohio Players ("Skin Tight," "Fire," "Love Rollercoaster") was usually seen onstage sporting a beachball-sized Afro and a Mosrite Joe Maphis doubleneck guitar.

More than one older Mosrite guitar made a national appearance in 1979, in the hands of Ricky Wilson, the founding guitarist of the B-52s, a quirky quintet from Athens, Georgia. The music the oddball aggregation purveyed what would come to be known as alternative rock, so perhaps it wasn't surprising that Wilson favored unusual tunings, including some with fewer than six strings on his instruments.

Wilson used several Mosrites, including a twelve-six doubleneck. His favorite instrument was a blue Ventures Model Mark V. The instrument figured prominently in early recordings.

Johnny Ramone in 1976 with his blue Mosrite Ventures II guitar. It was stolen in 1977.
Courtesy of Ralph Alfonso

The latter half of the 1970s also saw the first inkling of the Japanese guitar market beginning to seek out older Mosrite Ventures Model instruments. The Ventures were still icons in the Land of the Rising Sun, and were still touring there on a regular basis (often twice a year). Affluent Japanese businessmen also sought out Semie regarding new reproductions of classic Ventures Model guitars and basses, even though the band and the builder had parted ways a decade earlier.

Ventures founding guitarist Don Wilson recalled that Semie contacted the band, asking permission to put their logo on the headstock of his new instruments. The Ventures declined, but Wilson remembered that Moseley used the Ventures logo anyway.

As the Japanese demand for Ventures Model reissues increased, Semie would later proclaim that his new reissue guitars were named "in honor of the Ventures." Semantics aside, the placement of Ventures logos on such 1970s and 1980s instruments was not authorized by the band.

Semie also reintroduced the Vibramute vibrato system as an option for his guitars. While it was cruder than the standard Moseley vibrato, many collectors and players wanted a Vibramute to enhance the retro vibe if they were ordering a Mosrite reissue instrument.

Ramone onstage with his white Ventures II guitar.
Public Domain / Wikimedia Commons

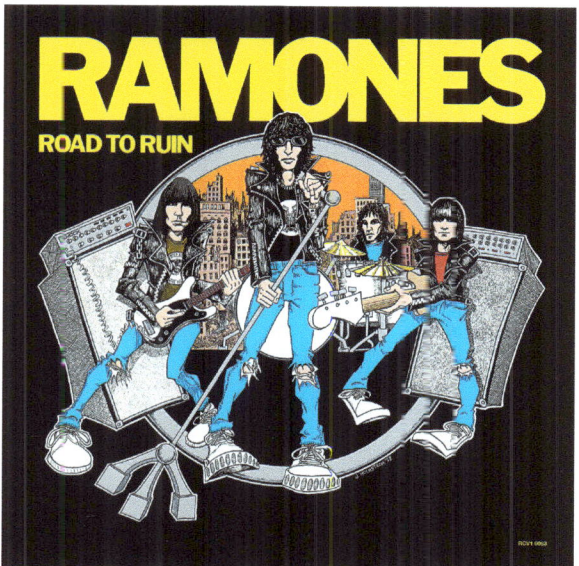

The caricature cover artwork for the Ramones' 1978 album Road to Ruin included Johnny's white Mosrite guitar

Surname Instruments and the 1970s

Early 1970s Gospel.
Courtesy of Heritage Auctions

1977 Gospel Bicentennial Celebrity Brass Rail.
Photo by Jeff Antkowiak/courtesy of Skinner Inc.

11
The Gospel Goes Onward

Semie continued to validate his aspirations as a Christian musician with his ongoing creation of Gospel-branded instruments as an ancillary line. Gospel instruments usually underwent changes similar to their Mosrite siblings, but many had unique features.

One early 1970s Gospel example that Moseley built was, like earlier Gospel guitars, based on the Celebrity hollowbody. Its electronics were different, in that the pickup toggle switch was installed on the treble cutaway, and the volume and tone knobs were installed from underneath the top (no control plate). The instrument had three-ply binding on the top, single-ply binding on the back, and unbound f-holes. The guitar also had humbucking pickups (note the two rows of polepieces) and was finished in a ghostlike color similar to Fender's "Antigua" finish. The pickguard on this instrument is also slightly different, with a "barb" near the bridge pickup.

A similar instrument with a clear pickguard was seen on the cover of an album by a young gospel performer named "Little David" Smith. The photo was actually taken inside the Mosrite factory, and the other prominent guitar appears to be a Cherryburst finish Mosrite Celebrity CE-I that was practically the same instrument as the Gospel.

One of Moseley's most unique Gospel creations ever was a "Bicentennial Celebrity" guitar that was crafted for a preacher named Beatty. The instrument utilized a Brass Rail neck that runs all the way to the bridge. The fretboard is made of rosewood and maple. The zero fret and nut are brass; the rosewood headstock overlay is 0.125-inch thick and has a 1977 date displayed.

The Bicentennial Celebrity's maple body has a figured top with no f-holes, and is 2.75 inches deep. It has eight-ply binding on the top and back. The bridge and tailpiece unit is similar to the one found on the Mosrite SM model.

Additional controls on this one-of-a-kind instrument include a push button for phase, and two mini-toggle coil-tap switches (one for each pickup). It is also one of the few instruments with Brass Rail neck construction to sport a vibrato.

Summing up the 1970s, Adam Tober cited the pluses and minuses of the history of Mosrite and related brands in that decade, including Semie's innovations:

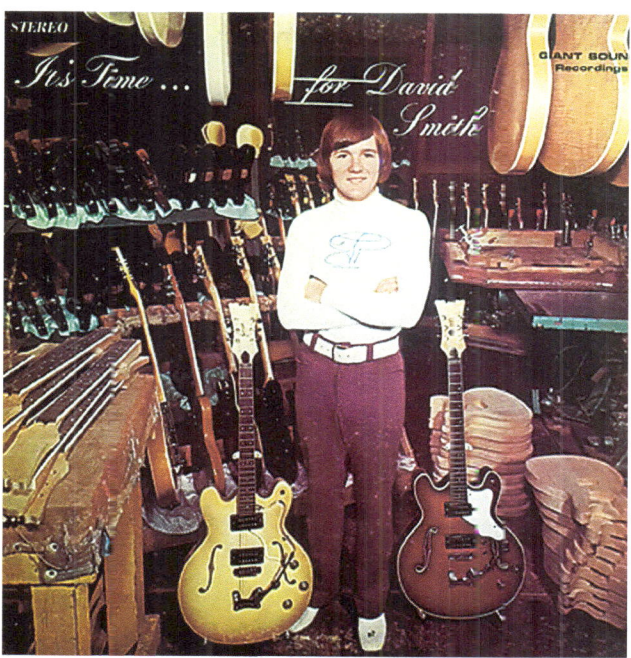

Early 1970s David Smith album cover; photo taken at the Mosrite factory.

> I find it interesting that Semie Moseley, a '50s gospel musician who broke it big making '60s surf guitars—the Ventures Model—was still being influenced by the wider guitar trends of the '70s "Brass Age." Wider necks, larger frets, and as much brass as possible. But as a decade of smaller batches and lower production, there tends to be greater variety, even among instruments of the same model.

1980 custom "Lost Wax Casting" instrument.
Photo by Jeff Antkowiak/
courtesy of Skinner Inc.

12
Further Migration

At the beginning of the 1980s, Semie moved his business to Carson City, Nevada. Before he left Bakersfield, however, he crafted what would become known among guitar aficionados as one of the most ornate instruments ever created.

The guitar has been dubbed the "Lost Wax Casting" instrument among collectors. Most of the metal parts are bronze, having been cast from molds. The molds themselves were made from hand-carved wood. The guitar has maple neck-through construction and walnut "wings." The sides are made of individual bookmatched pieces of walnut. The fretboard is not a solitary slab of wood—individual pieces of wood were installed between the brass frets.

The exquisite, one-of-a-kind guitar, which weighs sixteen pounds, is a work of art, and was apparently meant to demonstrate that around a decade after Mosrite's traumatic shutdown (and through his company's experiences in the 1970s), Semie was still viable as a luthier.

Not surprisingly, Semie began yearning to return to Bakersfield soon after his move to Carson City. The Mosrite founder was adamant that his brand belonged in the Golden State, considering the logo on the headstocks of his instruments.

Semie had, of course, created custom instruments during the 1970s. Proportionally, custom guitars and basses would become a larger percentage of his output during the 1980s as Mosrite struggled to find its footing. One instrument he crafted in Carson City was a blue sparkle doubleneck guitar for Barbara Mandrell, who was now an established superstar in country music.

Instead of moving back to Bakersfield, however, Mosrite would soon migrate all the way across the country to the unincorporated hamlet of Jonas Ridge, North Carolina, high in the Blue Ridge Mountains. Semie and his wife Loretta were planning on going into gospel music full-time, and he was planning on building custom Mosrite instruments to support their music plans. Jonas Ridge was Loretta's hometown.

Semie first set up shop in a vacant school. Soon after the move to Jonas Ridge, however, he was involved in an automobile wreck that severed his leg; he recalled that the car rolled over five times. The leg was reattached, and Moseley spent an extended time in therapy and in a wheelchair (but was still trying to build guitars). He would walk with a limp for the rest of his life.

Soon after Semie was up and about, his shop was the subject of a "Carolina Camera" news story broadcast on WBTV, a television station in Charlotte. A reporter and cameraman visited the school/guitar shop, which had a large sign on its facade proclaiming the front of the facility to be the "Gospel Encounters Music Hall," and the luthier was shown sawing a neck, sanding the German carve on a guitar body, and stringing up a "Gospel Encounters" Mosrite six-string guitar. Semie and Loretta were also seen performing a verse from a gospel tune with visiting musician Brian Lonbeck.

A disastrous fire on November 22, 1983, destroyed not only the original Jonas Ridge facility, but numerous completed guitars that were slated to be shipped to Japan.

Marshall Crenshaw, who had garnered a record deal that enabled him to expand his guitar-collecting proclivities, had detailed memories about his own early 1980s connections with Mosrite, following his purchase of a 1965 Ventures Model Mark I from Gruhn Guitars of Nashville:

> When it was delivered, I did a *really dumb* thing—I took it out of the case; it was Pearl White, really beautiful, and I decided to take it to a show that I was doing that night with Dave Edmunds at the Convention Center in Asbury Park [New Jersey]—an important gig.
>
> I took the Mosrite and an Epiphone twelve-string; that was it. When I got to the job site and plugged the Mosrite in, it was noisy; the pickups were unpotted [and] microphonic. I just struggled with it, a nightmare of my own making.

Somehow or another I got hold of Semie Moseley shortly after the Asbury show and talked to him on the phone. He was making another attempt at the time at getting back into the game, getting Mosrite back off the ground, and was interested in connecting with people who were on TV and on the charts, as I was just then. I told him my story about the pearl white Mosrite and he said, "Well, send it on down; we'll take a look at it."

I sent it to Jonas Ridge, waited a couple months, tried to reach him on the phone number that I had, got no answer. More time went by, no word from Semie. Finally I did get hold of him and he said, "Oh, terrible news! We had a huge fire; lost everything."

I was really perplexed; didn't know what to think. He didn't say anything about replacing my guitar or reimbursing me—not at first, anyway. But by the end of the conversation we were talking about him building me a new guitar. We talked a couple more times over the next few weeks but then I ran out of patience and asked my manager to call Semie and say whatever he needed to say to convince him to send me a brand new sunburst Ventures-style model *right now*, which he *did* do. I got that guitar and it was great! I bonded with it right away; it was one of my main guitars for the next couple years, '84 to '86. I used the sunburst Mosrite on my third album, *Downtown*, and in the movie *Peggy Sue Got Married*.

Soon afterward, Crenshaw also acquired a candy apple red twelve-string Mark XII and a blue Mark I. "I only used the twelve-string on a record once," he detailed, "on a track called 'This Street' on my fourth album. On all of the tour dates that I did in 1986, I only had those three Mosrites, no other guitars."

Crenshaw would get the opportunity to play a rare 1963 Joe Maphis model for two weeks in 1987: "I'm sad to say that the guitar never belonged to me; a nice fella in San Diego lent it to me for a few shows but wouldn't sell it to me, even though I begged him. That guitar is possibly my favorite electric guitar that I've ever played; it really came alive in my hands. 'Vibrant' is the word I'd use to describe it."

In 1989, Crenshaw acquired a Maphis doubleneck from "an elderly gentleman who was a friend of Semie's and had bought the guitar directly from him. The only record I ever used this one on is a Foster and Lloyd album track called 'She Knows What She Wants.' I used both necks; played the solo in octaves."

Marshall Crenshaw plays a 1963 Joe Maphis model Mosrite onstage in Santa Barbara, California.
Courtesy of the Bob Matheau Estate

Following the disastrous fire in late 1983, Semie would then erect several primitive shacks to house his operation. Some interior walls were made of unpainted particleboard and power lines were simply run in through windows. Reportedly, his paint facility was an old freight trailer.

Andy Moseley was residing in Nashville, and helped his younger brother with the attempt to revitalize Mosrite. Andy's post office box in Music City was the contact address on the publicity photos for instruments that were shown at a 1984 NAMM show.

Left: 1986 Mosrite Mark I with unauthorized Ventures logo.
Willie G. Moseley

Mark I style guitar promotional photo, 1984.
Courtesy of Bob Shade

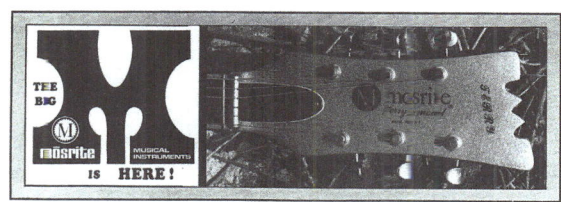

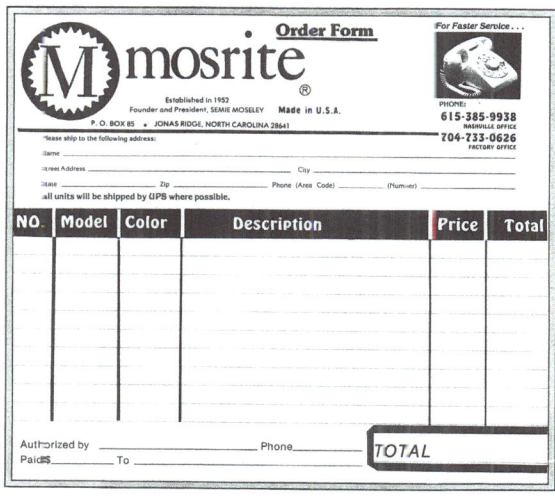

Jonas Ridge order form with photo of "Terry" model headstock.
Courtesy of Bob Shade

The Mosrite operation remained open but continued to struggle. Japanese orders for ("re-issue") Ventures Model instruments continued to drive the company's business, but Semie also built some slightly different instruments for Japanese guitarist Takeshi "Terry" Terauchi and his fans.

At one point, traditional-style Mosrite guitars briefly sported the "Vintage" designation, while more modern-looking variants were known as "Voltage" models.

In the middle of the decade, Semie had what he termed as "radical colon surgery."

The interest in Mosrite continued to grow, and Semie wrote an open letter to guitar buffs dated December 1, 1986. Therein, he addressed his recent problems, including the automobile wreck, the fire, and his surgery. He proclaimed that he was fully recovered and was planning to build the Ventures Model and the Joe Maphis doubleneck again, as well as a new model of Mosrite guitar.

Pierre Laflamme, a Canadian fan of Mosrite guitars, had ordered two instruments from Semie in December 1985. Around a year and a half later, he journeyed to Jonas Ridge, and was fascinated by how Mosrites were built under such primitive manufacturing conditions. Laflamme recalled:

> I first met Semie in June of '87. I found him to be tall, funny, energetic, very pleasant, and religious. . . . I had not seen a Mosrite in years, so looking at what he had was a real treat. They played great and looked great, too. I was impressed with his ingenuity and how he got things done with the tools at his disposal. [There was] a lot of handwork involved during that period.

Laflamme's visit firmed up a distribution agreement for distribution of Mosrites in Canada.

The year 1988 would turn out to be promising, as a guitar magazine article written by Elliot Easton, guitarist for a successful "New Wave" band called the Cars, brought Mosrite to the attention of many guitarists and collectors. Interest in Mosrite guitars mushroomed again.

Larry Collins was still active as a musician, and ordered another doubleneck from Semie. This one had a silhouette like his original 1955 guitar. "The body matches the shape of my original doubleneck," he detailed in 2020. "I tried several pickups in it over the years, and it currently has new Hallmark pickups, which are hot and crisp."

In the late 1980s, stereotypical guitar collectors were aging males—Japanese and Baby Boomer Americans—who had come of age during the 1960s and had coveted Mosrites because of the brand's association with the Ventures.

Semie in Jonas Ridge, mid-1980s.
Courtesy of Pierre Laflamme

Elliott Easton with Semie, September 1988.
Courtesy of Pierre Laflamme

Mosrite 88 guitar, Diamond Money finish (fine-flake sparkle), no vibrato.
Courtesy of Heritage Auctions

Late 1980s doubleneck made for Larry Collins.
Photo by David Silva

Now affluent adults, they could afford the guitars they could only dream about when they were teenagers. Such instruments were now considered "time warp machines."

Accordingly, Semie would begin showing his wares at vintage guitar shows, where the interest in his new products seemed to be as intense as the interest in vintage Mosrites. It didn't hurt that Japanese buyers also patronized such exhibitions.

Fred Newell, who was the staff lead guitarist for the long-running *Nashville Now* television show, met Semie at a guitar show in Dallas in 1988. "I first saw Mosrite guitars being played by Joe Maphis and Larry Collins on the *Town Hall Party* TV show," Newell recalled. "I was probably around thirteen years old, and they blew me away. Then, being a huge Ventures fan, I saw [Mosrite guitars] being played on album covers."

At the Dallas show, Fred and Semie were photographed with Semie's custom-made "Mr. President" doubleneck. Moseley would recall that the instrument—which had been made while Ronald Reagan was still president—was never delivered to President George Bush because of what Moseley called "political intervention."

Semie and Fred Newell at a vintage guitar show with the "Mr. President" doubleneck.
Courtesy of Brooke Newell

Semie also gave Fred a "Mosrite 88" guitar. Newell described it as

> a very well-made instrument; [it] played really well and had that famous "two-pickup Mosrite sound"—a sweet top end tone with a clean bottom on the lower strings. I suppose rock guitarists might prefer that bridge pickup growl instead of a "sweet" tone. . . . [U]s older country pickers probably can identify more with clean articulate sounds! He really presented good workmanship on it. The pearl white guitar that Semie gave to me at the Dallas Guitar Show had a maple neck with a maple fretboard, and a natural colored headstock.

Pierre Laflamme spent several months in Jonas Ridge in 1989, assisting Semie's efforts to make Mosrite a viable name in the guitar marketplace. In March of the same year, actor Mickey Rooney Jr. visited the Jonas Ridge facility. His production company was interested in making a biographical movie about Semie's life, but the deal was never consummated. Semie made a trip to Japan in October 1989, where he was able to gauge the interest in classic Mosrite instruments in that nation firsthand.

13
Gospels in the Blue Ridge Mountains

As noted earlier, some Mosrite "Gospel Encounters" instruments were made in Jonas Ridge, but straight-on Gospel-branded guitars were also built there. In fact, Semie made a concerted effort in 1990 to market the Christian-oriented line, advertising his wares in gospel music magazines.

The Gospel "Victory" series included the Victory I (plain pickups, no pickguard), the Victory II (pickups with polepieces, pickguard), and the Victory III (no German carve, flat body, no vibrato).

In addition to applying custom finishes and artwork to standard Mosrite instruments (see chapter 14), custom paint artist Wayne Jarrett of Greensboro, North Carolina, also painted Gospel guitars. The red Gospel guitar seen here is exemplary of Jarrett's capabilities, including pickup covers that were custom-painted. The figured maple fretboard is extremely rare for an instrument crafted by Semie Moseley.

Left to right: Victory I, Victory II, Victory III.
Courtesy of Steve Brown/vintaxe.com

Far right: 1980s Gospel custom-finished by Wayne Jarrett.
Courtesy of Michael G. Stewart

Courtesy of Steve Brown/vintaxe.com

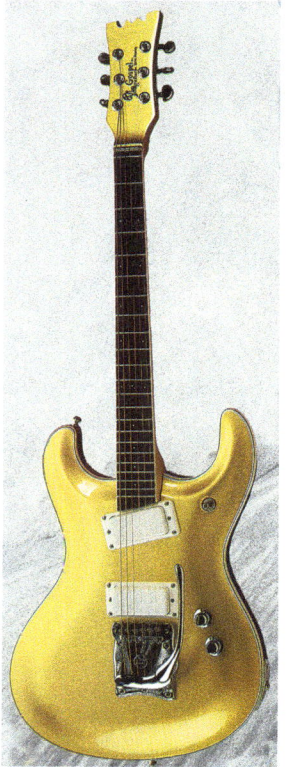   

Fourth Man advertisement photo.
Courtesy of the Andy Moseley Estate

Another Jonas Ridge Gospel model that was proffered was the Fourth Man, with a slightly different body configuration. The portrait of Jesus on this example was painted in oil. Semie offered details about this model in a separate brochure page:

The 'FOURTH MAN' Model Gospel Guitar was born through a dream that a dear friend of mine, Fred Moses, had one night. The dream was of a tall man standing on a mountain top playing a white guitar. Standing behind—and sort of leaning over this man's shoulders was . . . JESUS!

The next time I saw Fred he asked me if I could build him a guitar with a picture of Jesus. From this request the Fourth Man Gospel Guitar was created, and is dedicated to be used in the gospel music ministry.

Both Fred and I felt that this guitar should be shared with those people who would like to purchase the Fourth Man guitar if it were available.

We plan to build only one hundred (100) of this model—with the serial numbers being FM001 through FM100. The picture of Jesus will be hand painted in oils on each of the one hundred guitars, just as the original Fourth Man Guitar was.

Gospel-branded basses were also created in Jonas Ridge.
Semie's Gospel initiative was unsuccessful, so he reverted to concentrating on Mosrites.

1980s Gospel Bass.
Courtesy of Replay Guitar Exchange

Early 1980s original-style doubleneck.
Photo by Stanley Bystrowski / Courtesy of Skinner Inc.

Early 1980s "axe" bass.
Photo by Stanley Bystrowski / Courtesy of Skinner Inc.

14
Jonas Ridge Rarities

Since a minimal number of Mosrite instruments were crafted in Jonas Ridge, all of them might be considered somewhat "rare." There were, however, some unusual examples made in the Blue Ridge Mountains beside the production classic styles destined for Japan.

Semie began crafting special-order, one-of-a-kind instruments soon after Mosrite moved to Jonas Ridge. The original-style doubleneck (octave guitar over a standard guitar) and the axe-shaped bass shown here were made before the November 1983 fire.

The doubleneck's body is made of hollowed-out figured walnut with a figured maple top (the wood for the cap came from a church). It's a set-neck instrument, and the standard guitar neck appears to be a leftover item from the mid-1970s—note the slight difference in the headstock "M notches." Moreover, the neck pickup on the standard guitar is not angled.

The axe-shaped bass reportedly has a connection to a California gospel music promoter and Mosrite investor who was a friend of Semie's. Its whimsical legend chronicles that the promoter's son had referred to his own bass as his "axe" while Semie was visiting in California, and the term had to be explained to Moseley, who returned to North Carolina and built this bass for the son. It's made from the same piece of maple from a church that was used for the top of the early 1980s doubleneck.

The "Double Axe" was a three-pickup instrument that drew its influence from Mosrite's two "flame" guitars of the early 1960s. The irony is that the model was created after the destructive fire in 1983. The one shown in a 1984 publicity photo was reportedly the first one made. Its serial number was "AF 1"—"AF" stood for "After Fire." Double Axe models were on display at the 1984 NAMM show, but only a few of them were made during Mosrite's tenure in Jonas Ridge.

There was also an advertised model in a classic, standard-style guitar with three pickups called the Mark III.

In 1984, Semie made another custom guitar for Barbara Mandrell, who had been involved in an automobile accident herself. This one was a steel guitar made from a crutch.

As noted earlier, veteran commercial illustrator Wayne Jarrett was based out of Greensboro, and had been custom-painting motor vehicles since 1969. He credited the fact that he was raised in southern California during the advent of the hot rod culture for influencing his career direction.

Not surprisingly, Jarrett had an ongoing association with more than one NASCAR driver, but he had also worked on Pro Stock automobiles, drag racers, vans, and motorcycles. Among the guitars he painted were instruments owned by Jeff Cook of Alabama, Jeff Carlisi of 38 Special, and Mick Mars of Mötley Crüe.

Jarrett recalled that Cook introduced him to Semie at a California NAMM show. After discussions, they agreed

Double Axe promotional photo, 1984.
Courtesy of Bob Shade

to collaborate on high-quality, specialized finishes for Semie's custom guitars, figuring such an association would be relatively easy to coordinate since their shops were about two and a half hours' driving time from each other.

"He would bring a big ol' box of bodies," Jarrett recounted, "and I'd paint ten to twelve for him at a time. Most of the time he'd tell me to paint them something like candy blue or silver, or different 'bursts. He was real adamant about how he wanted the candy red [finish] done." The friendship between Moseley and Jarrett flourished because of their mutual focus on doing meticulous, high-quality work. Jarrett remembered,

> When he got sick, we started spending more time together because he would come from Jonas Ridge to get his treatments here in Greensboro—it would have been in a medical building over on Wendover Avenue—and he would spend the rest of the day with me. I enjoyed it when he'd come to the shop. We'd go over different things, talking about Gospel guitars and different colors. Sometimes he'd come here once a week.

Wayne was aware of the demand for Mosrite instruments in Japan and Semie's reliance on building instruments to be shipped to that country. "We actually did some custom guitars for some of the Japanese players," the artist remembered. "He really enjoyed doing those for the Japanese market." Some custom instruments even had pickups painted as part of the finish. Jarrett recalled that the idea was his. "I suggested that," he said, "and he said 'Let's try it.' I hate to see a pickup cover in the middle of a pretty paint job; it sticks out like a sore thumb."

Semie in Wayne Jarrett's shop in Greensboro, North Carolina.
Courtesy of Wayne Jarrett

Jonas Ridge-made Mosrite Ventures Model custom-painted by Wayne Jarrett for Mick Mars of Mötley Crüe.
Willie G. Moseley

SM model custom-painted by Wayne Jarrett.
Willie G. Moseley

Three Jonas Ridge Mosrites; the dominant instrument is a one-of-a-kind guitar with a black pickguard, body and headstock binding, humbucking pickups, and coil tap switches.
Courtesy of Pierre Laflamme

Some rare examples of standard-style Mosrite guitars had alternate features, compared to the so-called Ventures-style "reissues."

Semie had monitored John Cummings's (Johnny Ramone) ongoing iconic status regarding Mosrite guitars, and made three instruments for the guitarist—one in black, one in pearl white, and one in plain white.

However, Cummings reportedly didn't relate to the configuration of the guitars that Semie made for him—the Ramones guitarist still preferred a plain, student-style model, like his original Ventures II guitars, but Semie had made the guitars in a full-size Mark I style with a German carve, single large pickup, and only a volume control. Cummings would only play the new guitars on television appearances.

Semie also made a bass for Ramones bassist Christopher Ward (AKA C. J. Ramone). It, too, had a solitary knob for volume control.

A 1990 guitar made for Marty Stuart was a single-neck instrument that was obviously inspired by the original Joe Maphis doubleneck guitar, right down to the wood violin-style (and nonfunctioning) tailpiece, as well as the curlicues on the pickguard and arm guard. Other aesthetic influences were culled from both 1950s and 1960s versions of Joe Maphis Mosrites. It had humbucking pickups and a sand-cast Vibramute. The body contour was flatter on the top, to accommodate a flush-mount pickguard/control plate. The matching arm guard on the lower bout was elevated. The plaque on the top of the headstock reads "Custom Made for Marty Stuart by Semie Moseley—1990."

Pearl White single-pickup guitar made for Johnny Ramone. Semie-signed and dated (1990) on the back of the headstock.
Photo by Stanley Bystrowski / Courtesy of Skinner Inc.

Plain white one-pickup bass made for C. J. Ramone. Signed and dated (1990) by Semie on the back of the headstock.
Photo by Stanley Bystrowski / Courtesy of Skinner Inc.

1990 one-of-a-kind instrument, custom-made for Marty Stuart.
Photo by Stanley Bystrowski / Courtesy of Skinner Inc.

15
Finale in the Arkansas River Valley

In spite of the late-1980s resurgence of interest in Mosrite guitars, the tribulations for Semie's business were arduous, and government officials were now after his Jonas Ridge operation for fire code violations. As the 1990s arrived, Mosrite was getting close to being shut down (again).

Semie heard about a possible opportunity to relocate to Leachville, Arkansas, but his preliminary efforts didn't work out. Another Arkansas opportunity soon transpired, and appeared to be much more promising. A now-empty Wal-Mart building was available in Booneville, a small town in the Arkansas River Valley between the Ozark and Ouachita mountain ranges. Some models of Gretsch guitars had been built in Booneville some years earlier.

The Arkansas state government presented numerous incentives, including an offer to move the company's machinery, supplies, and inventory from Jonas Ridge to Booneville. A line of credit with local banks and a proposed state-financed employee training program were also included in the recruitment package.

Semie and Loretta accepted the offer. Incorporation documentation for the Unified Sound Association, Inc., which would be manufacturing Mosrite instruments, was filed in Arkansas on March 8, 1991. Semie quickly got involved in Booneville and the surrounding area, making speeches to local organizations and drumming up support for the new manufacturing enterprise. He was excited by the new opportunity, remarking that the mountainous rural location of Booneville reminded him of Jonas Ridge.

"Booneville was different," said Pierre Laflamme. "I personally felt that finally, things were going to happen in a big way, with someone else looking after the money and a decent factory, to boot. I went there at the beginning, to help Semie set up the plant."

Nokie Edwards got back on board as an endorser, and Semie began developing a high-end model called the "30th Anniversary Nokie" (to commemorate the guitarist's first visit to Semie's shop in Bakersfield). Also in 1991, Semie and Nokie performed at a concert in Japan with Japanese musicians backing them.

At the advent of 1992, new promotional items were created to commemorate Semie's fortieth anniversary as a guitar builder, as he had cited 1952 as the year he was hired at Rickenbacker. Mosrite's strategy was, of course, to continue to produce instruments primarily for the Japanese market. The Moseleys attended

Semie and Pierre Laflamme with Semie's personal guitar, fall 1991.
Photo by Pierre Laflamme

Japanese ad for a concert by Nokie and Semie in 1991.

Semie examines an instrument that a guitar enthusiast brought to the 1992 Dallas Guitar Show.
Willie G. Moseley

the Dallas Guitar Show in March 1992, where the Mosrite instruments on display at their booth commanded a lot of attention from American and Japanese buyers.

During the exhibition, Semie was interviewed extensively and exclusively for *Vintage Guitar Magazine*. The dialogue is reprinted here in its entirety:

I think a good way to pursue this is to more or less pick up where your first-person story left off in American Guitars *by Tom Wheeler; but before that, is there anything in that particular book that you'd like to clarify?*

Well, I haven't read that book in a long time, but there were some details in the Mosrite section that were a bit fuzzy, and the sequence of some things wasn't right. I'd like to state categorically that Mosrite has never been out of business, but there were times when we'd been out of the competitive, production part. When I was sick I just slowed down until I got well. Nowadays, we can't build enough guitars to fill all of the orders we have—there's that much demand for Mosrite.

Also, the "Ventures Model" guitar was named in honor of the Ventures; the Ventures do not endorse Mosrite, but they started playing Mosrites because the guitars made them sound like they wanted their band to sound.

Nokie Edwards *does* endorse Mosrite; he plays Mosrite today. He's the one who should really get the credit for Mosrite being introduced to the world; I think that needs to be noted.

During the harder times, were you ever approached to sell the Mosrite name?

Oh, yes—many, many times, and it even happens today. When I was sick, I was able to make a living by doing a few concerts and making a few custom guitars. At one time, I was disabled for three years. I could've retired, but I refused to do so.

My motives were two-fold: One, I wanted to make a living for my family, of course. And "Reason Number Two" may sound melodramatic, but when I lay down for the last time, I want Mosrite to be at the top again, and I want the crew to continue to build them to the quality standards I've set, after I'm gone. I don't want someone to have the Mosrite name and put it on mass-produced guitars that look and sound like everybody else's. My family is now involved with the company, so we can keep the name, and when I lay down for the last time, I can be at peace.

Most guitar enthusiasts consider the Mosrite body shape to be a "flipped-over Fender," but your experience with another guitar company before going out on your own was as an employee of Rickenbacker, not Fender, right?

Paul Barth owned one-third of Rickenbacker, and I went to work for him in the '50s. I'd played guitar since I was nine years old, and had been playing professionally since the seventh grade. So when I went to work there, I changed their guitar neck; I scraped it down and made it feel how a guitar player would want it to feel, and they still use the same shape now. I have a lot of respect for Rickenbacker; I really want to give them credit for taking in this young kid back then and putting up with him! [laughs] They've kept their business in their family, and that's what we're also doing here at Mosrite.

You referred to a guitar called the Brass Rail in American Guitars, *but the details regarding its construction weren't noted.*

There was a quarter-inch-wide exposed brass rail running down the center of the fretboard. Sustain was important to players back then, and there's been nothing *before or since* that offered so much natural sustain; the frets were bradded directly onto the rail. But it was so expensive to manufacture that we stopped making them; they're very rare and I think we made around 75 of them. However, we have full intentions of putting this type of guitar back into production sometime down the road.

Around that time, you were really having trouble with financing your efforts, weren't you?

Everyone that was going to help me with financing back then, including banks, said, "Prove you can build and sell your guitars, and we'll finance your orders." But when I'd get orders for several thousands of dollars' worth of instruments, then they'd decide they wanted to own part of the company. Even bankers took this approach! Some crazy things happened, so I went back to making custom instruments. For the last ten years, ninety-nine percent of my guitars have been bought by the Japanese. I also made instruments for Barbara Mandrell and Fred Newell.

How did you end up in Jonas Ridge, North Carolina? It isn't even on a map!

My wife is from there. We moved there planning on going into full-time gospel music, and I was going to build custom guitars to support that effort. We set up shop in an old schoolhouse. Soon I had orders for 500 guitars for Japan; some Japanese people wanted me to go to Japan and oversee the manufacturing of those guitars there, but I wouldn't do it, even though they offered to pay me $50,000. I decided to build them here, but on the way to California to work out some finances, I had a car wreck. I was rolling around the shop in a wheelchair for some time. The Japanese order got up to 700, of which we had 300 in production. Then we had a fire on November 22, 1983, that burned up the factory. We'd only shipped six of the guitars to Japan; we lost everything and were in debt. So we decided that we'd better get serious about making guitars.

In the late '80s, I made one for Elliot Easton of the Cars, and he wrote an article about me for *Guitar World* magazine. Later, the magazine sent a reporter and photographer to Jonas Ridge, and they did a centerspread story on Mosrite. We ran a small ad in that magazine and got about *3,000 letters* or inquiries from dealers and individuals, so I was inspired to keep going; I said "They still want Mosrite," so here we are!

What about the Gospel brand of guitar I saw advertised a while back in Gospel Music *magazine?*

My roots are in gospel music; when I was a kid I just wanted to make guitars for gospel musicians. I first registered the Gospel trademark in the late '60s. When we got going pretty good in the late '80s, I decided to try and offer something different to my original favorite musicians, so in 1990 we ran a four-page, full-color centerspread in *Gospel Music* magazine, showing three models. We had a low response; maybe only five guitars were sold off of that ad. So I said "Okay, we gave it a shot," and I went back to building Mosrites. By this time there were some Stateside buyers.

At the time you relocated from Jonas Ridge to Arkansas, how many were you making?

About 30 per month, all going to Japan.

Tell me about the move. 'Why' would be an obvious question.

Arkansas had offered me some incentives—an old Wal-Mart in Booneville that was 22,000 square feet, a line of credit, plus they offered to move me. We were thinking about it when the fire inspectors threatened to shut me down in Jonas Ridge . . . which is a bit strange, in that I operated for almost eight years in that particular setup, which included running the electrical lines into little sheds that I'd built. But now they were going to pull the plug, so I accepted Arkansas's offer. Otherwise, Mosrite would have been out of business.

They sent a state truck to move me, paid all of the costs, and they're financing a training program.

Since Gretsch used to be located there, another obvious question would be if you're using any of their old machinery.

No, but we *are* gleaning from some of their former employees. In fact, Gene Haugh, who's my production manager, was also a production manager with Gretsch. We're just getting underway there, but we hope to be making five to ten guitars per day by the end of the year.

Will you be making vintage styles only?

No, we'll be full-line. Vintage styles do take a little longer to make, though. We also plan to re-introduce accessories.

You commented a minute ago that you were getting some Stateside buyers by the late '80s. Do you think the percentage of domestic buyers of your products will increase?

Well, Japan will probably always be the major market for the Ventures Model. The Ventures have a great deal of respect over there, *and they should have.* The marriage between the Ventures and Mosrite was a natural. Nokie has re-united with us; he and I did a concert there last year and we're doing another in November.

The Japanese fans explain it like this: They want to re-live their youth; when they were young they wanted a Mosrite Ventures Model guitar. Now they're maybe 45 years old and they can afford one; they pay up to $20,000 for an old Mosrite.

But isn't the "re-living one's youth" an American phenomenon concerning old guitars as well, although US persons that age might seek many other brands besides Mosrite?

That's true with almost *any* person concerning his or her youth. When I was young, I wanted a pedal car and my folks couldn't afford one. After I was grown, a company once showed me a "pedal car for grownups"; they called it a "People Car." I bought the franchise for it! [laughs]

Have you made any special instruments recently that you want to note?

I made a guitar for myself to celebrate my fortieth year in the business. It's made from burl rosewood from Brazil, and it's got an old-style vibrato on it that I hand-shaved from aluminum. The fretboard is scalloped, since I do a lot of bending when I play.

I also made a couple of guitars in an unusual shape; we called it the "Double Axe." We made those just to show everyone that we could make a guitar with a strange shape if we wanted to. One rare feature is that they have is six-on-a-side tuners. I painted one pink for my wife.

Not to sound like a marketing cliché, but is it your contention that "Mosrite is back and better than ever"?

Definitely! My health is better than it's ever been, except for maybe the day I was born. [chuckles] I'm gratified that something I made for myself ultimately turned out to be wanted by other players. I did some things by accident in the '60s, but I had to have learned *something* in 40 years! [laughs]

The irony in some of Semie's remarks would soon become self-evident. The initial Booneville training program was promising, as was the quality of initial production instruments. However, in early summer, Semie began to feel woozy. The dizziness and disorientation increased, and he was hospitalized. The diagnosis quickly came back as multiple myeloma, a type of blood cancer that attacks plasma cells in bone marrow. Semie's health rapidly deteriorated, and he breathed his last on August 7, 1992. His body was transported to Jonas Ridge, where he was buried in his wife's family cemetery.

Wayne Jarrett reflected on Semie's passing, noting, "I know a lot of people in the music business, and there's a lot of arrogance out there. Most people don't start out like that, but it becomes part of their lifestyle. But Semie was always a good, down-to-earth guy; the kind of person you'd see in Walmart."

The Booneville operation continued, trying to salvage some kind of motivation following the relatively abrupt death of the Mosrite founder.

By the end of the year, a downsized version of the Combo model was being developed. It was dubbed, not surprisingly, the Mini-Combo. Former Gretsch employee Gene Haugh was involved with the Mini-Combo's design.

There was also a one-pickup "Ramones'" model in the works, as well as a budget two-pickup guitar without a vibrato, German carve, or binding. Pickups were being hand-wound by Semie's daughter Dana and Loretta's daughter Merinda Kacsmaryk. Almost all of the Booneville Mosrites were being shipped to Japan. Part of the Booneville facility's interior had been walled off and was being converted into an auditorium when Semie died. It was now considered—by employees and visitors alike—to be a shrine. "Semie was joking that we would get so big we'd have to convert the *entire* old Wal-Mart into an auditorium and move down the road into the old Gretsch facilities," Loretta said in a late 1992 interview.

The rigorous training program stayed in effect following Semie's passing, as the company endeavored to create the highest-quality Mosrites that had ever been made.

"That's not to say anything negative about Semie," company vice-president Jerry Standridge clarified at the time, "but now that he's gone, customers are going to be even more meticulous about Mosrite instruments, since

Stack of bodies with German carve in the Booneville factory.
Willie G. Moseley

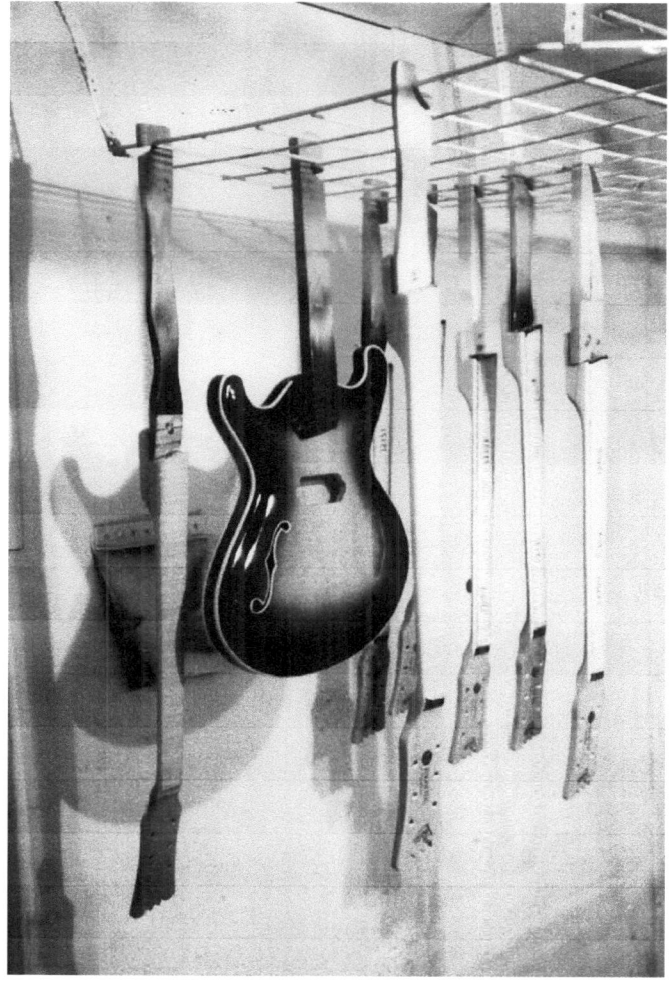

Experimental Mini-Combo body in drying chamber.
Willie G. Moseley

Finale in the Arkansas River Valley 99

he won't be making them. They'll go over each instrument with a fine tooth comb. We've got a tremendous responsibility to live up to."

Loretta averred that in spite of Semie's passing earlier in the year, the employees and management were still building instruments with the Mosrite founder in mind.

"We'll find ourselves saying things like 'Semie would like that' or 'Semie *wouldn't* like that,'" she said. "We fully intend to keep his name at the forefront of this company when we do our marketing, because this company was his life."

A Semie Moseley memorial concert was held in the factory auditorium in late April 1993, as a benefit to help out with residual medical expenses. Attendees included Semie's mother, Irene, Nokie Edwards, Andy Moseley, Andy's son Mark (who was a noted producer in Nashville) and author Del Halterman. One of Mosrite's biggest Japanese business associates, Keiichi Takaya, brought several fans from that nation. However, the travails of the company continued. Arkansas state records indicate that the incorporation of the Unified Sound Association was terminated on January 5, 1995.

Courtesy of Del Halterman

Part 2
Hallmark

Early-1960s Sterling doubleneck.
Courtesy of Jeremy Gullotto

Early-1960s Sterling guitar.
Courtesy of Bob Shade

16
Starting Solo with Sterling Instruments

The chronicle of Joe Hall's surname-referenced brand, Hallmark, is unique, and is decidedly different from the multiple-state history of Mosrite. What's more, its two main storylines are separated by decades.

Like Semie Moseley, Hall was a native of Oklahoma, and had been one of the Mosrite builder's earliest Bakersfield associates. As noted earlier, Hall had moved to Bakersfield in 1959, and had hooked up with Moseley soon after Semie had returned to the southern San Joaquin Valley from the Los Angeles area.

Hall was also one of the first Mosrite associates to depart. He contended that Semie had promised him an opportunity to be a part-owner of the company, but such a business deal didn't happen. So Joe left Mosrite in 1962, soon after working with Semie on the primeval (Standel) solidbody guitar that would evolve into the iconic Mosrite Ventures Model. He'd picked up plenty of information about guitar building, however, and set about making his own way in luthiery.

Joe's rare first creations went by the Sterling brand name, and he meticulously handcrafted each instrument, just like Semie. A lot of the metalwork was hand-formed aluminum, and the string guide on some guitars was a piece of slotted fret wire, aluminum, or Plexiglas. Most Sterling instruments had carved tops, laminated woods, and scroll work. They were well-made and sturdy.

The six-on-a-side headstock silhouettes on one early doubleneck matched the headstocks seen on some mid-1950s Mosrite guitars, and the pickguard silhouette matched those found on the "scroll" guitars Semie had made around 1960 (and Hall had purchased one of those).

The early Sterling doubleneck instrument had an angled bass/neck pickup on the standard guitar, and zero frets on both necks. Most of Hall's early handwound pickups had adjustable polepieces and two flat alnico magnets under the coil. Many had wood covers, as was the case on the early doubleneck seen here. The instrument also had plastic fret marker stripes. The body was finished in a light sunburst color and had a scroll on the lower bout only, as well as two maple strips inlaid on the top.

A single-neck Sterling guitar had a silhouette that seemed to reference a reversal of the original Mosrite design by Semie and Joe—the upper bass cutaway horn was longer than the lower treble cutaway horn. It also had a bound body, side jack, and fret markers on the bass side of the fretboard.

There was also a blond, double-scrolled instrument with a prominent German carve and a light-colored headstock overlay.

Early-1960s Sterling guitar, blond double-scroll body.
Courtesy of Bob Shade

Sterling doubleneck, ca. 1964.
Willie G. Moseley

Early-1960s Sterling octave guitar.
Courtesy of Bob Shade

Hall also crafted an octave guitar that had a decorative wood stripe in the middle of its fretboard. It also had symmetrical cutaway horns and a wood pickup cover.

One of Hall's latter-day Sterling doublenecks had an electric mandolin as its upper instrument, as well as 3 + 3 and 4 + 4 tuner layouts on its headstocks. The Mosrite Vibramute on this example's standard guitar is intriguing—there was originally a Hall-made vibrato on the instrument; the Vibramute was added later but the arm is different from most Vibramutes. The vibrato still has the "harp" center outline of the Guild/Mosrite vibrato, but there's no ground-out area that has been painted black.

Artie Niesen's encounters with Sterling guitars—as both a musician and guitar dealer—have been rare occurrences, even in Bakersfield. However, he corroborated Hall's own recollection about Semie's allowance of ancillary building projects.

"I've only seen three or four Sterlings in my life," he said. "I didn't know Joe Hall at the time, but I knew that the guy who had made Sterlings had worked for Semie. I'd always thought that Sterling was built by Semie's employees, and that Semie had allowed them to build their own guitars alongside Mosrites."

Transitional double-branded instrument with Hallmark and Standel logos.
Courtesy of Bill Ingalls Jr.

17
The Standel Interlude

Joe's next initiative would be brief, and would involve another placement of the Standel moniker on Bakersfield-made instruments. The Temple City amplifier company was still seeking to get into the guitar business, and Hall signed on to make instruments branded with Standel's snakelike logo.

The resulting two-pickup guitar and short scale, one-pickup bass were arguably more balanced and more comfortable to play than Mosrite classic-style solidbodies. The headstock silhouette was asymmetrical and seemed to have a vague allusion to Mosrite. Hall's Standel-branded guitars and basses also had, like Mosrites, zero frets and angled neck pickups.

Joe's own innovations included a large die-cast plate on the guitar that housed both pickups and the bridge all in one unit. The Standel logo appeared on a medallion that was placed between the two pickups. The vibrato was Hall's own design, and he would also install an arm from one of these units on his large Mosrite "scroll" guitar he had ordered from Semie around 1960. The bass was simpler, and its Standel medallion was installed directly on the body.

An ad in the July 1, 1965, issue of *Downbeat* magazine heralded the instruments' connection to the quality of Standel amplifiers, as well as their light weight, balance, and features such as an innovative roller bridge. The guitar and bass shown in the ad were in a sunburst finish, but three solid-color options were also available.

Unfortunately, the advertisement was about as far as Standel went with the Hall-built instruments. Joe recalled that the business relationship ended abruptly, and he would consider the Standel-branded instruments he'd made to have been prototypes.

Hall would later build a few "floor-sweep" instruments made from left-over bodies, necks, and parts that were originally intended to be Standel instruments. Some of them were double-branded, with a Hallmark brand name on the headstock and a Standel logo medallion still located in the middle of the die-cast plate. These were the first instruments to bear the early Hallmark logo, albeit with another brand's logo. Hall estimated that, all told, only around twenty-five Hall-made Standel and Standel/Hallmark guitars and basses were built.

Standel guitar ad, seen in the July 1, 1965, issue of *Downbeat*.

Brochure illustration of Marlin guitar.
Courtesy of Del Halterman

Brochure illustration of Ocelot guitar.
Courtesy of Del Halterman

Brochure illustration of El Toro guitar.
Courtesy of Del Halterman

18
The Encor Initiative

Interestingly, the history of Encor brand instruments, a very brief 1965 venture (no pun intended) between Joe Hall and Bob Bogle, contains more information than might be expected. The total number of Encors made in 1965 consisted, according to Hall, of only two handcrafted instruments—one guitar prototype and one bass prototype.

Having divested himself of his business association with the Ventures/Mosrite guitar enterprise, Bogle had been watching from somewhat of a "sidelines" perspective as the success of Mosrite in the electric guitar marketplace continued to grow. Ultimately, he decided to embark on his own musical instrument business sojourn, and partnered with an electronics factory in the Canoga Park section of Los Angeles.

Bogle named the new company Encor. The company was supposed to manufacture and market amplifiers as well as guitars from the get-go. While the initial emphasis for the new business was to be on amps, the Ventures' bassist hired an automobile designer to create a modernistic solidbody design that was somewhat wedge-shaped with deep cutaways.

Two two-pickup guitars, the Marlin and the Ocelot, were envisioned, along with a two-pickup bass, the El Toro. Artwork of such instruments was seen in a four-page, three-color brochure alongside numerous piggyback amplifiers with names like the Bermuda, the Malibu, and the Waikiki (which had a "built-in Reverb-Echo Chamber").

Encor lined up Joe Hall, who was still building guitars in Bakersfield, to create prototype salesman's samples of Encor instruments. Hall recounted that one Marlin guitar and one El Toro bass were made. Several prototype amplifiers were made in Canoga Park. The aforementioned brochure was reportedly printed while the Ventures were on a lengthy tour of Japan during the first half of 1965. In addition to their space-age body configuration, the prototype Encor instruments sported modernistic asymmetrical headstocks.

The Ocelot and the Marlin were to be designed as exactly alike except for the width and depth of their respective necks. The Marlin was to have a relatively chunky neck "for average to large hands," according to the brochure, while the Ocelot's slimmer neck was touted as "[e]specially designed for small to average hands." Both guitars had a "4-way adjustable bridge" and a vibrato system.

The El Toro bass was unique in that its design included a vibrato. While bass vibrato systems would turn up in future decades on brands such as Peavey and G & L such a device would certainly have been considered cutting-edge in the mid-1960s.

Other features for the guitars and bass included "ultra-high-sensitive pick-ups with individual magnets," "selector switches for activating or combining pick-ups," an "adjustable truss-rod neck," and a rosewood fretboard. Cosmetics included an "attractive shell pickguard." Body colors proffered were Arctic Ice Blue, Pearl White, Mustang Red, Ebony Black, Sunburst, and Candy Apple Red. The brochure illustrations were advance images, so it's interesting to note that the treble cutaways on all three instruments differed from each other.

A letter purported to have been written and signed by Bob Bogle was part of the brochure. More than one road salesman was hired, and the initial reception by dealers to the new line was said to be encouraging. However, the Encor enterprise never got off the launching pad, because of alleged financial impropriety by Bogle's business partner. In early September, the bassist returned from that year's second tour of Japan to find the Canoga Park facility deserted. Bogle abandoned the Encor project, and decided to exit the musical instrument manufacturing business.

Willie G. Moseley

In 2018, Bob Shade discovered that the Encor El Toro bass prototype was for sale in Montana. Its potentiometers did indeed date from 1965, but some of the instrument's aesthetics were decidedly different from what an artist had imagined in the Encor brochure. Gone were the envisioned numerous switches and small pickups.

The neck is one-piece maple with an Indian rosewood fretboard sporting twenty frets. The instrument's scale is 30.5 inches. The body is alder. The contour of the upper bass cutaway horn differs slightly from the brochure illustration, but the lower treble cutaway seems to match. The pickups were made by Hall, and didn't resemble the pickups in the brochure illustration at all. What looked like bar-style pickups in the pamphlet turned out to be large rectangular units with individual alnico magnet polepieces poking through.

Some observers might think the pickups were Gibson items, as found on that company's then-frontline basses such as the EB-O, EB-2, and EB-3. However, the polepieces on these Encor units aren't adjustable or threaded, as was the case for similar-looking Gibson pickups. Moreover, the large rectangular housings of this prototype's pickups are half an inch wider than a Gibson bass pickup (dimensions were 4 inches by 2 inches for Encor and 3.5 inches by 2 inches for Gibson).

The Gibson pickup was a humbucking design, while the Hall-created pickups were hotly wound, single-coil units. The sheer size of the Hall pickups implies that they were more potent than the bar-type pickups seen on the instrument illustrations in the Encor brochure.

The prototype El Toro's pickguard is similar to the catalog illustration, but is made from brushed aluminum instead of "attractive shell." Hall was developing the use of aluminum on his instruments in those days; parts made from that metal had also appeared on Sterling and Standel-branded instruments he crafted.

The bass vibrato mechanism was under the chrome plate, and was hand-fabricated. As a primeval example of such a gizmo, its design was quite crude and its operation wasn't particularly reliable. The Encor brochure illustrations had displayed all three instruments with an industry-standard layout of one dot marker on all designated frets except the twelfth, which had two.

Willie G. Moseley

On this prototype, however, the fret markers are laid out in pairs on the first octave, three dots on the twelfth fret and single dots in the higher register, à la Mosrite. Curiously, the fret markers and the nut are made from clear acrylic. There's no white or bright-colored filler under the transparent plugs on the fretboard. Hall was also experimenting with acrylic material around the time this prototype was made (as were Semie Moseley and Bill Gruggett, in their own respective endeavors).

The Encor enterprise was a fulguration in the history of California guitar and amplifier manufacturing, and its instrument inventory consisted of no more than two prototype instruments. Nevertheless, their aesthetics would motivate Joe Hall in the near future.

19
The Swept-Wing Takes Flight

Joe Hall remained ambitious in spite of his two short-lived 1965 attempts to build contracted instruments. He decided to create instruments bearing a brand name that referenced his own surname, and moved about fifteen miles south of Bakersfield to a town called Arvin. His guitar facility was located on Derby Street.

At the beginning of the Hallmark enterprise, Don Stanley, who was in charge of tooling at Mosrite, left that company to work for Joe Hall, who remembered the highly respected Stanley as a huge asset to his fledgling business. And to say that the introductory model of the new 1966 Hallmark line was radical was an understatement, particularly since those guitars and basses were created in an area that had become known as "Nashville West," thanks to the local music scene.

At first glance, the aerodynamic silhouette of the Hallmark Swept-Wing's body seemed to resemble the "scoop" on the side of a 1959 Chevrolet Corvette. An aesthetic this revolutionary on an American guitar seemed to roar *Whoosh!* to anyone who simply *looked* at the instrument.

Joe brought in fellow luthier Bill Gruggett, another former Mosrite employee, who would work with Hall in Arvin during the development of the Swept-Wing. Gruggett assisted in the design of other potential models, and also began the initial stages of creating a proprietary line that bore his own surname. Swept-Wing bodies were made of mahogany or alder, and the neck was a two-piece bolt-on style. A piece of maple would be sliced in two, and one piece would be reversed as the two pieces would be glued together. The neck was then cut out with the juncture of the two pieces as the centerline. The stability was as good as that of a quartersawn neck. The fretboard was rosewood and had a zero fret. The guitar had a Fender-like scale of 25.5 inches (vs. Mosrite's 24.5 inches), and the bass had a 30-inch scale.

Hall had originally built his pickups with alnico magnets running from the top of the cover to the bottom of the pickup, similar to Fender pickups of the same era. However, after being threatened with legal action because of the design, Hall reverted to the adjustable-polepieces, two-alnico-magnet style he'd been using since his early days as a builder (he'd used them on his Sterling and Standel instruments).

Curiously, the pickups on Swept-Wing basses retained the exposed, nonadjustable alnico rods. Hall's pickups had black, white, or tortoise-shell covers. Swept-Wing guitars used a lot of hardware from the same suppliers that serviced Mosrite. Parts included bridges, strap buttons, and wood-trimmed tailpieces. The earliest vibrato (and bridge) unit to be installed on a Swept-Wing was made by the Kapa company of Hyattsville, Maryland. Hall then opted to use a Japanese vibrato tailpiece that was similar to a Fender design, and later ordered vibratos made by a local machinist that replicated the Japanese vibrato. The local vibratos were heavier and turned out to be more stable.

Swept-Wing prototype with Kapa vibrato.
Courtesy of the Joe Hall Estate

The Swept-Wing lineup was originally marketed in a 1966 brochure, proffering a "Deluxe" model with a vibrato as well as a hardtail "Professional" or "Pro" model. A single-pickup, hardtail "Student" model was listed, as was a twelve-string model. The bass was offered with one pickup or two.

Standard colors listed included Cardinal Red, Regal Blue, Raven (black), and (pearl) White, but the brochure also noted, "Pearlescent colors available at a slight additional charge." Custom colors included sparkle finishes dubbed Metallic Blue and Metallic Red. At least one sunburst-finish Swept-Wing was built, but most of its finish was hidden by the large, flush-mounted control plate pickguard, which covered most of the front surface of the body.

The front cover of the 1966 brochure showed a 12/6 double-neck guitar. The toggle switch that controlled the pickups on twelve-string neck was on the upper bass cutaway horn, the toggle switch that controlled the neck on–off function was on the body between the two neck butts, and the toggle switch that controlled the six-string pickups was on the lower treble cutaway horn—a simple and practical arrangement.

Three Swept-Wing doublenecks would be made. On the back cover of the 1966 brochure, Joe was shown with Eric "The Doctor" Hord, an LA session musician who was the lead guitarist for the group of studio musicians that backed up the Mamas and the Papas. Hallmark had agreed to a "tie-in" advertising and catalog collaboration with the Jordan amplifier company of Pasadena, California, and one of those amplifiers appeared on the back of the brochure.

Bill Gruggett soon opted to go out on his own again, but this time with a full-blown line. He and Hall would remain friends and collaborators regarding their respective brands. In 1967, Hall decided to expand his line with an "Electric Acoustic" series of semihollow instruments. The semihollow process began by simply routing out sections out of the alder bodies of solid-body examples of the same model, to create a skeleton-like frame. A lift was then glued to the center of the front and back of the frame to support the arch of the top and back, which was constructed of marine-grade plywood. The top veneer on such plywood was birch or a similar wood that had a decent grain pattern and was capable of having a quality finish applied to it. The completed semihollow body was 12.5 inches wide and two inches deep.

Production models of the "Electric Acoustic" series were available in "Sunburst" and "Cherry Burst" finishes. Asymmetrical oddities on the semihollow

1966 brochure, front cover.
Courtesy of Bob Shade

1966 brochure, back cover featuring Joe Hall posing with Eric "The Doctor" Hord.
Courtesy of Bob Shade

Top left: Swept-Wing Deluxe, (pearl) White finish.

Top center: Swept-Wing Deluxe. Raven (black)—this unusual example has one original-style Hallmark (neck) pickup and one-latter style (bridge) pickup, and is autographed by surf music icon Dick Dale.

Top right: Swept-Wing Deluxe, custom Blue Metallic (sparkle) finish.

Bottom left: Swept-Wing Deluxe, Cardinal Red finish.

Bottom right: Swept-Wing Pro, custom Red Metallic (sparkle) finish.

Courtesy of Michael G. Stewart

Swept-Wing bass, (pearl) White finish front and back. Note the matching back of the headstock.
Willie G. Moseley

Top left: Swept-Wing "Electric Acoustic" semihollow, three-tone sunburst, 1967.

Top right: Swept-Wing "Electric Acoustic" semihollow, three-tone sunburst which appears to have faded to two-tone. 1967. This phenomenon, due to exposure to ultraviolet light rays, was also seen on other sunburst finishes on other brands of instruments.

Bottom left: Swept-Wing "Electric Acoustic" semihollow twelve-string, 1967 front (refinished in sparkleburst decades later by Bill Gruggett).

Bottom center: Swept-Wing "Electric Acoustic" semihollow twelve-string back.

Bottom right: Swept-Wing "Electric Acoustic" two-pickup semihollow bass, serial #003127 (1967).

Courtesy of Michael G. Stewart

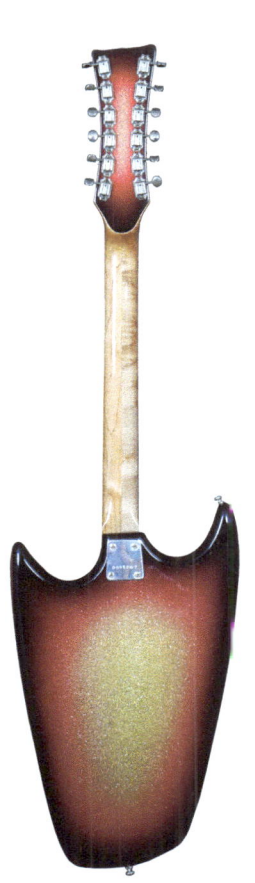

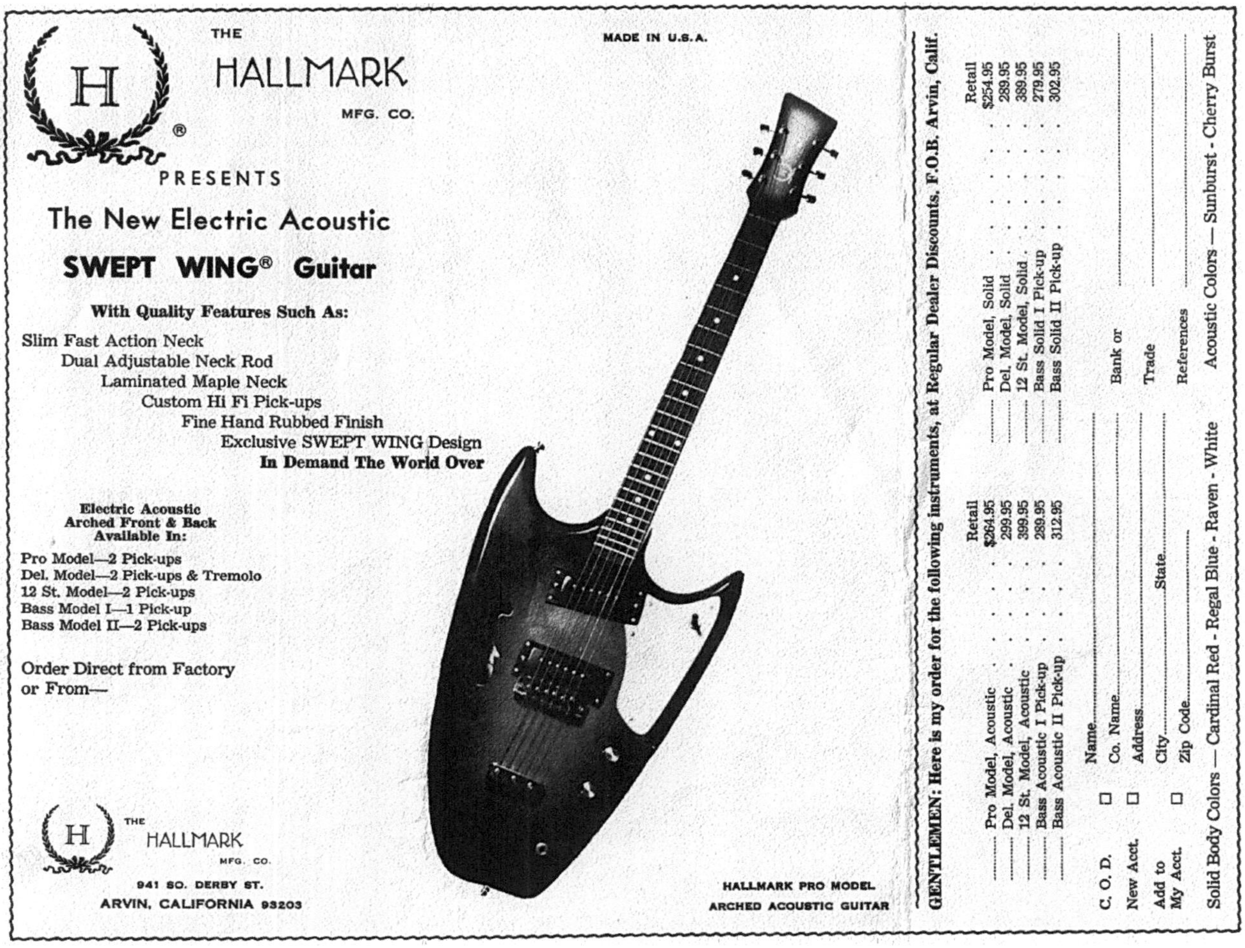

THE HALLMARK MFG. CO.

PRESENTS

The New Electric Acoustic SWEPT WING® Guitar

MADE IN U.S.A.

With Quality Features Such As:

- Slim Fast Action Neck
- Dual Adjustable Neck Rod
- Laminated Maple Neck
- Custom Hi Fi Pick-ups
- Fine Hand Rubbed Finish
- Exclusive SWEPT WING Design
- **In Demand The World Over**

Electric Acoustic Arched Front & Back Available In:

- Pro Model—2 Pick-ups
- Del. Model—2 Pick-ups & Tremolo
- 12 St. Model—2 Pick-ups
- Bass Model I—1 Pick-up
- Bass Model II—2 Pick-ups

Order Direct from Factory or From—

THE HALLMARK MFG. CO.
941 SO. DERBY ST.
ARVIN, CALIFORNIA 93203

HALLMARK PRO MODEL
ARCHED ACOUSTIC GUITAR

GENTLEMEN: Here is my order for the following instruments, at Regular Dealer Discounts. F.O.B. Arvin, Calif.

	Retail			Retail
Pro Model, Acoustic	$264.95	Pro Model, Solid		$254.95
Del. Model, Acoustic	299.95	Del. Model, Solid		289.95
12 St. Model, Acoustic	389.95	12 St. Model, Solid		389.95
Bass Acoustic I Pick-up	289.95	Bass Solid I Pick-up		279.95
Bass Acoustic II Pick-up	312.95	Bass Solid II Pick-up		302.95

C.O.D. ☐   Name ....
New Acct. ☐   Co. Name ....
Add to My Acct. ☐   Address ....
City .... State ....
Zip Code ....
Bank or Trade References ....

Solid Body Colors — Cardinal Red - Regal Blue - Raven - White
Acoustic Colors — Sunburst - Cherry Burst

NAMM SHOW 1967

Hallmark and Gruggett instruments on display in Chicago in 1967. That's the El Dorado prototype in the right foreground.
Courtesy of Bob Shade

Swept-Wings included a three-layer, white–black–white pickguard with a silhouette that looked like the blade of a battleaxe, as well as a small and unusual looking f-hole.

Two-pickup "Electric Acoustic" basses were exceedingly rare, so much so that Hall recalled that the example seen here may have been special-order. Moreover, this bass serves as an example of Hallmark's serial number coding system.

The serial numbers of Hallmark instruments were found on the neck mounting plate. The serial number on the two-pickup "Electric Acoustic" bass, 003127, indicates that it was the third instrument ("003") made in the twelfth week ("12") of 1967 ("7"). Simple as that.

"For the most part, the Swept-Wing was about the only model produced in the Hallmark plant," Hall recalled. "We designed and built the prototype for what we called the El Dorado, which looked like a double-cutaway, semihollow Gibson, with a formed arched top and double f-holes."

A 1967 order form for both solidbody and semihollow versions of the Swept-Wing was illustrated with a six-string "Electric Acoustic" model. At one point, Andy Moseley was a partner with Joe's company. Moseley recalled to Bob Shade that he was brought in when one of Joe's partners was bought out.

The ongoing friendship between Bill Gruggett and Joe Hall prompted the two builders to share a booth to exhibit their wares at the 1967 NAMM show in Chicago.

Hoping to generate interest in the line, a sales representative began distributing Hallmark Swept-Wings to musicians in the greater Los Angeles area. One recipient of a guitar was reportedly Robby Krieger of the Doors, and an ad was published in a 1967 issue of *Hullabaloo* magazine that strongly implied that the Doors used the brand and model. However, Krieger apparently never endorsed Hallmark, and there is also no record of him having played his Swept-Wing in public. A Swept-Wing "Electric Acoustic" was shown in the ad.

Bakersfield musicians who noticed and perhaps coveted Hallmark Swept-Wings probably included a disproportionate number of teenagers. "Hallmarks were in the area," said Artie Niesen. "I knew people that had those. They were radical-looking. When I was a paper boy, I went into a club down the street, and they had a big poster-size photo over the bar of a guy in a full Indian headdress playing a Hallmark Swept-Wing."

At least one pro player became an enthusiastic performer with his Swept-Wing. John Morton was the lead guitarist for a band from the Pacific Northwest called Hunger. That aggregation had relocated to Hollywood, and Morton remembered his acquisition of his guitar and the audience reaction to it. He considered his Swept-Wing to be "a Mosrite-configured instrument with a changed body, thanks to Joe Hall."

The band's equipment had been stolen in late 1967, and management lined up a meeting with Hall to discuss the possibility of Morton playing and endorsing Hallmark. Morton recalled,

> I met Joe Hall with our manager, and Joe opened that case and I was blown away. I loved the blue sparkle, black pickups, thin neck and out-of-this-world body design. I smiled at Joe and said "I'll endorse the hell out this guitar as my go-to instrument—onstage, recording and wherever we play!"
>
> Joe was thrilled that I would expose his Swept-Wing to a worldwide audience, and looked at me and said "We're going to give Fender and Gibson a run for their money!"
>
> Everywhere I played people would ask me what kind of strange new guitar I was playing. It was ideal for me with the antics I did onstage. It was easy to play, with a thin fast neck and with its design—ideal for playing wide strokes and hand movements as I strutted across the stage.

As for the sound and operation of his guitar, Morton remembered that

> the pickups were strong on the Swept-Wing. They had very good response and were ideal for our psychedelic sound. The only change I had made was a cut-off switch put on the guitar so there'd be no feedback between songs. Other than that, the electronics were great. The guitar never failed me with the heavy use I put through it. I liked the position of the controls—totally out of the way with the right hand picking for lead or rhythm. It had the ideal sound, too—a cross between a Fender and Gibson guitar, but yet very unique with its *own* sound.

The Hunger guitarist was also enthusiastic about the Swept-Wing's sonic attributes in the studio: "The Swept-Wing was great for recording. I needed only one take on the guitar tracks. . . . My favorite song is 'Workshop in My Mind.' The subtlety of the lead is simple yet powerful in its delivery."

Courtesy of Bob Shade

Hullabaloo Club News

At least another 25 Hullabaloos will be opened by the end of the year. At this point John Angel has been launching new ones so fast — sometimes four and five a week — it's hard to keep track. Take for example one week last month. We were all over the ball park. Kansas City, Mo.; Gulfport, Fla.; Aurora, Ill.; Wind Gap, Pa.; and Norwalk, Conn.

Down in little 'ole Wind Gap, population just a little over 2,000 at last count, the great music of "The First Grade" whipped it up for the first nighters. Over in the Chicago suburb of Aurora, "The Little Boy Blues" had the local YADS yelling for more after they played their hit recording of "I'm Ready," "The Train Robbery" and "I Can Give You Everything". In Gulfport it was "The Jades" a group well-known to Floridian YADS, who broke it up. And out in the former badlands of the West, Kansas City, "The Chessmen" and Hullabaloo Dancers Michelle and Peggy, got things off to a smashing start.

So keep your boots on, wherever you may be. Before you know it, a Hullabaloo will be opening near you . . . sooner than you think.

Over the past couple of months we've been getting loads of queries on where all the Hullabaloos are. Some of the correspondents point out that they are allowed to travel up to 30 miles from their homesteads if there is a Hullabaloo at the end of the rainbow.

So, get out your Atlases. You might find one in the following list that is even closer. You know the old saying: "Sometimes you don't even know what's going on in your own back yard."

Hullabaloo Clubs Now Open

ALABAMA
HUNTSVILLE
3413 Memorial Parkway
ARIZONA
PHOENIX
3030 North 7th Street
COLORADO
COLORADO SPRINGS
3200 North Nevada Ave
CONNECTICUT
ANSONIA
212/220 Main Street
MIDDLETOWN
590 Washington Street
NORWALK
195 Main Street
ROCKY HILL
1930 Silas Dean Highway
WATERBURY
373 Thomaston Avenue
WATERFORD
Rope Ferry Road
FLORIDA
CLEARWATER
225 North Fort Harrison
GULFORT
1839 49th St., South
SANFORD
2613 Orlando Drive
SARASOTA
70 Azar Plaza
GEORGIA
COLUMBIA
4411 River Road
DECATUR
1240 Columbia
MACON
482 Walnut Street
ILLINOIS
AURORA
950 East New York St.
INDIANA
FORT WAYNE
5711 Hatfield Road
PORTAGE
Portage Mall
LOUISIANA
NEW ORLEANS
2047 Airline Highway
MARYLAND
GLEN BURNIE
130 Crain Highway, N.W.
SALISBURY
South Division St. Ext
MASSACHUSETTS
DUDLEY
Hall Road
SOUTH DEERFIELD
Route #5
MICHIGAN
CLARKSTON
6696 Dixie Highway
DEARBORN
25125 Ford Road
MINNESOTA
ST. LOUIS PARK
Cambridge Street
MISSISSIPPI
JACKSON
Old Sugar Bowl,
Lane Building
MISSOURI
KANSAS CITY
2740 East 85th Street
NEW HAMPSHIRE
SALEM
154-158 Main Street
NEW JERSEY
ASBURY
Asbury Park
BORDENTOWN
Route 130
BROADWAY
Route 24
MANVILLE
729 South Main Street
MIDDLETOWN
The Oaks
PLEASANTVILLE
Cardiff Circle
RAHWAY
1488 Irving Street
NEW YORK
BREWSTER
Main Street
EAST ROCHESTER
499 West Commercial St
LINDENHURST
200 Bangor Street
NEW WINDSOR
Walnut Street
NORTHPORT
Wing Foot Roller Drome
Route 25A
PINE CITY
1505 Pennsylvania Ave
ROME
Route 37
UTICA
1305 Conkling Avenue
COLLEGE POINT
Fourteenth Street
OHIO
CLEVELAND
16110 Lorain Road
DAYTON
4371 Forest Park
Lower Mall
MENTOR
7681 Mentor Avenue
OREGON
2665 Navarre Avenue
PENNSYLVANIA
CONSHOHOCKEN
7th Avenue &
Freedley Street
MOOSIC
Rocky Glen Park
TEMPLE
4900 5th Avenue
Highway
WIND GAP
Penn. Can.Interchange
& Rt. 152
Wind Gap, Penna.
TEXAS
DALLAS
142 Webb-Royal
Shopping Center
FORT WORTH
2520 White
Settlement Road
VERMONT
BURLINGTON
183 Williston Road
VIRGINIA
NEWPORT NEWS
Denbigh Blvd.
RICHMOND
5001 West Lee
Street
WISCONSIN
RACINE
3072 Douglas Avenue

Didn't find one near you? How about dropping us a line where "Nearyou" is. If we get enough letters from that spot, we might be able to find someone who will realize, like you, that a Hullabaloo is definitely in the need.

THE DOORS are on top with HALLMARK SWEPT-WING GUITARS.
Like **THE DOORS**, you will appreciate the fast, smooth low action. The full range of uncompromising SOUND, made possible by our custom wound pick-ups. Our stainless steel bridge and our two piece maple neck, PLUS a new Concept in modern design. Weighs only 6½ LBS.
Ask your nearest Dealer about HALLMARK SWEPT-WING GUITARS.

Available in 6st. 12st. and Bass.

THE HALLMARK MFG. CO.
941 SO. DERBY ST., ARVIN, CAL.
PH. 805-774-5153

Ed King of the Strawberry Alarm Clock briefly played and recorded with Hunger in early 1968, and the band released an album. Morton's Swept-Wing was stolen in September of that year. Decades later, he still had fond memories of it: "That Hallmark Swept-Wing served me well, and I'm sure Joe Hall never dreamed about the rigors that instrument would go through."

Hunger was history by the end of 1968, and around the same time, Hallmark was also nearing the end of its brief run. A late 1967 attempt for a traveling salesman's private label line hadn't developed (see chapter 20), and Hallmark's wares weren't garnering enough business to keep the operation viable.

20
The Epcor Project

A brief and pretty-much-final series of instruments to emerge from the Hallmark plant in Arvin was the Epcor line, a private label. The brand was the dream of Ed Preager, a successful manufacturer's representative whose lines included Mosrite. He resided in Beverly Hills, and was reportedly a spiffy dresser who also drove a Cadillac and sported a Rolex watch.

Preager was seeking a guitar line to sell somewhat on the side; his own brand would not conflict with the lines that had contributed to his success in sales. The rep approached Joe Hall in September 1967, wanting to create a budget-priced series of hollowbody instruments, which was somewhat contradictory since hollowbody guitars and basses are inherently more expensive to produce than solidbody instruments. Nevertheless, Hall and Preager came to an agreement to create the Epcor line (the brand name combined Preager's initials with the first three letters of "corporation"). They set a goal of producing two hundred instruments per month, to include six-string guitars, twelve-string guitars, and basses.

One idea that saved manufacturing time and expense was the importation of prefinished instrument bodies from Italy, leaving the creation of the necks and pickups to Hallmark. The laminated body was the same for all instruments, and came in two finishes, red or three-tone sunburst. It featured five-ply white-black-white-black-white binding on the top, and three-ply white-black-white binding on the rear edge, as well as plugged-in "binding" on the f-holes, as found on Mosrite Celebrity and Combo series bodies.

The headstock had two contoured portions that meant the silhouette was supposed to allude to an "E" if viewed sideways, in a playing position. Most guitar enthusiasts would probably surmise that this idea was plagiarized from the "M" headstock design of the nearby Mosrite company.

The two-piece, bolt-on maple neck was unbound, with a Brazilian or Indian rosewood fretboard.

Close-up of Epcor bass headstock.
Courtesy of Michael C. Stewart

Epcor guitar, sunburst finish.
Courtesy of Michael G. Stewart

Epcor bass, sunburst finish.
Courtesy of Michael G. Stewart

Epcor bass, red finish.
Willie G. Moseley

Swept-Wing with Epcor brand on its headstock.
Courtesy of Michael G. Stewart

Hardware and other parts included vibrato tailpieces and bridges made by the Bigsby company, Kluson tuners, and Hallmark strap buttons and knobs. Pickups were Hallmark's own design. One prototype was a Hallmark Swept-Wing "Electric Acoustic" guitar with an Epcor-branded, natural-finish headstock.

Some thirty Epcor instruments of all configurations had been made by Hallmark when the deal fell apart for financial reasons. Bill Gruggett was reportedly able to assemble a few more instruments, perhaps utilizing other brand names, from leftover parts. No shipping records are available, but it's been estimated that around thirty-five Epcor-style instruments were made.

Joe Hall loved designing and building guitars, and many of his innovations were laudable. However, he was disillusioned with the results of more than one of his efforts in the electric guitar industry, so he took a job in the oil industry after Hallmark went out of business. "I took assignments overseas for a few years," he detailed. "When I returned, I continued to work, and studied for a petroleum engineering degree."

Hall would remain in that career field for decades as a consulting engineer. A guitar that ended up as Joe Hall's personal instrument may have actually started out as the prototype for the Epcor line. It had a Swept-Wing-style neck, Hallmark pickups, and a Bigsby vibrato tailpiece (which were to have been standard on Epcor guitars). The pickguard resembles the design for Epcor, and the headstock has pencil marks where the "E" contouring was to be routed out. Hall must have liked the instrument, as he kept it for decades. It has visible wear from playing.

Joe Hall in later life with his personal guitar.
Courtesy of the Joe Hall Estate

As the interest in vintage guitars began to develop in the late twentieth century, Hallmark's place in the history of American guitar building would be the subject of mysterious lore and conjecture. One reason for such speculation was because Joe Hall's whereabouts were unknown.

However, any "flash-in-the-pan" or "peripheral" perceptions about Joe Hall and the history of his Hallmark guitar line would ultimately be brought to the public eye some three and a half decades after Hall's enterprise went out of business. The Bakersfield-born designs of Hall and other builders would return to the guitar marketplace (under the Hallmark banner) on the other side of the country.

21
"Rebirth," in Maryland

For someone who had experience as a drummer in a progressive rock band, Bob Shade's alliance with guitar brands that had been made in Bakersfield might seem somewhat improbable. Originally from Hyattsville, Maryland, Shade was single-digit age when he saw the Beatles on *The Ed Sullivan Show* in 1964. His father subsequently bought him a budget guitar from Montgomery Ward. Bob remembered,

> He must have paid all of $12 for it because it sure *felt* that way. I couldn't play it; the action was so high that it hurt my fingers.
>
> The only thing they offered in school that had to do with the Beatles was drums, so I immediately fell into that and went all the way to the top, playing concert snare and tympani. But I never really wanted to be a drummer; my passion was guitar.

Shade had taken high school courses in woodworking and metalworking, and played in area rock bands, one of which opened a concert for progressive rock icons Emerson, Lake & Palmer. He also worked at area music stores, and began getting back into guitar. This time around, his interest included taking them apart. "All of a sudden I became a repairman," he recalled. He found himself drawn toward Mosrite instruments. He recounted,

> The first record I remember seeing with a Mosrite on it was *The Ventures Knock Me Out!* with those big headstocks. I flipped it over, and thought the guitar on the back was the coolest thing I'd ever seen. The album was in the cut-out bin and I bought it for 50 cents. I was thinking that the music probably wasn't very good, but it actually blew my mind about how the Mosrite guitars sounded and how cool the Ventures' music was. I realized later how many other players had cited the Ventures.

Shade's Mosrite jones was later reinforced when he became a fan of the Ramones. He bought his first Mosrite in the mid-1970s at Washington Music Center (and later worked at that store). "It was in the used section for $135," he remembered. "I put $45 down and paid off the rest in about a month. It was a Metallic Blue Mark I, made in late 1965. I'd heard about Johnny Ramone, but got curious as to why Mosrite never really made it as a guitar company, other than as a flash-in-the-pan. They were very popular for a short time. No pros really used them after that."

Bob studied luthiery with builder Bill Loveless for three and a half years, and by the late 1990s had decided that he wanted to build guitars instead of just repairing them. He dedicated himself to learning anything and everything about the history of Bakersfield-made instruments, and put out the word that he specialized in Mosrite repairs and restorations.

"I got to know where the instruments' weak spots were, and how to improve them," he said. "I also wanted to make an affordable guitar that could play any style of music with the same vibe and sound of the originals."

Shade visited Artie Niesen's store in Bakersfield, and also befriended legendary luthier Bill Gruggett as well as former Mosrite employee Ed Sanner. His discussions with Gruggett and Sanner about the history of guitar production in Bakersfield reinforced his determination to revitalize some of that locale's classic and underappreciated designs from the 1960s.

"I thought it would be a great idea if I could start something that would keep Bill busy, making a living doing what he liked to do," Shade remembered. "I thought about starting Hallmark guitars back up again and offering the [originally Gruggett-branded] Stradette and the [originally Hallmark-branded] Swept-Wing." Around the time Shade began to formulate his game plan, he managed to locate Joe Hall.

"Nobody knew where Joe Hall was," he recalled with a chuckle. "He had left Bakersfield, apparently never to be seen again. The oil business took him to Kansas, and a Hallmark collector connected me with him. Joe was very receptive to the idea of Hallmark guitars being made again." Hall was residing in Independence, Kansas, and was retired from the oil business.

Shade could probably have acquired the rights to the expired Hallmark name and trademark on his own volition, but noted,

> I didn't want to do it without Joe's blessing. I wanted him to be a part of it, to oversee certain facets. He thought it was a great idea, and sent me original necks, an original Swept-Wing body, pickups and parts, and told me about other guitars he'd made before Hallmark. He was a talker, and we had a lot of conversations. Once I developed parts for the new line I sent them to Joe to see what he thought. He gave me feedback and was very impressed by the way things were progressing, as well as some of the modern improvements that I employed.

Under Shade's aegis, the Hallmark guitar brand name reappeared in 2002.

"The reason I restarted Hallmark is because I knew I couldn't restart Mosrite," Shade said. "That name was already owned by somebody, but people were fighting over it. I thought Hallmark never had a chance anyway. Swept-Wings were ahead of their time, like the Gibson Flying V, so I thought I should start there."

The new Hallmark company did indeed begin its efforts with the Swept-Wing model and Stradette instruments handcrafted by Gruggett and Shade. However, Bob opted to combine features from more than one Bakersfield brand, interpolating modern refinements that still paid tribute to the original California instruments. One example was his trademarked Shade vibrato. The Maryland luthier said,

> Everybody loves the feel of the Moseley vibrato, so that's what I started with, but the bridge on mine is separate from the vibrato, unlike the Mosrite, where they were usually together on one plate. By moving the vibrato plate forward, I got more string tension. Moving it backwards reduces string tension, which would be good for something like an archtop [guitar]. It wasn't a big innovation, but Mosrite didn't use the same principle that I wanted to do, in terms of string pressure. My intention was to be able to use it on all of my guitars.

Other parts such as the bridge deck were refined. The original Mosrite configuration had been made of folded sheet metal, whereas the new Shade deck was solid—and thicker—brass. The cylindrical bridge saddles on Mosrites were hollow; on a Shade vibrato, they're solid brass, which Shade says results in more sustain and no buzzing. The saddles are also capable of being locked, to ensure stable tuning.

To prevent his pickups from becoming microphonic, Shade designed them with "enough windings to get the kind of tone that Nokie [Edwards] got, and better grounding and potting for less noise." Shade also went somewhat retro-but-improved regarding the truss rod on the new line—the adjustment point was at the butt end of the neck and, like the earliest Mosrites, the neck–bass pickup had to be popped off to access the truss rod. He explained that he interpolated the throw-back truss rod system "for aesthetic reasons. I never liked that 'spade' [truss rod cover] look on the headstocks of Mosrites. On my instruments, the [neck] pickup can be removed and the truss rod can be adjusted in five minutes, without removing the strings."

The Swept-Wing Vintage series lived up to its moniker, with retro looks that included a large pickguard on the front face of the body, just like its Arvin-built predecessors. The guitar's scale was 25.5 inches, and the bass's scale was 30 inches.

Compared to the original Swept-Wings from the mid-1960s, the new models had slightly larger fret wire, a slightly wider fingerboard at the heel, a one-piece maple (and still relatively thin) neck, and hotter pickups.

The upgrade Swept-Wing Custom series had a modern take on the aerodynamic silhouette, with figured wood caps on bodies with no pickguards. The guitar scale was 24.75 inches, as would become the scale on all subsequent standard-production Hallmark guitars. Swept-Wing Custom guitars came in a hardtail version (CS-6) or with a vibrato (CS-6V).

Both series of Swept-Wings had mahogany bodies. As for Shade's association with Bill Gruggett on a (Hallmark-branded) Stradette model, the veteran Bakersfield luthier was enthusiastic about building and overseeing the reintroduction of his signature instrument (see part 3, "Gruggett").

Swept-Wing Vintage model, gold sparkle finish.
Courtesy of Michael G. Stewart

Swept-Wing Vintage series bass, blue sparkle finish.
Courtesy of Michael G. Stewart

Left-handed Swept-Wing Vintage model, made for Elliott Easton.
Willie G. Moseley

"At the beginning—or maybe I should say 're-birth'—the Stradettes were completely handcrafted by Bill," Shade detailed, "using hardware, pickup covers, etc. that I handmade. We had no tooling at that point. We made about ten of those, all of which had one-of-a-kind finishes and pickup cover materials."

The new Hallmark line would debut at the 2003 Winter NAMM show in Anaheim, California. The display consisted mostly of prototypes and handmade instruments. Bill Gruggett was in attendance, and was proud of his new handcrafted pearl white Stradette, which had gold hardware and a scrolled headstock.

Among the players who checked out Hallmark instruments at the Anaheim show were Alabama's Jeff Cook; Lee Rocker of the Stray Cats; and Mike Dirnt, bassist for Green Day. Joe Hall would attend the 2003 Summer NAMM show in Nashville, as would Andy Moseley and Bakersfield dealer Artie Niesen.

CS-6V in Honey Sunburst.
Courtesy of Michael G. Stewart

Swept-Wing Custom bass, cherry sunburst finish.
Courtesy of Michael G. Stewart

Stephan Jenkins of Third Eye Blind plays a Swept-Wing Custom CS-6 in concert.
Courtesy of Bob Shade

"This was my first time meeting Joe, outside of phone conversations," Shade remembered. "He was as genuine and up front and honest as they come. He was very proud of the company being restarted and carrying on. We had a great time, and he was full of stories about the old days. He got a very early Swept-Wing off the production line and said it was 'awesome.'"

Hallmark proffered an "Art series" of instruments and custom finishes almost from the get-go. Customers could special-order custom-painted instruments that were decorated by professionals such as the redoubtable Wayne Jarrett, who already had considerable experience with such artwork.

"Rebirth" in Maryland

Early Hallmark Stradette with scroll headstock, handcrafted by Bill Gruggett.
Courtesy of Michael G. Stewart

Stradette standard model, three-tone sunburst. A Shade vibrato was standard on production instruments.
Courtesy of Michael G. Stewart

Bob Shade and Joe Hall at the 2003 Summer NAMM.
Courtesy of John Lackey

Bakersfield time warp: Artie Niesen and Andy Moseley check out the new Hallmark line in 2003.
Courtesy of Bob Shade

Top left: Eric Bloom of the Blue Oyster Cult with his "Godzilla" Swept-Wing, custom painted by Wayne Jarrett.

Bottom left: Wayne Jarrett works on a Swept-Wing with a Washington Redskins motif.
Courtesy of Bob Shade

Stradette with a Wayne Jarrett flame paint job.
Courtesy of Michael G. Stewart

As is the case with many guitar companies, overseas manufacturers have been utilized by the new Hallmark company in the creation of what Shade termed as American–South Korean "hybrid" guitars, which are created from parts made in both countries.

Shade would work on custom orders, as well, including one that had some "reversed" facets. "A customer wanted a Stradette with a stop tailpiece," he recalled, "so being as how the Stradette is symmetrical, I took a left-handed body that I had and converted it to a 'righty.' I inlaid the pearloid stars to hide the original volume and tone holes, as well as the jack. I also rescreened the logo." The right-handed conversion to the body also meant that the neck pickup was angled in the opposite direction from standard right-handed Stradette bodies.

Another one-of-a-kind Stradette had a white pearl finish (with matching pickup covers), gold hardware, and a clear pickguard with a screened-on logo.

While Swept-Wings and Stradettes were indeed the initial models introduced by the revitalized Hallmark brand, Shade quickly realized that he needed something

Stradette—gold sparkle, left-handed converted to right-handed.
Courtesy of Heritage Auctions

Stradette—Pearl White custom-made.
Courtesy of the Chicago Music Exchange

more "traditionally popular," so he designed and built instruments that emulated the classic Mosrite body silhouette. The "60 Custom" is a set-neck model with body and neck binding and a top-mounted jack. The neck is painted the same color as the body, as were the original Mosrites.

One custom-made variant of the 60 Custom was built for Bob Spalding, a member of the then-current touring incarnation of the Ventures (and Spalding has been an associate musician with the Ventures for decades). Spalding's instrument had a set neck, a side jack, triple-ply binding, and a parchment aged pickguard that attached with three screws. Spalding used the guitar on the Ventures 2018 and 2019 tours and still uses it today.

The "65 Custom" has an unbound body (but still has neck binding); a top-mounted jack; and a natural-finish, bolt-on neck.

60 Custom, three-tone sunburst.
Courtesy of Michael G. Stewart

60 Custom, Fire Sparkle.
Courtesy of Michael G. Stewart

Bob Spalding onstage in Japan in 2018 with his custom-made Hallmark guitar.
Courtesy of Yasushi Tachikawa

65 Custom in tealburst finish and artwork by Wayne Jarrett.
Courtesy of Michael G. Stewart

65 Custom, three-tone sunburst.
Courtesy of Michael G. Stewart

65 Custom with patriotic sparkle finish.
Courtesy of Michael G. Stewart

65 Custom in bowling ball finish.
Courtesy of Michael G. Stewart

65 Custom with artwork by Wayne Jarrett.
Courtesy of Michael G. Stewart

63 Custom bass, three-tone sunburst.
Courtesy of Michael G. Stewart

63 Custom bass, Sky Blue.
Courtesy of Michael G. Stewart

65 Custom bass, Fire Sparkle.
Courtesy of Michael G. Stewart

65 Custom bass, Pearl White.
Courtesy of Michael G. Stewart

63 Custom bass with military-style paint scheme.
Courtesy of Bob Shade

Shade confirmed that the 60 Custom and the 65 Custom became his best-selling models. They are available with custom finishes and artwork by Wayne Jarrett.

The "63 Custom bass" (one-pickup) and "65 Custom bass" (two-pickup) basses had a scale of 32 inches, considered to be "medium" bass scale, which offers a richer sound and more resonance to players. Medium-scale basses had not previously been marketed by Mosrite.

Not all of Jarrett's artwork on Hallmark instruments was fancy. In 2020, the North Carolina artist painted a 63 Custom bass in a flat green, military-style finish on an instrument that was special-ordered by a Marine on active duty. The rank that was illustrated on the headstock was Staff Sergeant/E-6.

The "59 Custom" model would take the term "retro" to an extreme, with a bound body that displayed a German carve that was historically accurate for the era, white headstock trim, a side jack, an aluminum compensated bridge, and a sandcast vibrato with a flip-up mute. There was even a faux "mistake plate" around the base of the vibrato that was cosmetic only.

Hallmark also opted to create and market a series of instruments that referenced another stereotypically California phenomenon—hot rods and custom cars. Shade remembered being inspired in his childhood by hot rod magazines and model cars, and found himself attracted to "those zany, crazy show cars built by guys like Ed Roth and George Barris. I contacted George, expecting to get a cold shoulder, but he was very receptive."

At his first meeting with Barris Kustom Industries, Bob presented a custom-made black Swept-Wing with red trim that alluded to Barris's iconic Batmobile, built in 1966 for the *Batman* television series. That vehicle had been Barris's most famous creation. Shade had installed a voice module in the instrument that announced, "To the Batmobile!"

The two artisans signed a five-year contract but would end up collaborating for eight years. One of Hallmark's earliest Barris-connection instruments was the Fireball 500 guitar, which was inspired by a 1966 stock car racing movie from American International Pictures. The instrument shown here was made for Larry Collins, and was custom-painted by Wayne Jarrett.

"We were introduced to Bob by [roots rocker]) Deke Dickerson," Larry recalled. "[Shade] told Lorrie and me he wanted to make guitars for us, and asked us what we wanted. I said, 'Well, a doubleneck would be nice.'"

59 Custom, sunburst.
Courtesy of Jim Page

Custom-made Swept-Wing presented to George Barris.
Courtesy of Michael G. Stewart

Fireball 500 doubleneck made for Larry Collins. Note the Barris "Krest" in the upper middle portion of the body.
Courtesy of Michael G. Stewart

Lorrie Collins's Stradette.
Courtesy of Michael G. Stewart

Ad photo of the Collins Kids with their Hallmark instruments.
Photo by Jeff Dow

The instrument made for Collins had an octave neck and a standard guitar neck, just like his Mosrites. It, too, had a special sound effects module that Shade had installed. The Collins Kids received their instruments at a car show in Culver City, California. Barris was also in attendance, as was hot rod enthusiast Billy Gibbons of ZZ Top.

"They did a good job," Larry said of the Hallmark instruments. "My Fireball 500 sounded quite a bit like my Mosrite, and it had a pushbutton on it that would make a sound like a drag race. George really liked that!"

Lorrie Collins received a custom Stradette at the same event. "Lorrie needed a light guitar, so I made a Stradette for her and dolled it up with pinstriping and custom paint," said Shade. "She was just delighted with it," Larry recalled with a smile.

Another Hallmark–Barris instrument was the Dragula, an homage to a 1964 Barris creation for *The Munsters* television show.

Dragula.
Courtesy of Michael G. Stewart

Barris Krest prototype.
Courtesy of Michael G. Stewart

Wing-Bat.
Courtesy of Michael G. Stewart

George Barris displays the Barris Krest model, while Bob Shade shows off the Wing-Bat model at a Chicago automobile show. They're positioned in front of a then-recent Barris creation called the Red Demon.
Courtesy of John Lackey

Barris and Shade schmooze at an automobile show in London, Ontario, Canada, with Adam West, star of the "Batman" television series in the 1960s. Julie "Catwoman" Newmar looks on at the far right.
Courtesy of John Lackey

Prior to a second meeting at the Barris shop in California, Shade made a guitar with a body that was an enlarged Barris crest and presented it to the custom car legend as a gift. The single-pickup instrument had gold hardware. "I never gave any thought to it actually becoming a model," Shade recounted. "George was impressed, to say the least. He kind of flipped out over it and said, 'You have to make that a Barris guitar!'"

The Maryland luthier continued to develop another instrument inspired by the Barris Batmobile, and ultimately created a prototype for a guitar that would be known as the Wing-Bat. "I worked really hard on the Wing-Bat to make it a guitar all its own, not just a dressed up Swept-Wing," said Shade. "So it got heavy scallops, neon pinstriping, and, of all things, a 'turbine.'"

The Wing-Bat was striking, and would become Hallmark's most popular "automotive" model. It had a mahogany body, an ebony fingerboard and no zero fret. All twenty-two frets on the neck were clear of the body. Its "turbine power boost" was a light-up visual effect (a red "rocket nozzle" on the end of the body that illuminated).

Shade began attending car shows with Barris, displaying some of his instruments. "The Wing-Bat and the Barris Krest got a lot of interest in the car circuit," Shade recalled, "and both ended up going into production."

One custom variant of the Wing-Bat, dubbed the "Wing Walker," was made for Larry Collins, as part of a short-lived attempt to venture into other entertainment media. "We were going to make a movie, a game controller, and a comic book," said Collins, "but it didn't work out."

Barris would introduce Shade to other custom car builders, including Chuck Miller, Bob Larivee, and Gene

Collins manipulates his Wing Walker guitar in this rare publicity photo.
Courtesy of Larry Collins

"Rebirth" in Maryland 145

Red Baron.
Courtesy of Michael G. Stewart

Chuck Miller with his iconic automotive creation, accompanied by a Red Baron guitar and a one-of-a-kind Red Baron amplifier made by Shade.
Courtesy of Dave Chapman

Bob Larivee, Miller, and Shade display the Red Baron during the Autorama car show at Cobo Hall in Detroit in 2015.
Courtesy of John Lackey

Winfield. Shade subsequently created a guitar based on Miller's Red Baron show car (which had been a Monogram model car kit before the actual automobile was created in the late 1960s). The Red Baron instrument had an alder body and maple neck. In addition to its Iron Cross body silhouette, there were numerous innovations on the guitar that had a direct connection to the show car—the truss rod cover was shaped like a World War I Pickelhaube spiked German helmet, the volume and tone controls each had an Iron Cross "wheel" in the center surrounded by a miniature rubber drag slick tire, and the pickup selector was a skull with ruby eyes. The pickup switch was five-way, offering humbucking and single-coil tones. The jack was located on the back of the body.

A special auto-centric Swept-Wing had a 1950s-style, two-tone paint job, and was presented to the iconic band Paul Revere and the Raiders. "I delivered it at a gig in Canada with Barris," Shade recounted, "and we had a blast."

Swept-Wing "57" two-tone.
Courtesy of Michael G. Stewart

Darren Dowler (left) plays the Swept-Wing "57" two-tone onstage with Paul Revere & the Raiders.
Courtesy of Bob Shade

Hallmark diversified into the endorsement guitar realm with a Deke Dickerson signature model guitar. Dickerson had first aligned himself with Shade in the early history of the new Hallmark enterprise, when Shade built a double-neck Swept-Wing model that had a six-string bass on top and a standard guitar on the bottom. Moreover, Dickerson's name was placed on both necks, à la Joe Maphis, but the letters of Dickerson's name lit up. It almost goes without saying that Shade considered the instrument's creation to be the hardest project he's ever undertaken.

The first Deke Dickerson signature model was a full-blown time machine, particularly for fans of Joe Maphis and Larry

Deke Dickerson with his custom doubleneck.
Courtesy of Bob Shade

Collins. It featured a hollowed-out, chambered alder body with a maple cap and maple back, a set-in maple neck with a bound rosewood fretboard, a bone nut, a standard Shade locking saddle roller bridge and vibrato (with a longer arm), walnut headstock overlay with pearl and abalone inlay, Grover Imperial tuners, and the expected ornate trim. The pickups were Hallmark JM-6 custom-wound units, which looked like the old Carvin pickups that were originally on Maphis's iconic doubleneck. In the initial production run of one hundred, ninety were in a sunburst finish and ten were in a natural finish.

An endorsement model sanctioned by Brian "Star Crunch" Causey of the surf-punk band Man or Astroman? was basically a Pearl White–finished 65 Custom with a medallion on the headstock and an actual printed circuit board for a pickguard. In a nod to modern times, "case candy" for this model included a visitor's badge and a download code for the band's latest album.

In 2011, Hallmark scored a coup when the company signed an agreement with the estate of John "Johnny Ramone" Cummings to create a signature model in honor of the deceased guitarist. The instrument referenced Ramone's Mosrite Ventures II in a respectful manner, including a narrow headstock and vintage-style tuners. It featured special alnico pickups and was one of the rare production Hallmark models that didn't have a vibrato.

Top left: Deke Dickerson signature model.
Courtesy of Michael G. Stewart

Top right: Man or Astroman? signature model.
Courtesy of Michael G. Stewart

Brian "Star Crunch" Causey.
Courtesy of Bob Shade

At the same time, the company introduced the Hallmark II, an upgraded version of the Ramone tribute guitar. It sported unique contouring (not a German carve) on its body, and a vibrato was also standard.

The Deke Dickerson Model Two, patterned after the 1969 Moseley-branded guitar that Semie Moseley made for Don Rich, was less fancy and lower priced compared to the first Dickerson endorsement model. Its construction appointments were similar to the original example, with the exception of a body was all alder with no f-hole (but still chambered), and a different headstock silhouette that had plain tuners. The pickups were still JM-6s, but they were housed in surplus/new-old-stock (NOS) Mosrite pickup surrounds from the 1960s (the same pickup frames that were on Rich's guitar).

Other custom guitars Shade created included an instrument based on the "Boy Howdy!" logo of *Creem* magazine, an iconic Michigan-based rock-and-roll periodical.

There was also a patriotic shield-shaped guitar that was obviously inspired by the Captain America comic and movie character—but the then-current version of the superhero used a round shield.

Former Mosrite and Rosac employee Ed Sanner had retired to the small community of Lake Isabella, California, located in the Greenhorn Mountains northeast of Bakersfield. He established an affiliation with Shade's company to handbuild Hallmark-branded reproductions of his Rosac Nu-Fuzz distortion unit (see chapter 30,

Johnny Ramone signature guitar. The model was also available in a white finish as a nod to Ramone's other iconic Ventures II guitar.
Courtesy of Michael G. Stewart

Hallmark II.
Courtesy of Michael G. Stewart

Deke Dickerson Model Two.
Courtesy of Michael G. Stewart

"Boy Howdy!" guitar.
Courtesy of Michael G. Stewart

Patriotic shield guitar.
Courtesy of Michael G. Stewart

Ed Sanner at his workbench.
Courtesy of Bob Shade

"Melobar"), using NOS Rosac knobs and stainless steel chassis. Sanner signed each unit when it was completed.

The modern Hallmark company also emulated Mosrite in another facet of the music business by releasing *The Kustom Kings*, a CD of music recorded with Hallmark guitars and basses by endorsers. Performers included the Collins Kids, Deke Dickerson, the Dynotones, the Neanderthals, the Ghastly Ones, the Kilaueas, and the Untamed Youth. In addition to two songs recorded with his sister, Larry Collins contributed two solo tunes titled—perhaps not surprisingly—"Fireball 500" and "Wing Walker."

Joe Hall was ultimately pleased with—and he probably felt somewhat vindicated by—the success of the modern Hallmark company, and Bill Gruggett felt the same, according to Hall. "Bill thinks a lot of Bob's guitar-building talent," the Hallmark founder said in 2004. "If Bill Gruggett says you're a master luthier, that's good enough for me." Hall died in 2011.

Courtesy of Bob Shade

As the twenty-first century entered its third decade, Bob Shade found his company in a unique position, compared to the Bakersfield builders whose history had first motivated him in the late 1990s—Hallmark Guitars had been in business for almost twenty years without interruption, and was producing products that were selling well and were respected by players. That kind of longevity never happened to any guitar company in Bakersfield.

Not surprisingly, much of the company's success was due to the internet and social media. One post on the www.reverb.com website intoned, "In the late '90s, the brand was revitalized by Maryland-based builder Bob Shade, who produces a whole range of guitars based on ultra-rare original Hallmarks as well as some Mosrite-inspired designs. Based on their popularity, it appears the current generation of Hallmarks have earned a spot as the go-to make for anyone looking for a 'Mosrite-esque' guitar."

And to say that Hallmark's Buckaroo model looked all the way back to Bakersfield is an understatement. Introduced in late 2020, the model took its inspiration from a similar guitar made by Semie Moseley around the advent of the 1970s (think Buck Owens and *Hee Haw*). In addition to the patriotic color scheme, the modern model featured a slab body, controls on a small plate, and NOS Mosrite/Dobro pickup rings. Another aesthetic and sonic reference to Owens's guitar was the angled bridge treble pickup.

Courtesy of Michael G. Stewart

Buckaroo.
Courtesy of Bob Shade

Former Mosrite associate Pierre Laflamme paid perhaps the ultimate compliment to Hallmark when he recalled playing a 60 Custom model for the first time.

> Wow, it was weird. The tone, the feel—it was all there . . . the frets were pristine on the Hallmark. I still have the 60 Custom plus a Red Baron guitar and a bass. I am totally thrilled with them. The sound, action, feel, [and] build quality is top notch.

You could say that Bob Shade has captured the essence of Mosrite.

22
The Gospel According to Bob

In October 2008, Bob Shade's company acquired the name rights and the registered trademark for the Gospel brand of guitars and basses.

Like Semie Moseley's original Gospel line, many modern Gospel instruments were one of a kind with special-ordered finishes and pickups. The first production Gospel models offered after Shade secured the brand rights were based on the Hallmark Custom 60 series, with three-ply body binding as well as neck binding, and pearloid pickguards and pickup covers. Pearl white examples had gold hardware; gloss black examples had chrome hardware. The instruments usually had pearloid pickup covers that matched the pickguard.

Left: Early Hallmark/Gospel guitar.
Courtesy of John Majdalani

Right: Pearl White Gospel with "Stained Class" pickup covers.
Courtesy of Michael G. Stewart

153

Left: This Gospel instrument features a hound's tooth motif on the pickguard and pickup covers.
Courtesy of Michael G. Stewart

Right: Sunburst Mark V.
Courtesy of Michael G. Stewart

One variant of Shade's Gospel-branded instruments was a pearl white example with chrome hardware. It had a white pearloid pickguard and colorful "Stained Class" pickup covers. Shade himself makes the covers one at a time.

Another model was a sunburst limited edition that tipped its headstock to the Ventures Mark V Gospel variants from the late 1960s. Accordingly, it was a subliminal tip of the headstock to the late Kurt Cobain, as well.

Part 3
Gruggett

Early Gruggett solidbody guitar with pickups installed under pickguard (protruding polepieces).
Willie G. Mcseley

23

Native Californian

Bill Gruggett stuck it out.

As noted previously, not only did Gruggett work for Mosrite on more than one occasion, he also helped Joe Hall build Hallmark instruments during that brand's brief existence in the 1960s. Moreover, he crafted his own brand of instruments for decades, including the unique "Stradette" line in the late 1960s, and was also affiliated with the new Hallmark company in Maryland.

And he never moved from the Bakersfield area. Gruggett was born in Tulare. He recalled that his childhood had a great deal of itineration, as his father was a minister who specialized in starting new churches and helping churches that were struggling. Ultimately, his family returned to Tulare. Bill graduated from high school, and a few years later, moved to Bakersfield and began working as an auto mechanic. Around the same time, he began picking up used guitars, mandolins, and violins at local yard sales and garage sales to restore and sell.

"The first instrument I fixed up was a little mandolin-banjo," Gruggett recalled in a 1997 interview. "I painted it candy apple red." The mechanic soon began building his own stringed instruments. Initial customers included fellow employees at his auto shop.

"I began to accumulate tools, and built guitars in my garage at night, after work hours," he recounted. "After two years at the auto shop, I quit, and concentrated on building guitars full-time. My first guitars were sold to local musicians playing in clubs throughout the [San Joaquin] Valley. I also put my instruments on consignment in music stores as far away as Fresno."

One of Bill's earliest notable instruments was a two-pickup guitar made around 1960 for Bakersfield music icon Bill Woods. The instrument's body was almost exactly the same as some single-cutaway Mosrites of the same era (Gruggett may have traced a template or perhaps he acquired a body from Semie and trimmed it slightly). The side edge of Woods's guitar had two grooves of fluting, like a leg on a piece of furniture. The body was finished in a brown sunburst, and Woods's name was inlaid on the fretboard.

The headstock was an exaggeration of the headstocks found on early Mosrites, but some guitar buffs might also reference Bigsby and Fender guitars in the Woods guitar's headstock silhouette. The original pickups appear to have been Carvin units.

Woods later returned the instrument to Gruggett, who refinished the body in red,

Bill Woods with his Gruggett electric guitar in its first configuration. This image was seen on a poster advertising an upcoming concert and dance.
Courtesy of the Bill Gruggett Estate

157

white, and blue. The luthier also replaced the original pickups with a set of his own hand-wound pickups. Somewhere along the line, a replacement pickguard was installed on the instrument, with different knobs and placement of controls.

The time spent by Gruggett in developing his own instruments was considerable, and was reportedly a contributing factor to the dissolution of his first marriage. Bill's aspirations went into a tailspin, but then he hooked up with Mosrite as a bona fide employee.

Gruggett displays an early electric guitar and mandolin, 1962.
Courtesy of the Bill Gruggett Estate

Bill Woods's Gruggett-made guitar in its ultimate configuration.
Willie G. Moseley

158   Chapter 23

24
Mosrite (Part 1) and Hallmark

"I knew Semie Moseley was working in a tin barn out in the country, on Panama Lane," Gruggett remembered.

> He was working by himself, like I was, so I started working for him. The first Ventures guitars were made there. The orders started coming in to the point that Semie called his brother, Andy, in Tennessee to help with the company; Andy was to be Vice-President. We hired help, and Semie also hired several men from prison who needed a job to gain parole. Eventually, the tin barn became too small, and we moved to a larger facility on P Street, in downtown Bakersfield.

Gruggett's primary duty during the first year at the P Street factory was to paint all of the instruments, which involved long hours until he was able to train two associates. He recalled that he was ultimately in charge of the painting, wet sanding, neck dressing, and buffing sections, as well as assembly and checkout.

"Later, we initiated a custom department that I was also in charge of," he noted. "I worked for four years without a vacation."

While at Mosrite, Bill built the first instrument, which had a body silhouette that would be seen several years later on his most noteworthy instrument series, the Stradette line. His initial creation, built in Semie's factory, was a solidbody bass. While it had a unique shape, it still had a German carve à la Mosrite. Bill recalled that once he *did* take a well-earned three-week paid vacation, trouble was in the cards when he returned.

"Semie had bought out the Dobro company, and had to hire Mr. Dopyera and a sidekick of his for one year," Gruggett said. "So they made Mr. Dopyera the maintenance manager, and they gave his sidekick one of my departments, but he would come into the departments that I had left and try to boss my supervisors around. This wasn't working out, so I began looking for another job."

Bill recalled that Don Stanley had gone to work for Joe Hall's new Hallmark company in Arvin. Hall's organization then approached Gruggett, and he went to work for Hallmark as the company's production manager. Like Semie Moseley had done at Mosrite, Hall okayed employees working on their own projects when they weren't on the clock, and Bill would take advantage of such an opportunity while he worked at Hallmark.

1960s thinline with unique pickup switch plate, made with Epcor body and Hallmark/Mosrite bridge. Gruggett handmade the maple neck with rosewood fretboard.
Willie G. Moseley

1966 Gruggett Stradette guitar with scrolled headstock, one of a kind.
Willie G. Moseley

25

The (Short-lived) Saga of the Stradette

Bill's short-lived effort with Hallmark motivated him to begin making his own instruments once again, particularly since he had also been allowed to "do his own thing"—albeit off the clock—while working for Joe Hall.

One of his projects was a special-order series of guitars for a band called the Raindrops, but since such instruments were painted red, they looked more like blood drops. Having built a unique-looking bass at Mosrite, Bill had further developed his ideas regarding electric basses while still employed at Hallmark. When Bill went out on his own, he moved into a shop on Chester Avenue in downtown Bakersfield, and hired four employees to help him create his new line.

Gruggett Stradettes have a unique place in the pantheon of vintage guitars because of their definitely different style. Bill intentionally designed the Stradette line to look like—well, like nothing else of its time. To many guitar buffs, the hybrid aesthetics of Stradettes are probably their most endearing feature, as the luthier was envisioning an instrument that incorporated a classical, violin-like shape with a modern, double-cutaway electric guitar shape.

Bill reportedly wanted to make only basses, but the first example of a Stradette guitar was made in early 1966 while he was still working for Joe Hall. It had a rosewood top, standard f-holes, a scroll headstock, pickup rings from Mosrite's Dobro D-100, and a Moseley vibrato with a portion cut out of it. The instrument ended up in the hands of Gerald Claunch, guitarist for a local band called the Savage Sound (founded by Inez and Don Savage). A few very early basses and just that first guitar had a scroll headstock, according to Gruggett.

The production version of "The All New Stradette Model Guitar" was introduced by the Gruggett Manufacturing Company in 1967. The series was proffered in six-string guitar, bass and twelve-string guitar models (brochures from those days included the phrase "For the Mod Generation").

In addition to the unique body silhouette, the Stradette's aesthetics also included unusual-looking soundholes, which interpolated a classic f-hole design with a zigzag lightning bolt outline (to allude to electricity), underlining the Stradette's combined modern-classic vibe.

Stradette (single-neck) bodies were 12.25 inches wide and 3.5 inches deep. They were made from alder, with a laminated arched top and back. Their semihollow construction utilized a center block (to which the neck attached) running through the middle of the body. Binding was three-ply, front and rear. Necks were made of maple, with a bound rosewood fretboard.

Scales for the guitars was 25.5 inches, and the bass scale was 30.5 inches.

In an interesting effort to economize, both Gruggett and Joe Hall would slice up white knitting needles to

Gruggett brochure, front, 1967.
Courtesy Bill Gruggett Estate

make dots for their respective instruments' fretboards. "We had to use anything we could find that would work," Bill recalled to Bob Shade. "There were no guitar supply shops in those days."

Like Joe Hall, Bill remembered the 1967 NAMM show in Chicago, where he and Hall shared an exhibition space. "We put Gruggett guitars on one side, and Hallmarks on the other," Gruggett recalled. "We didn't have money to rent a room, so at night we put our display tables together, got a mattress and blanket, and put them on the tables. That's where Joe and I slept!"

Advertised finishes for the Stradette series were Goldenburst and Cherryburst, but several instruments were finished in a rare Cardinal Red color, and were displayed at the Chicago show. Accordingly, the bright red bass shown here may have been one of the instruments displayed at that exposition, and may be one of a kind. It had reportedly been in the possession of the owner of a bar and restaurant in Bakersfield for decades. The restaurateur passed it on to his son, who sold it to the present owner (as of this writing).

Bill Gruggett and Joe Hall in Chicago for the 1967 NAMM show.
Courtesy of the Joe Hall Estate

Stradette, Goldenburst finish.
Courtesy of Michael G. Stewart

Stradette, Cherryburst finish.
Willie G. Moseley

Stradette bass, Cherryburst finish.
Willie G. Moseley

Stradette bass, rare Cardinal Red finish.
Courtesy of Michael G. Stewart

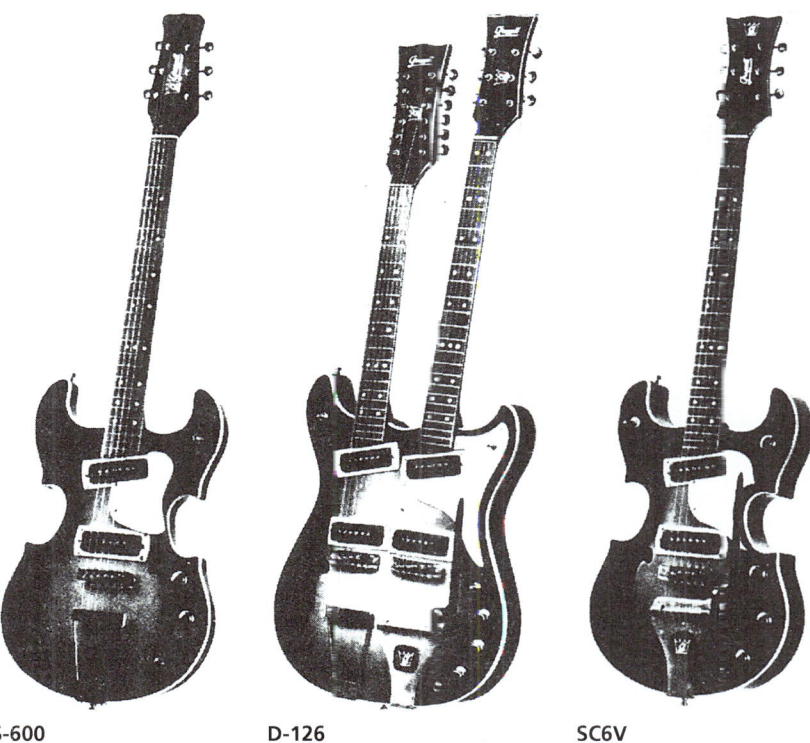

S-600   D-126   SC6V

Later Gruggett Stradette models, as seen in a follow-up flyer ad.
Courtesy of the Bill Gruggett Estate

Gruggett later introduced three new instruments. The S-600 had a trapeze tailpiece instead of a vibrato, and the slightly deeper-bodied SC6V was Bill's attempt at a "jazz box" guitar configuration. It had a different control system with an extra master volume knob on the treble cutaway. The pickup switch was located on the upper cutaway.

The new doubleneck model was particularly unusual. The D-126's twelve-string neck had a shorter scale than the instrument's six-string neck. "I cut off the first two frets," Gruggett explained. "It sounded brighter." The doubleneck was also proffered with other neck combinations, but such variants weren't shown on brochures.

Sharp-eyed guitar lovers may also note that some of the hardware on Stradette models looks familiar. According to Gruggett, a local metalworking company, Metaltech, had been supplying the Mosrite company with parts, such as bridges. Bill recalled that Semie Moseley opted to change suppliers, and Gruggett bought some of the remaining parts from Metaltech.

Moreover, Stradette guitars were advertised as being available with optional Bigsby vibratos, but the vibratos shown in the brochures were left over from the third Standel builder in Bakersfield (see chapter 32, "Standel: The Mysterious Third Manufacturer"). Gruggett acquired those items at a Standel bankruptcy sale; he removed the Standel "snake logo" medallion and placed his own crown-motif medallion on them.

The Stradette would not be successful as a new and innovative frontline model, and the Gruggett Manufacturing Company closed its doors in 1968. Bill yearned to continue building guitars, however, even if he had to handcraft them one at a time.

Post-Gruggett Manufacturing Co. hollowbody guitar.
Courtesy of Michael G. Stewart

The (Short-lived) Saga of the Stradette 163

Solidbody electric, late 1970s—(leftover Mosrite?) basswood Brass Rail/ Bluesbender–style body, maple neck with rosewood fingerboard, Gibson bridge, DiMarzio bridge pickup, Gibson neck pickup, and handmade tailpiece.
Willie G. Moseley

26

Custom Luthiery, Mosrite (Part 2), Back to Custom Luthiery

In 1969, Gruggett's father became ill and turned responsibility for running his pipe and cable business over to his son. Bill's effort to continue his luthiery was put on hold, and he closed his shop. He ran his father's business until the elder Gruggett passed away in 1974, after which he began doing repair work for Bakersfield-area music stores and musicians.

In the mid-1970s, Semie Moseley returned to Bakersfield from Oklahoma, and hired Gruggett to manage his shop. Among the instruments the Mosrite company built in that era was the innovative Brass Rail, and while Gruggett was reportedly heavily involved in its design, his second association with Moseley only lasted six months.

Gruggett returned to making his self-monikered instruments, including his own Brass Rail–style models, some of which had a solid piece of brass stock running through the entire neck and body. He also continued doing repairs and restorations, and would maintain his independent luthiery and repair work for the last three and a half decades of his life.

Curiously, Bill usually declined to give esoteric or artsy names to his guitar models, other than the Stradette series. He preferred to let the look, feel, and sound of each individual instrument speak for itself. Gruggett's instruments usually had hand-carved tops and set necks. The use of highly figured woods was also an important facet of Bill's craft. Since he made almost all of his instruments one at a time, it's fair to say that his work was almost always made to order, although some retailers displayed and sold his wares.

Another intriguing aesthetic amenity on Gruggett instruments were wood-covered pickups. Veneers were hand-sanded to the thickness of a sheet of paper, so plenty of signal could get through. Some guitars had pickup covers and pickup rings made from gorgeous bird's-eye maple.

Numerous Bakersfield musicians and guitar enthusiasts were fans of his repair work. Chuck Seaton recalled,

Bill displays one of his own Brass Rail–style guitars in the late 1970s.
Courtesy of the Bill Gruggett Estate

> I was in my mid-twenties when I met Bill Gruggett. He was my "go-to" whenever I had a guitar problem, and when he set up your [guitar's] action you always knew you were going to be happy because it always played great.
>
> He was very easy to talk to, and he would show us the special pieces of wood he had been saving for the right project. Even when I didn't need guitar work done I would go by and just hang out while Bill was working. He had a lot going on back then, and for a man of few words, he had a lot to say. He worked on everybody's guitars, and you could catch up on what he had done to who's guitar, and who he was building one for.

Peter Scaffidi noted that his mother, legendary jazz guitarist Mary Osborne, utilized Gruggett for repair work.

Above: 1982 Gruggett (HB-S-HB) guitar.
Willie G. Moseley

Top right: Body of a "Velvet Touch" model made in the 1990s features wood-covered pickups and wood knobs.
Courtesy of Bob Shade

Bottom right: During the 1990s Bill was reunited with the original Stradette-shaped bass he made when he was employed at Mosrite in the 1960s.
Courtesy of the Bill Gruggett Estate

He was our mother's first choice when she needed work on her guitars. In the mid-1980s, while visiting my parents' home one evening, Bill learned that my mother had a 1952 sunburst Gibson L-5 that had been severely damaged in a car accident—the guitar had been smashed and splintered. Bill asked to see the guitar, and when he examined it, he told my mother he could repair it.

In less than three months, Bill astonished my mother with a fully restored, now-mint-condition instrument. The wood grain was visible underneath the lightest part of the sunburst; there was no visible evidence of any cracking, splintering or other damage—a testimony to Bill's artistry and talent.

Bill befriended Marc Lipco, whose family had owned a local pawn shop that "morphed into a music store," according to Lipco, "back in the day when there were no 'big box' music stores; dealers were all independents."

Among the brands that Alan's Kern Guitar World retailed in its time were Magnatone and Yamaha. Marc started working at his father's business around the age of thirteen. He was aware of local builders like Mosrite and Gruggett, but recalled that local guitar manufacturing was "kind of like cars in Michigan. People don't really think about 'Hey, we're making cars here' because they're shipping them somewhere else." Lipco's admiration for Gruggett's luthiery lasted for decades, and he considered Bill to be an artisan rather than merely a craftsman.

Gruggett was always trying out new shapes, styles, pickup layouts and circuitry innovations, as well. A 1982 guitar crafted by Bill and his apprentice at the time, Chuck Long, had a humbucker–single coil–humbucker pickup configuration with a downsized headstock and cutaways, plus wood pickup covers, pickup surrounds, and knobs. All three knobs were a push-pull style to interpolate splitting the coils or reversing the phase on the humbucking pickups. Long also applied the finish to the instrument.

One of Gruggett's most elegant creations was a guitar commissioned by Marc Lipco around the end of the millennium. It featured a uniquely shaped, chambered body made with figured woods, a figured wood tailpiece, a figured maple Brass Rail–style neck, a single f-hole, and gold hardware.

Around the same time Gruggett crafted the Brass Rail–style instrument for Lipco, the luthier began his new relationship with Bob Shade of the revitalized Hallmark brand, as previously chronicled.

Brass Rail–style guitar, ca. 2000—one of a kind, front and back.
Willie G. Moseley

Gruggett with handcrafted Hallmark Stradette #6.
Courtesy of the Bill Gruggett Estate

Custom Luthiery, Mosrite (Part 2), Back to Custom Luthiery   167

Gruggett was gratified that his earlier designs and creations had attained enough respect in the burgeoning vintage guitar market that Shade's company was creating and selling updated versions of the Stradette. However, Bill also continued to create new instruments, even as his health began to decline because of a malignancy.

As the new century progressed, Gruggett crafted several instruments for Marc Lipco there were based on classic guitar styles. Three examples are shown here.

Tele-style guitar, leather pickguard, early 2000s.
Willie G. Moseley

Esquire-style guitar, sparkleburst finish, early 2000s.
Willie G. Moseley

Les Paul–style guitar, saddle-stitch binding, early 2000s.
Willie G. Moseley

One of his higher-end models, the elegant Corvette, was codesigned with Lonnie Hyde, who had worked at Mosrite in the 1970s and was a close friend of Gruggett. This three-pickup example has an alder body with a maple top and neck, and wood pickup covers. The entire instrument was handmade by Bill except for hardware, including a vibrato supplied by the Hallmark company.

Early in the new century, Bill made at least two Telecaster-style instruments with a "waving flag" motif. They was commissioned by a Bakersfield businessman, Stan Ellis, who played in a local band called Stampede. That aggregation performed regularly at Buck Owens's Crystal Palace, an entertainment venue, restaurant, and museum. Ellis recounted,

Gruggett is reunited with a two-pickup, twelve-string Raindrop guitar that he built in the mid-1960s.
Courtesy of the Bill Gruggett Estate

Corvette.
Courtesy of Michael G. Stewart

Years ago, Buck hired our band to be the Friday and Saturday night band after the Buckaroos. We were really honored to be playing after one of the world's greatest music legends. We weren't the best musicians around, but Buck liked us because we worked really hard and always maintained a very professional attitude no matter what the situation. We all had day jobs and realized we were a service to the Crystal Palace; we felt anyone who came in there deserved the best for their money. Sometimes we wouldn't even take a break, never drank on stage, were always timely, and treated the staff with the utmost respect.

While browsing in an out-of-town music store, Ellis encountered an Ovation acoustic guitar with an illustration of an American flag waving in the breeze on its top. He ordered a guitar from Gruggett to be styled like a Telecaster and finished with a similar image on the body as a gift for Owens. "The paint job was done by Jason Janes at his shop in Bakersfield," Ellis said of his special order, "and it wasn't identical to the Ovation, but [the Ovation] gave Jason an idea of what we wanted."

Owens used his new instrument extensively. Ellis recalled that the guitar got a unique workout at the Crystal Palace on May 25, 2005, when Garth Brooks played it at a special outdoor concert to celebrate the unveiling of ten bronze statues of country music legends.

Owens had informed Ellis that after his death, he wanted the Gruggett guitar to be displayed in the Crystal Palace museum. The Bakersfield icon succumbed to a heart attack on March 25, 2006. "When he passed, [Buck's nephew and CEO of Buck Owens Productions] Mel Owens called and asked if I wanted it back," Ellis remembered. "I told him Buck wanted it displayed and it was to go to the museum." Ellis later had Gruggett build another flag guitar for his own collection.

Gruggett made a few acoustic instruments over the decades. The last Gruggett instrument of that type sports his signature on the neck block. It can be seen through the soundhole and is dated June 19, 2008. The guitar has a small parlor guitar configuration, and is 13.75 inches wide. The neck is mahogany and the fingerboard is rosewood with mother-of-pearl inlay. The scale is 25.34 inches and the "lower belly" bridge is ebony.

It has a spruce top with multiple-layer soundhole trim that has a herringbone marquetry center ring. The rims and back are lacewood, and the top edge and the center back strip also have elaborate multilayer and herringbone marquetry, while the back edge is single-ply white.

The strap button on the end of the body is also a jack, as the instrument has a piezo-type pickup built into the bridge.

Mark Lipco recalled one of Gruggett's last electric instruments as an original-style guitar with a single-cutaway body shape:

Above: Bill with a flag-motif, Telecaster-style instrument.
Courtesy of the Bill Gruggett Estate

Left: Gruggett acoustic guitar, 2008, front and rear.
Courtesy of Tony Brown

Below: Gruggett's signature as seen through the soundhole.
Courtesy of Tony Brown

Single-cutaway model with figured maple fretboard.
Willie G. Moseley

Single-cutaway model, rear view showing mahogany neck.
Willie G. Moseley

The body was his design, the neck and headstock was a design I made in the '80s. He used the headstock design on this guitar as well as one other he made for me; [I'm] not sure why but he surprised me with it. The neck is mahogany with a bird's-eye maple fretboard. The body looks to be alder with a bookmatched flame maple hand carved top that is bound. The pickups are from Dave Wintz at Rio Grande Pickups. This was kind of a typical style guitar he made with some random mix of woods and styles, usually what he had in his garage; no serial number, just his hand-drawn name on the back of the neck.

Bill Gruggett, the soft-spoken luthier who handcrafted guitars in Bakersfield for decades, died in October 2012 at the age of seventy-five. "Billy was a really good builder," Artie Niesen remembered. "It was easy for him to envision something and turn it into a finished product. He was more reserved than Semie; he generally did great work, either in building his own custom guitars or doing repairs."

Courtesy of Bob Shade

Part 4
Ancillary Brands

Acoustic Black Widow guitar—back view showing "hourglass" pad and "peanut" neck attachment plate.
Willie G. Moseley

27
Acoustic

Unlike Semie Moseley's offshoot Gospel line, Acoustic brand guitars and basses built by Mosrite in the early 1970s weren't originally envisioned or designed by Bakersfield's frontline guitar builder or any of his former or then-current associates.

Around a decade after Mosrite had built Standel-branded instruments, the company worked with the Acoustic Control Corporation of Van Nuys, California, creating guitars and basses for another Golden State amplifier company that had wanted to get into the guitar business. Among the famous bands that were users of Acoustic amplifiers were the Doors and Spirit.

Acoustic's short-lived attempt at a guitar line consisted of one guitar and one bass, dubbed the "Black Widow" series. Reportedly, most Acoustic Black Widows were made in Japan. Mosrite would finish out Acoustic's guitar initiative, and Semie would recount that he built about two hundred Acoustic-branded instruments.

Mosrite-made Black Widows were easy to discern, as they had the distinctive Mosrite bridge and a reverse "peanut" neck attachment plate. The smaller humbucking pickups with twelve polepieces fit inside the same metal frame as used on the pickups that were on Dobro D-100 electric resonator guitars and the "Moseley"-branded custom guitar made for Don Rich. Knobs on Mosrite-made Acoustic Black Widows were the same style

Acoustic Black Widow guitar.
Willie G. Moseley

as found on Acoustic amplifiers. The scale of the guitar was an unusual 27 inches, while the bass had a scale of 31 inches.

Innovative jazz guitarist Larry Coryell was a latter-day endorser, and an ad showed him playing a Mosrite-made variant. Another reported Black Widow player was Jimmy Nolen, the machine-like funk guitarist for James Brown's band.

The body had symmetrical cutaways and a German carve. Wood bodies were made of maple, but some Black Widow bodies had a different (and bizarre) composition. In an effort to develop a lightweight body, Mosrite briefly experimented with a technique involving a molded epoxy "shell" and a Styrofoam core. While the weight reduction was accomplished, such bodies were too flimsy to support the instruments' hardware. There were reports of control knobs and tailpieces falling off while instruments with molded bodies were being played. It was an intriguing initiative that didn't work, and dozens of such bodies reportedly ended up being destroyed.

The coolest cosmetic feature of many Acoustic Black Widows was actually on the flat back of the body. A red vinyl pad emulated the "hourglass" marking found on the arachnid from which the model took its name.

Acoustic exited the guitar marketplace in the mid-1970s.

Acoustic Black Widow bass.
Willie G. Moseley

Mosrite-Dobro "Uncle Josh" model, built in Gardena, California; note both brand names on the headstock.
Courtesy of Olivia's Vintage

28

Dobro

"Dobro" is a contracted term for "Dopyera Brothers"; the surname is of Czechoslovakian heritage. The Dopyera siblings and other family members were involved with the innovation, development, and marketing of resonator guitars with such brand names as National and, not surprisingly, Dobro.

The large, round resonator on such acoustic instruments amplifies strings and is stereotypically placed underneath a hubcap-like plate. Resonator guitars come in a Hawaiian style (elevated strings, played horizontally with a handheld slide) or a Spanish style (played like a regular acoustic guitar). The instruments have their own unique sound in either configuration. Indeed, "dobro" (lower case) has become a generic term for any resonator guitar, regardless of its brand name.

Feeling its oats because of the huge success of the Ventures Model guitars, Mosrite purchased the Dobro company, located in Gardena, California, in the mid-1960s. Factory machinery as well as guitars that had already been built in Gardena were transported to Bakersfield. Ed Sanner recalled that while resonator guitars had the potential to be an asset to the Mosrite line, Semie had another motive for buying the company:

> When Semie bought the Dobro company—the inventory *and* the name, lock, stock and barrel—he put me in charge of putting those (instruments) together. A lot of them were already completed when he bought the company, but they weren't set up too well. They all had to be adjusted. But the main reason he bought Dobro was because they had the machines to make the sides for the bodies, which we could also use to make flat-top guitars.

The earliest Mosrite-Dobros were indeed guitars that had been built in Gardena. The only Mosrite facet on such instruments was a logo that was added to their headstocks.

It wasn't any surprise that Mosrite-era Dobros—whether built in Gardena or Bakersfield—were soon nicknamed "Mobros" within the Mosrite organization and among musicians. As noted earlier, the nickname would briefly become a legitimate appellation in 1972.

A nineteen-page, full-color Dobro catalog was distributed in 1966. Therein, an introductory essay chronicled the history of the resonator instrument and the Dopyera family. It concluded by noting that the increasing demand for Dobros had motivated Emil Dopyera, a son of one of the Dobro founders, "to set about organizing and arranging financing for a new company which was formed in December of 1964."

The 1966 catalog listed Dobro's address as 1424 P Street in Bakersfield, which was the address of the Mosrite factory. There was no mention in the Dobro catalog of Mosrite guitars, Mosrite Distributing Company in Los Angeles, or the Ventures. The catalog also differentiated between instruments that had a Type D resonator (the "Original resonator identified with the 'Dobro sound'") and a "new in concept and design" resonator known as the Type C.

Instrument models had a simple coding system. The "D" or "C" prefix indicated the type of resonator that the instrument had. An "S" suffix noted that instrument had a square neck and was designed to be played in a Hawaiian style, while an "E" suffix indicated that the guitar had an added pickup to make it an acoustic-electric variant.

The necks of the Spanish-style instruments featured a tilt-neck adjustment, which the catalog proclaimed as a Dobro exclusive for American guitars. This tilt-neck concept had actually been introduced a few years earlier on budget instruments made by Danelectro, but the Mosrite-Dobro version did precede the introduction of this type of configuration by the gargantuan Fender company by approximately six years.

D-12E Columbia.
Photo by Stefani Mills

C-3 Monterey model. This example, owned by Eugene Moles, has an aftermarket DeArmond pickup and controls added.
Willie G. Moseley

Standard production Dobro models made by Mosrite included:

D-12 Columbia twelve-string
D-12S Lexington twelve-string
C-65 Plainsman
D-50 Richmond
D-50S Uncle Josh
C-60 Avalon
D-40 Texarkana
D-40S Blue Grass
C-3 Monterey

All models were available with the added pickup "E" option. Scale on the lineup was 24.63 inches, with the exception of the downsized C-3 Monterey, which had a scale of 23.25 inches.

Several noted musicians were seen in the 1966 catalog, admiring the new instruments.

While the lineup of Dobro models was presented in a logical manner, the keystone instrument in the 1966 catalog was a completely new guitar model that had been developed in Bakersfield by Mosrite.

The D-100 Californian was a thinline-style electric guitar with two pickups as well as resonator guitar appointments. The black instrument shown in the catalog, in a photo as well as line drawings, was apparently a prototype. It had somewhat odd-looking symmetrical cutaway horns that flared out from a right-angle juncture at the neck. The body was bound front and rear, and was advertised as being available in cherry and black finishes. The body depth was 3.5 inches, and the scale was, like most other Mosrite Dobros, 24.63 inches.

The resonator on the new model was a Type D. Controls included four knobs mounted around the lower bout. The pickup toggle switch installed in a somewhat awkward location near the neck pickup and treble cutaway horn.

Apparently the prototype's body was too weird-looking, or maybe it would have been too complicated to manufacture. By the time production commenced, the body style had switched to the configuration and dimensions as found on Mosrite Celebrity thinline electric guitar models. The use of Celebrity bodies would have been more efficient, production-wise. The production D-100's controls, including two knobs (master volume and tone), a toggle switch, and a jack, were installed on a banana-shaped plate.

Guitarist Jimmy Bryant and war hero, actor, music publisher, and songwriter Audie Murphy examine a D-40E Texarkana in the 1966 catalog.
Courtesy of Steve Brown/vintaxe.com

Singer-songwriter Hoyt Axton with a D-50SE Uncle Josh model in the 1966 catalog.
Courtesy of Steve Brown/vintaxe.com

Original-style D-100 Californian seen in 1966 catalog.
Courtesy of Steve Brown/vintaxe.com

D-100 Californian (double-branded). This example has been cited as the first production model completed.
Willie G. Moseley

D-100 made for Joe Maphis. Note that the style of the lettering on the fretboard differs from the Glen Campbell example.
Courtesy of the Country Music Hall of Fame® and Museum

Custom-order Dobros were also offered. Options listed included gold or silver plating, hand-engraved resonator plates, special colors, and inlaid fingerboards.

Joe Maphis and Glen Campbell were recipients of D-100 Californians with their names inlaid on the fretboard. Their instruments were aberrations, as the controls were installed from underneath the top (no control plate).

Both Campbell and fellow guitarist James Burton were seen with D-100s in late 1960s "Change-Overs" ads. By this time, "Mosrite" had become the dominant brand name regarding the instrument's promotion.

As noted earlier, the Dobro name was acquired by a Los Angeles company not long after the Mosrite factory was closed.

29
GM Custom

Following the closure of the Mosrite factory in 1969, Gene Moles took a different tack compared to other professional and amateur guitar builders who had patronized the bankruptcy sale. For many years—even before he went to work at Mosrite—Moles had occasionally experimented with making his own instruments when his schedule allowed him to do such. Many times, he collaborated with Bill Gruggett in the design and construction of such instruments, which he designated as the "GM Custom" brand. "They were real close," Eugene Moles said of his father's friendship with Gruggett. "Almost like fraternity brothers. [My father] was good pals with Ed Sanner, too."

Other GM Custom instruments were, not unexpectedly, built primarily from leftover Mosrite parts. However, Eugene recalled that his father didn't want any of his instruments to be perceived as a phony Mosrite, so Gene initiated a policy of affixing a small "GM" medallion to the back of a headstock that had a Mosrite logo on the front. He also used other parts from other erstwhile Bakersfield guitar companies.

Moles continued to perform in the Bakersfield area, using his Mosrite Mark I guitar for which he had traded in his original Mosrite pre-Ventures solidbody. One memorable 1970 performance was at the California Correctional Institution in nearby Tehachapi. "I was there," said Eugene Moles. "It's a maximum security prison. He played there with some other local guys from Bakersfield. Ronnie Sessions was on that show; Jimmy Thomason, Jelly Sanders."

However, the occupation that would sustain Moles for the rest of his life was running his Doctor of Guitars repair and refinishing business, which he started in his own garage. Numerous famous players utilized his services, and an occasional GM Custom guitar would also be created. Eugene recalled that his father also enjoyed picking up guitar licks from Doctor of Guitars customers.

Eugene had begun to perform with his father at a young age. He would often use a GM Custom instrument with a unique body shape.

Early GM Custom guitar—compare this instrument's aesthetics to the instruments Bill Gruggett is displaying in a 1962 photograph in the Gruggett section.
Willie G. Moseley

This GM Custom guitar is made mostly from Mosrite parts.
Courtesy of Bob Shade

Wearing bib overalls, Eugene Moles performs behind his father with the Roadrunners at an early 1970s CB radio convention in Las Vegas, using a guitar that Gene made.
Courtesy of Eugene Moles

Merle Haggard, Gene Moles, and Roy Nichols perform at the grand opening for Moles's new Doctor of Guitars shop.
Courtesy of Bryce Martin

Moles in his shop, 1976.
Courtesy of Bryce Martin

The Doctor of Guitars would move to larger facilities more than once. At one grand opening, Moles fans Merle Haggard and Roy Nichols (then-lead guitarist for Haggard's band the Strangers) participated in an on-site concert. Moles used the same GM Custom guitar that Eugene often played.

In later years, Gene was proud of the accomplishments of his son. Eugene was a member of the house band at the Palomino Club in North Hollywood, and actually worked briefly with both Buck Owens and Merle Haggard. "I was a temporary member of the Buckaroos and the Strangers," said Eugene. "I had been to Nashville in 1979 and '80 to do *Hee Haw* shows with Buck, then many of the good players I knew in California began migrating to Nashville. I was a fan of (legendary Nashville guitarist) Reggie Young, and I moved to Nashville in '87."

Another GM Custom guitar, ca. mid-1970s.
Willie G. Moseley

"The apple didn't fall far from the tree," Marc Lipco said of Eugene's musicianship. "One of the best I've ever heard." Gene continued to perform in the Bakersfield area, in addition to maintaining his repair and refinishing shop. He also continued to build guitars.

One latter-day GM Custom was another Bill Gruggett collaboration. It featured extra-wide binding, and a plaque on the back of the headstock notes that the guitar was made in 2001, the same year Moles died. "He got behind on some of his repairs because of his illness, pulmonary fibrosis, so I went out there and helped him catch up," said Eugene. "He had the shop up until he passed away."

2001 GM Custom. This angled view shows the instrument's extra-wide binding.
Willie G. Moseley

Mid-1960s Melobar promotional flyer showing Walt Smith with his unique instrument.
Courtesy of Ted Smith

30

Melobar

Walt Smith was born in northern California in 1920. The son of an insurance salesman, he took up piano lessons at a young age and became a childhood prodigy on multiple instruments. Smith developed a love of the Big Band and Western Swing musical genres, and purveyed his talents on guitar and steel guitar, trying to make his longtime dreams of becoming a cowboy musician a reality.

Rebelling against his father's plans for his son to pursue a career in business, Walt chose an agrarian lifestyle instead, moving to an Arizona ranch in 1939 with his new bride to raise long staple cotton. He would eventually return to California, settling in Ojai to run a nearby large ranch. Smith was an inveterate tinkerer, and in the mid-1950s, he began to develop an idea for a hybrid instrument—a lap steel guitar that could be played comfortably standing up. He began to visit and exchange ideas with southern California guitar builders such as Leo Fender in Fullerton and the Dopyera brothers, Ed and Rudy, in Gardena.

By the mid-1960s, Smith's idea had resulted in the construction of a few experimental instruments, which were first given an official brand name of Mel-O-Chord, which later evolved into Mel-O-Bar. Ultimately, the moniker of the stand-up steel was usually referred to *sans* hyphens (Melobar).

To most observers, the Melobar was an odd-looking solidbody instrument that resembled a standard (Spanish) electric guitar, but its neck (which usually had ten strings) was attached at an approximately 45-degree angle to the body.

Melobars abruptly came into strong public focus when Smith contracted with Mosrite to have his innovative instrument manufactured in Bakersfield. "Back then, Dad wanted a real quality instrument," recalled John Selby Smith, one of Smith's five sons, "and that's what Mosrite represented. I think it had to do with wanting top pickups, too."

The Melobar production agreement gave Mosrite the opportunity to use up the leftover plain basswood guitar bodies that Semie had rejected for use on the Ventures II electric guitar model in 1965. However, the angled neck of the Melobar had to be installed differently, so Mosrite fashioned a wood block to seal off the open end of the body's neck joint cavity.

This disassembled Melobar includes a body that was originally designated for a Mosrite Ventures II guitar.
Courtesy of Ted Smith

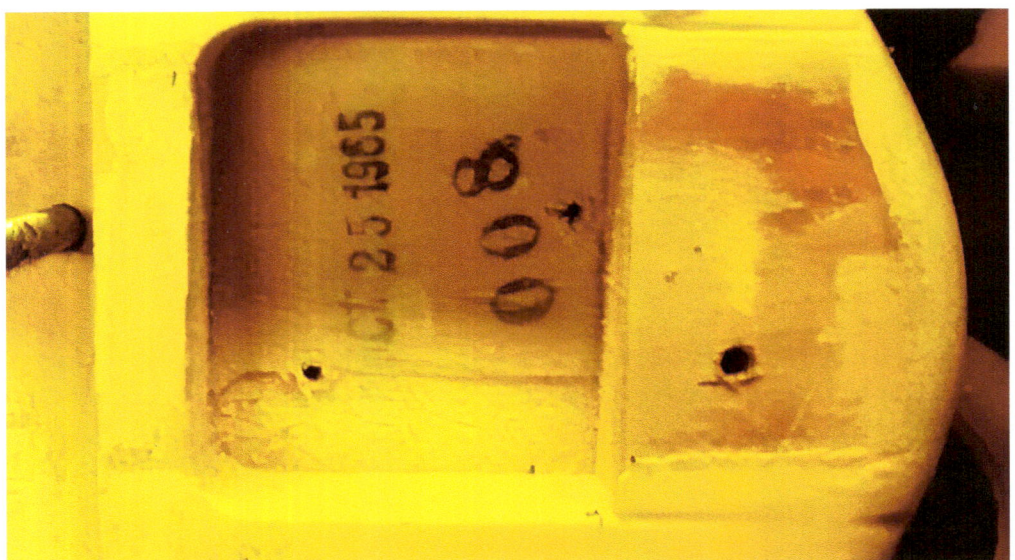

Close-up of the Mosrite-made Melobar body, exhibiting the wood block installed in the neck joint (right). It had been stamped with a production date of October 25, 1965, but it languished in the factory for an extended time before being used as a Melobar body ca. 1967.
Courtesy of Ted Smith

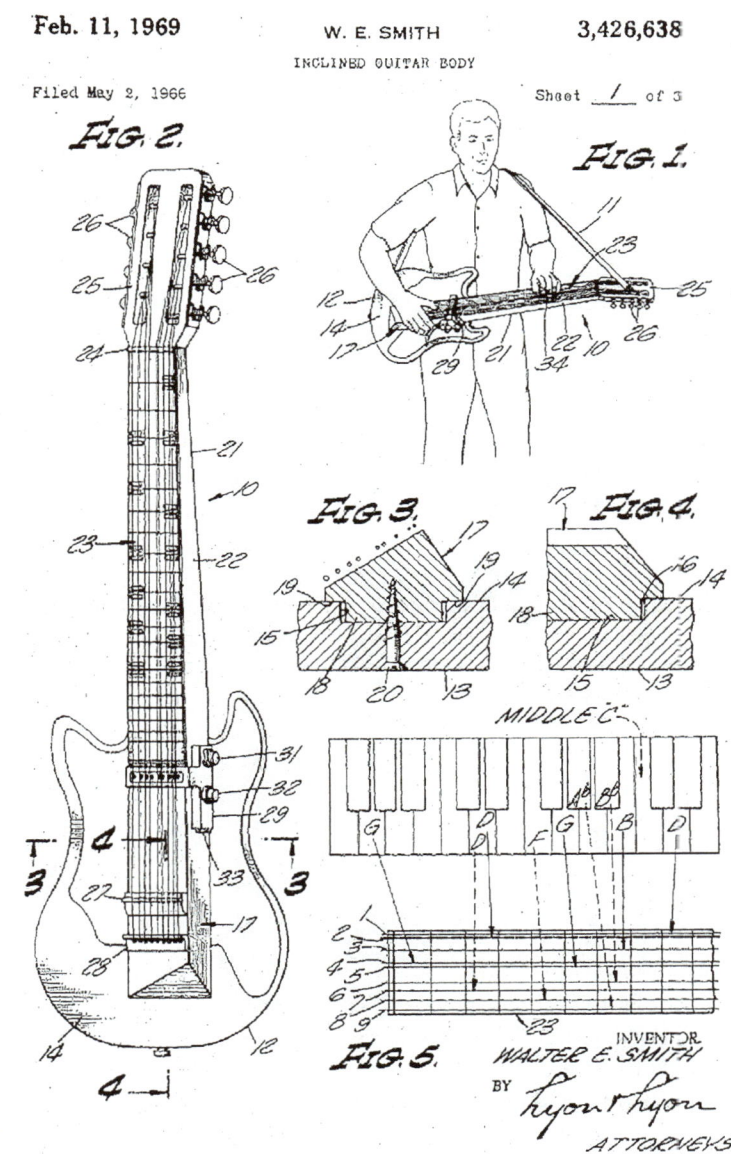

Patent for Melobar electric steel guitar.
Courtesy of Ted Smith

Smith applied for a patent for his instrument on May 2, 1966, and it's probably not accidental that the line drawing had a body silhouette that resembled a Mosrite guitar.

In the summer of 1967, the so-called Summer of Love in popular music lore, John Selby Smith, then a student at Princeton, visited San Francisco and Los Angeles in an effort to get his father's instrument into the hands of frontline rock musicians.

"In June, I'd been sent to San Francisco by the head of my psychedelic research institute in New Jersey to report on what was happening in Haight-Ashbury," he recounted (Haight-Ashbury was a district in the city that was Ground Zero for the "hippie" movement). "After a crazy three weeks, I hitched down to L.A., and through friends, just naturally slipped into showing the Melobar to rock bands—the [Jefferson] Airplane for a week, the Mamas and the Papas, the [Grateful] Dead for a few days, a few others."

Smith detailed his encounter with the Jefferson Airplane at the RCA studio in Hollywood, where the band had begun recording music for their third album, *After Bathing at Baxter's*. He described the facility as "a giant gym of a room. We showed up with the guitar and they were very nice; we spent the whole day there with them while they recorded, me teaching Jorma [Kaukonen, lead guitarist] the ins and outs of some Melobar licks during breaks in recording sessions."

Kaukonen concurred with Smith's assessment of the studio. "It was a huge room with perfect accustics," the legendary guitarist recalled. "They knew what they were doing back then; they recorded symphony orchestras there."

Kaukonen had not seen or heard of a Melobar prior to Smith's visit to the RCA studio. He detailed,

Slide guitar was never my thing, and it is quite different from playing a steel guitar. I remember thinking that the Melobar was the coolest-looking guitar ever—the fact that you could wear it like a guitar and the slanted neck allowed you play it like a steel was absolutely brilliant! I thought the aesthetics were tops!

I had played a little dobro in an "old-timey band" in New York in 1960 so I was comfortable holding the bar like a steel guitar player or a dobro player. At the time, the only tuning I knew was GBDBGD. I had yet to experience steel guitar tunings like C6 or E13. And I was still busy transitioning from being a fingerpicker to being a rock guitarist, even though *Baxter's* was our third album.

Kaukonen had tried Mosrite guitars earlier in his career, and recalled, "I thought they were cool but they did not have the sound I was looking for."

And the guitarist was also aware that the strange instrument Smith had brought to the studio was Mosrite-made. "The aesthetic was definitely Mosrite-esque," Kaukonen said, "even to the crass non-knower."

"Jorma ended up inviting us back the next day, and then the next," Smith recounted. "It was an amazing time, because they were experimenting with wild music like I'd never heard before."

Kaukonen also reflected on having Smith around to show him how to play a ten-string instrument:

Again, I didn't know much about steel guitars and their typical usage. I didn't know what to do with a ten-string instrument—six- and occasionally a twelve-string guitar was all I knew. I wish I had known then what I know now. That said, it was easy to play, and sounded like . . . well, a steel guitar. [Smith] was a really nice guy and I truly appreciated the gifts of the instruments.

Kaukonen ultimately put a Melobar to use on Jefferson Airplane recordings. "You hear the Melobar here and there, when there's slide or strange glissando licks," said Smith. "*Crown of Creation* [the Airplane's fourth album] had several Melobar leads."

Walt Smith noticed that the list of instruments credited to Jorma Kaukonen on that 1968 release included something dubbed the "electric chicken" and presumed it was a reference to a Melobar. "Dad was *not* happy about that," said Walt Smith's youngest son, Ted. However, Kaukonen clarified that the curious instrument citation wasn't about Smith's invention. "'Electric chicken' is just nonsensical '60s Dada-esque stuff,' the guitarist said, "and I'm sure it had nothing to do with the Melobar."

One curious "endorsement" for Melobar germinated during John Selby's LA sojourn. While walking through a residential area of Beverly Hills, he saw a woman in distress rushing out of her house. Shirley Boone, wife of crooner and actor Pat Boone, explained to John Selby that her dog was having puppies, and she didn't know what to do. John Selby assisted in the delivery of the pups, and his midwifery begat a friendship with the Boone family. A few years later, Pat would work on a unique endorsement project for the Melobar company.

Following his attempt at spreading the word about the new instrument in San Francisco and Los Angeles, John Selby was compelled by his father to visit the Mosrite factory in Bakersfield for an extended time. "Dad sent me over to Bakersfield," he said, "to oversee how things were going. I felt very much a part of Melobar then, and went to Bakersfield as requested."

Over fifty years after the "Summer of Love," John Selby still had vivid memories of the Mosrite factory and its personnel, including how any initial misgivings of his were assuaged:

> I felt at first that everything was out of hand and undermanaged. Decisions were made differently than I was used to, but their logic *did* work. They had an attitude—the employees—that was laid back, fun, irreverent, and masterful at the same time.
>
> I reported back to Dad that the situation was working well. Excellent precision and quality control. Almost all the people working on our project were in a corner of a big, big factory, and they were almost all women. I remember they talked with a strong Okie accent, which I'd also grown up with. And I slipped back into that accent with them, and right then was when I started singing with the Okie accent that's my singing voice of preference.
>
> I also realized I'd picked up a prejudice against that accent related to good, fast work—and I quickly learned to throw away that attitude, because those women were *really good* at their work! They all took me on with humor, played word games with me, laughed an exorbitant amount, and taught me a lot about growing up in the process. I loved being there!

Brian Jones of the Rolling Stones was also reputed to have experimented with a Melobar in 1967. One legend about that particular instrument recounts that Jones gave it to Jimmy Page, who was playing with the Yardbirds.

Ted Smith recalled that Page called Walt Smith's residence some years later seeking information and playing tips. Page's call came in late at night and woke Walt up from a sound sleep. The company founder turned over the call to Ted, who did his best to accommodate the iconic rock guitarist. Page called Ted later, and was able to impart that the Melobar in question was a Mosrite-made example that Jones had used with some kind of unknown effects box. Reportedly, Jones had loaned it to Page just before Jones died.

Walt Smith had specified that Melobars were to have alder bodies, but the leftover flat Ventures II guitar bodies on most—if not all—of the Mosrite-made Melobars were made of basswood. The scale of the instrument was 23 inches. As for the angle at which the necks were mounted, "Mosrite models varied a little," according to Ted Smith. The Mosrite Melobars were usually finished in the bright, three-tone sunburst color that was popular on Mosrite's own instruments at the time. Some other rare finishes were also seen.

Walt Smith's patent application was granted on February 11, 1969, three days before Mosrite's financial problems culminated with the factory being closed on Valentine's Day. An estimated three hundred Melobar instruments were built by Mosrite.

Morris Rosenberg and Ben Sacco had founded the Sierra Bag Company in Bakersfield in 1947, making sacks for agricultural workers. They expanded their business interests in 1959, creating the Sierra Iron and Metal company as a primeval recycling facility for salvaged metal.

In September 1968, they met with former Mosrite representative Ralph Scaffidi, and partnered with him in a new company, Sierra Electronics. That moniker was changed before the end of 1968 to Rosac Electronics & Manufacturing, "Rosac" being an amalgam of the first syllables of the last names of Rosenberg and Sacco. A number of former Mosrite employees went to work at Sierra/Rosac.

The original idea for Rosac was for the company to start out by making amplifiers and guitar effects. Former Mosrite electronics supervisor Ed Sanner was one of the earliest Rosac employees, and was right at home with crafting electronic items. Sanner would design a device called the Nu-Fuzz, an improvement over his Mosrite FUZZrite design, as well as the Distortion Blender, which had a third knob designated as a "blender" control. Other Rosac foot-operated devices included the Nu-Wa and Nu-Wa Fuzz.

Standard Mosrite-made Melobar, front and rear.
Willie G. Moseley

Rosac's Distortion Blender by Nu-Fuzz.
Willie G. Moseley

Jazz guitarist Mary Osborne, wife of Ralph Scaffidi, was known to stop by the Rosac production facility to check out amplifiers. "From time to time she would go to the Rosac factory and play through the finished amps, checking for sound quality and response," said her son, Ralph Scaffidi Jr.

Ed Sanner recalled that around the time Rosac opened, the company briefly manufactured Melobars in one section of the company's factory. Rosac-made Melobars were made of alder, and had a different body silhouette from their Mosrite progenitors—the Rosac instrument body had stubbier cutaway horns that flared outward. The neck was mounted at an angle of 45 degrees, and the scale was 22.75 inches. Cheaper tuners were used on Rosacs, and the pickup rings were left over from the Mosrite-made Dobro D-100. Once again, the most popular color was a bright three-tone sunburst.

When the Rosac-made Melobars were introduced, Pat Boone recorded an introduction for the instructional record included with each new instrument.

Around the end of 1970, however, Walt Smith "pulled the plug" (to quote his son Ted) on Melobar. The patriarch had tired of the lifestyle of the greater Los Angeles area, and relocated to Idaho. Prior to moving to the Gem State, Walt built a one-pickup Melobar in a purple finish and gave it to his Ojai neighbor, singer Sheb Wooley (of "Purple People Eater" fame). Rosac's production of Melobar instruments totaled around three hundred, according to John Selby Smith and Ted Smith.

Moreover, Rosenberg and Sacco's electronics initiative didn't last long, closing in 1975. Mary Osborne and Ralph Scaffidi would quickly branch out on their own with a company that also focused more on amplifiers instead of guitars (see chapter 31, "Osborne").

John Selby Smith managed to acquire six Rosac instruments around the time of the Rosac closure, and converted them to what he called a "blues" configuration with six strings, which was more oriented toward rock musicians. Stripping the sunburst finishes, he painted three white and three red. One of the white ones ended up in the possession of Poco's Rusty Young, who nicknamed his instrument "the Bear." He would use it extensively in concert.

Melobar went into stasis for a number of years, and was later resurrected. Instruments were manufactured in locales other than Bakersfield, and the newer models included radical body silhouettes resembling Gibson Explorer and Flying V guitars.

Walt Smith died in 1990.

Rosac-made Melobar, ca. 1970.
Courtesy of Ted Smith

31

Osborne

To Mary Osborne, her husband Ralph Scaffidi, and their three children, the differences between Long Island, New York, and Bakersfield were numerous, as would be the observation of almost anyone making such a move. When the family moved across the country in 1968, Ralph Jr. was thirteen, Susan was eleven, and Peter was nine.

Their father had been a professional trumpet player and sales associate for the C. Bruno & Sons company, a large musical instrument distributor. Their mother was a legendary jazz guitarist who had gigged and recorded with Billie Holliday, Louis Armstrong, Mel Torme, and numerous other jazz giants. She was also an endorser of Gretsch guitars.

Mary and Ralph had spent years in the New York music scene, but it took a while for the Scaffidi kids to become aware that they were growing up in a musical family environment. Susan recalled,

> Given that so many of our parents' friends were also musicians and they took us to so many of the events at which they performed, I'm not sure that it sunk in that my parents had unique occupations until we moved to Bakersfield. My father was also the director of bands for the Diocese of Rockville Center on Long Island, and Ralph and I were students in those ensembles—that was just Dad's job.

Ralph Jr. remembered,

> Our dad had been working as a business representative for C. Bruno and Sons since 1960. He had developed a very good professional reputation while with Bruno—first as a customer relations rep for problem resolution, then later as a sales rep, in many cases for customers who he had originally met via addressing their concerns and resolving their problems.

Phil Brenner was Mosrite's national sales manager, and hired Scaffidi on the recommendations of several knowledgeable music business acquaintances. The move to California also meant that Mary and Ralph also planned to look to Los Angeles for potential recording and performance opportunities. Of Bakersfield, Ralph Jr. said,

> It was very different in many ways. Some differences were very obvious, like the climate. We were in the Central Valley—very hot and semi-arid—and not near the beach, as we had been on Long Island. The culture was a bit more casual, and certainly Western in nature. We were quite aware of the impact of Country and Western music, especially the "Bakersfield Sound." At the same time, Bakersfield offered a bit more conservative way of life—a true "small town" atmosphere.

"On the other hand, Bakersfield's size and the downtown area were somewhat similar to our hometown on Long Island," said Susan. "Besides the Country and Western culture that was new to us, there was the addition of Basque and Mexican cultures that were not really present on the Eastern Seaboard in the 1960s."

Peter recounted the differences between Mosrite guitars and his mother's endorsement brand, Gretsch, noting, "Not only were the guitars visually different, they played differently. The Mosrite neck was thin, and was very fast with low action. The Gretsch neck was wider, and offered more 'resistance,' characteristic of the classic jazz guitar."

About the only time Mary assisted Ralph during his brief Mosrite tenure was to informally demonstrate the Mosrite line at a 1968 NAMM show in Chicago. As noted previously, Ralph Scaffidi would become one of the earliest associates of the Rosac company, which built amplifiers, footswitch effects, and a run of Melobars.

While the Los Angeles jazz music scene was welcoming to Mary, she—like Gene Moles—soon tired of commuting, preferring to play regularly with local musicians. She would later teach jazz guitar at Bakersfield College and California State University at Bakersfield (CSUB). However, she still occasionally performed elsewhere across the country with other veteran musicians at jazz festivals.

After the dissolution of Rosac in 1975, Mary and Ralph set about creating their own enterprise, the Osborne Guitar Company. Its moniker averred that Osborne-branded products would include stringed instruments in addition to amplifiers and effects. Not surprisingly, Mary would personally test each completed amplifier.

"Kerry Savee was the lead luthier at the startup of the company," said Susan. "Some of the Rosac staff who had been making amplifiers when Rosac closed were hired for the same roles at Osborne Guitar." A factory was located in Lamont, several miles south of Bakersfield (near Arvin). Mary collaborated with Savee on the design of the instrument, particularly the neck. According to Peter, the unlabeled guitar seen on page 199 is an early instrument, and differs from production instruments regarding neck width. Peter explained,

> It has a slightly wider, flatter neck. In addition to being a talented luthier, Kerry also played classical guitar. He incorporated a neck into his design that was very much like a classical guitar. Due to the shape and greater width of the fingerboard, this model is great for chording, especially for players with large hands.
>
> Ultimately this design gave way to a neck and fingerboard more like most electric guitars on the market, making it a one-of-a-kind instrument—truly unique and a pleasure to play.

Peter described the Osborne-monikered guitar shown on page 199 as a prototype that was close to a production model. "An upscale model," he said of the instrument, "featuring Hi-A pickups—[which were] the first generation Bartolini pickups—a Leo Quan Badass bridge and tailpiece, and Schaller tuners, standard on all models."

Guitar bodies and necks were made of hard rock maple. The center stripe was rosewood, and ran through the entire body (not an inlay) with the maple portions glued onto either side. Fingerboards were rosewood, but one exception was a sunburst instrument that Mary used in performance, which had a walnut fretboard.

A bass was envisioned but the prototype was never completed. Peter commented,

> The [bass] design was ahead of its time, as far as I'm concerned. The piece of rosewood runs not only through center of the body, but throughout the entire neck. Two thicker pieces of wood run through the body on either side of the rosewood stripes—I believe they are redwood.
>
> It was apparent from my conversations with Kerry that he was a great admirer of [Bay Area–made] Alembic instruments, and I believe they inspired his work. The natural finish, vertical rosewood layers, and rosewood tips at the head were unique at the time; the design is closer to the basses that are being built today. It is unfortunate that this bass design never got to the production stage and introduced to the market. With its unique concept and design, I think that it would have hit big.

An estimated forty Osborne guitars were built before guitar development and production was abandoned around the end of 1976. The company changed its name to Osborne Sound Laboratories, and continued its work in electronic gear. Susan said,

> While I do not know all of the details, one factor was economics; another was personnel. Economically speaking, it was more profitable to make amplifiers. The guitars were almost custom pieces, which were beautiful and met the quality standards worthy of carrying our mother's name, but not enough could be made in enough time to meet costs. The other answer would have been to find more luthiers of similar skill, but that search was not successful.

Ralph Jr. added,

> When the company was first conceived, it was intended to be a maker of guitars, amplifiers, and electronics. So even though the original name was Osborne Guitar Company, amplifiers and electronics were always a part of the initial production efforts. With the ending of the guitar production plans, the name was changed to Osborne Sound Laboratories to properly reflect the focus of production.

Osborne guitars, ca. 1976.
Photo by Stefani Mills

Unfinished Osborne bass prototype.
Photo by Stefani Mills

Osborne Sound Laboratories closed in 1980. Ralph Sr. retired from further business ventures, but resumed teaching trumpet lessons. He, too, became an instructor at Bakersfield College and CSUB, teaching individual students and leading ensembles. He played with local bands and Mary's combo. He organized a dance band that played throughout central California.

Mary continued to play until shortly before her death in 1992. Her children would often join her. Peter performed with her extensively on upright bass and electric bass from 1976 through 1992. Susan was a vocalist and Ralph Jr. played drums; they performed with their mother periodically beginning in the mid-1980s. All three performed regularly with Ralph Sr.'s big dance band until his passing in 1996.

The Osborne Guitar Company was apparently the last attempt at founding a stringed instrument manufacturer in Bakersfield and the surrounding area. Two of the Scaffidi children eloquently summed up the city, its music scene, and their participation in it. Ralph Jr. said,

Bakersfield offered a very different living experience for us. A stand-alone small city not directly connected to a large metropolitan area . . . it truly was a small town. Additionally, the agriculture industry was very prominent. I made a number of friends whose families were engaged in the agriculture and ranching industries. This all became a very important factor in my developing a deep and life-long appreciation and respect for agriculture and rural America.

Another aspect of being in California was that it opened many opportunities for me to be directly exposed to—and experience many in-person encounters with—a number of the remaining mainstream jazz and big band musicians, many of whom I was a huge fan. For me, these encounters—in-person meetings and musical performances—started my journey to continue developing my musical knowledge and abilities as both a personal interest and semiprofessional avocation. The involvement of Dad and Mom in their new endeavors in California made this exposure possible. I do not believe that I would have had these opportunities if we had remained in New York on Long Island—at least not in the frequent and significant ways as they occurred in California at that particular time.

Beyond this, I certainly developed a greater appreciation and awareness of the broader reach and variety of the then-current rock, pop and County and Western music scenes. . . . I think we all did. For me, I was somewhat aware of, and had a passing appreciation for, earlier country performers, but in Bakersfield I developed a new direct knowledge of the then-more-current country performers, including Buck Owens, Glen Campbell, Roy Clark, Johnny Cash, Merle Haggard, Porter Wagoner—with a very young Dolly Parton—and Willie Nelson. This was certainly due to the fact that Dad had been involved with Mosrite and continued with Rosac.

Susan reflected,

There were two very strong music movements in the 1960s to the '90s in Bakersfield. One was jazz, which got a big boost when my parents came to town, and also by the flourishing of the jazz programs at some of the high schools, at Bakersfield College, and the addition of one at California State University Bakersfield. Many name musicians performed in Kern County, especially for clinics and school festivals; this movement would eventually lead to some high-profile jazz concerts—Ray Charles, Chick Corea, Wynton Marsalis, Spyro Gyra—and the start of the Bakersfield Jazz Festival, which my parents helped found. That festival would last for thirty-two years.

The other, of course, was the "Bakersfield Sound," which was an actual musical movement. These musicians developed their own style of country music—combining country music elements with rock music, especially the use of the electric bass, the back beat and the occasional blue notes in the solo sections, but without tipping over into rock and roll.

I worked for Buck Owens in the 1980s; by then, he was an institution, and an astute businessman. Fans used to drive to Bakersfield just to visit his radio station, and maybe get a few souvenirs if not catching a glimpse of him. Buck already had his costumes and awards—there were many—on display at the studio. It was a short leap to add the rest when Buck Owens Enterprises moved to their current location.

Buck, who never neglected his fans, performed at his Crystal Palace every weekend until his death, and brought in name acts every month. His death, and more recently Merle Haggard's death, certainly muffled the presence of the Bakersfield Sound, which was by then being researched and written about as history by scholars and reporters. Some of the last founding musicians, such as Red Simpson, Lefty Frizzell and Rose Maddox, have now passed away, and attempts to memorialize them all have not become permanent. On the other hand, Bakersfield is more and more an alternate recording site for many name artists. The lower cost, excellent producers and studio space, and greater availability have made the local recording industry viable.

I believe all this is part of the legacy of the Bakersfield Sound—as well as the activity of Mosrite, Rosac, Osborne Guitar and Sound Laboratories, Buck Owens Enterprises, and other companies, as well as individuals such as our parents.

The Scaffidi family was perhaps an exception to how musicians are stereotyped. Mary and Ralph remained married for decades and raised their children in a traditional lifestyle. "Dad and Mom were committed to us having the best life and upbringing that they could provide," said Ralph Jr. "They were very talented people, and were also people of faith. They could have done a lot more with music and the music instrument business, but they were willing to make the career sacrifices necessary to ensure that we were always together as a family—always safe and always loved."

Custom, sunburst, front.
Courtesy of Heritage Auctions

Custom, sunburst, back; note the disproportionately larger yellow field.
Courtesy of Heritage Auctions

32

Standel: The Mysterious "Third" Manufacturer

The history of the last Standel-branded instruments that were made in Bakersfield is apparently caught in an ultimately impenetrable time warp. Not much information is available about the brief but prolific production of such guitars and basses in 1966 and 1967, but price lists exist from both of those years (and only the address of Standel headquarters in Temple City is found on them).

The building that housed the Bakersfield production facility no longer exists. "It was over on Union Avenue, near 21st Street," said Artie Niesen. "The place is gone now; it's an overpass over the (railroad) tracks. I don't know if they ever even had a name on the outside."

The third Standel manufacturer produced some unique—if not particularly inspiring—instruments. The only guitar lineup cited on the 1966 price list was the solidbody Custom series, consisting of a two-pickup guitar, a one-pickup short scale bass, an upgrade Custom Deluxe two-pickup guitar and a Custom Deluxe twelve-string guitar.

The silhouette of the Custom series was somewhat different from other guitars of that era (and its aesthetics were different from other Bakersfield guitars, for that matter). The headstock had three "barbs" and vaguely resembled a bush axe. The guitar's bolt-on maple neck had a bound, twenty-two-fret rosewood fingerboard with a zero fret.

The relatively thin body appeared to be a bit elongated, and sported prominent, pointed cutaway horns. To some observers, the instrument probably looked like a Gibson SG model guitar that had been run over by a steamroller.

Hardware included Grover Sta-Tite tuners, although Kluson tuners have been seen on some examples. A unique-to-the-model arched bridge and a vibrato were installed on a brushed aluminum plate. The individual bridge saddles were intonatable. Curiously, the basic Custom guitar's vibrato was standard (and the vibrato was cited in advertising) but only the Custom Deluxe was mentioned on the price list as having such a device. Electronics on the guitar included two not-so-potent pickups, with a Standel logo medallion affixed between them. Each pickup was controlled by a slider switch, and the two knobs were master volume and tone controls.

Colors offered included sunburst, pearl white, black, and metallic red. The sunburst finish had a disproportionate amount of yellow in its three-color coating. A later standard color was a lavender finish.

Custom, black.
Courtesy of Bill Ingalls Jr

Some potential customers may have wondered why the Custom Deluxe model listed for twice the price of the standard Custom ($399.50 vs. $199.50), but the differences were indeed numerous. Custom Deluxes featured matching headstocks with upgrade Grover tuners. The bodies had an all-around-the-top German carve. A different aluminum mounting plate and plastic pickguard layout were also seen.

However, one of the primary differences in the Custom Deluxe was its electronic capabilities, abetted by better pickups with adjustable polepieces. The controls included three rocker switches near the treble cutaway horn. The two black switches were off/on for each pickup, and the red rocker switch, hyped in company literature as a "rhythm and lead switch," allowed two different presets of volume and/or tone, much like a Fender Jazzmaster guitar, which was the industry standard for guitars with onboard switchable sounds. Accordingly, the four knobs were not volume and tone controls for each pickup. Instead, they were master volume and tone controls for either preset position.

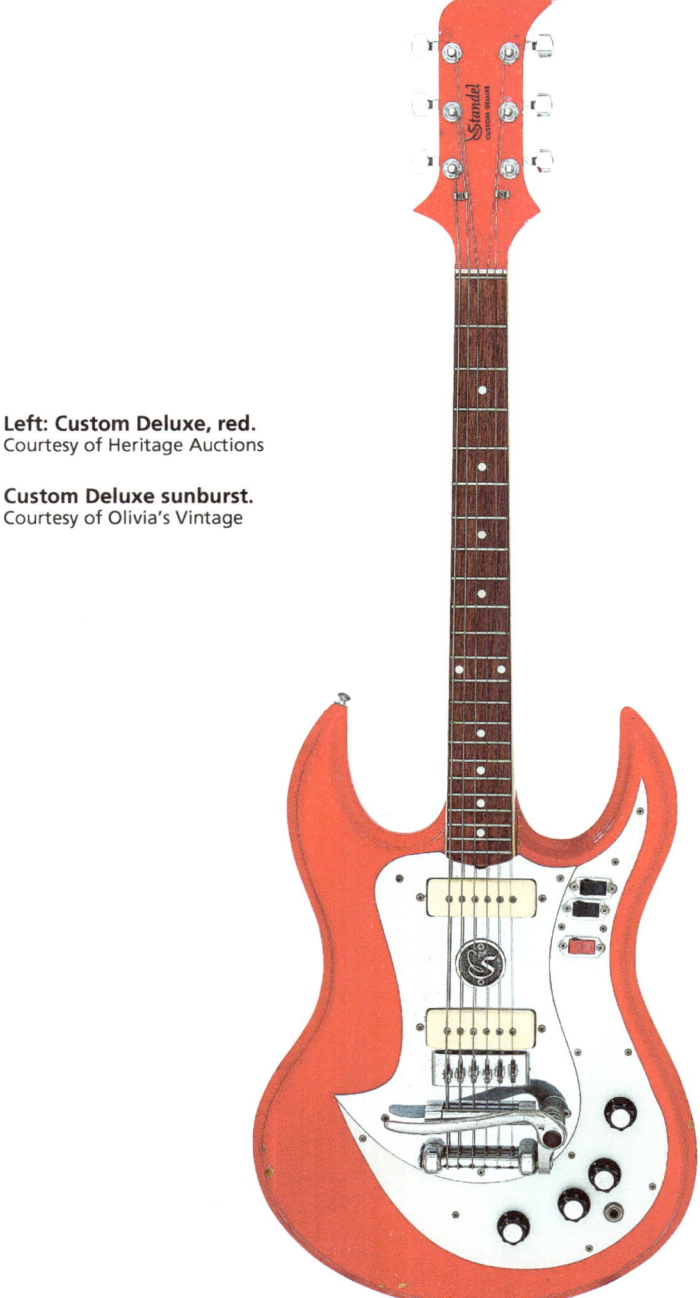

Left: Custom Deluxe, red.
Courtesy of Heritage Auctions

Custom Deluxe sunburst.
Courtesy of Olivia's Vintage

Refinements and additions to the solidbody line for the 1967 price list included nonvibrato models as well as a Custom Deluxe two-pickup bass. However, the big news for Standel in 1967 was the introduction of an entirely different series known as the "Thin Body Acoustic" guitar line. Interestingly, the new series was not acoustic at all. The bodies were made from molded fiberglass, and what appeared to be f-holes on the top were actually decals. Standel medallions were affixed to vibrato tailpieces, which differed from the vibratos found on the solidbody Custom series.

Once again, the six-string guitar models came in Custom and Custom Deluxe styles, with similar features to their solidbody predecessors. The Custom Deluxe variant of the Thin Body Acoustic featured faux body binding, front and rear. They were offered in "5 solid colors and sunburst," according to an ad.

Thin Body Acoustic Custom, black.
Courtesy of Olivia's Vintage

Thin Body Acoustic Custom, red.
Courtesy of Michael Wright

Thin Body Acoustic Custom, white.
Courtesy of Michael Wright

Thin Body Acoustic Custom, sunburst. Unusual variant—standard instrument with matching headstock.
Courtesy of Olivia's Vintage

Among the more curious and enduring aspects of the last Standel guitars and basses made in Bakersfield are the two series' respective construction regarding neck attachment. The necks on the solidbody series attached with three bolts. However, there were also two threaded screws on the bottom of the neck plate, if viewed vertically, that could change the angle of the neck to the body. As noted earlier, this idea had first been utilized by the Danelectro company. Standel's version was made around the same time Mosrite-made Dobros with tilt-neck adjustment were being built.

Thin Body Acoustic Custom bass, light blue.
Willie G. Moseley

Thin Body Acoustic Custom Deluxe, white. Note the black "binding" decoration and the matching headstock with a brand name only (no model designation).
Courtesy of Heritage Auctions

On the other hand, the neck joint on the fiberglass instruments had no discernible means of attachment or adjustment at all. Such an incongruity probably baffled many guitar players and repairmen back in the day.

There were also cynical comments about the fiberglass bodies of the Thin Body Acoustic series—one guitar buff wisecracked that the body could be cleaned with Windex or Corvette polish.

The last Bakersfield-made Standel line just didn't have enough going for it to merit the serious attention of professional musicians. "Those Standels were not really players' instruments," said Marc Lipco. "The [neck] radius didn't seem right, nor did the rollers on the vibrato tailpiece. They looked really cool, but it was hard for a 'real' guitar player to play them. And nobody wanted them; at the time you couldn't give them away."

"I never saw anybody playing them, and I remember the pawn shops here had plenty of them," said Artie Niesen, who acknowledged that while the design and quality of the line had a somewhat dubious reputation, "the ones I've had seemed to be okay."

When the final Standel factory went out of business, an auction was conducted to dispose of

Neck joints on a Custom solidbody guitar (three bolts, two tilt-adjustment screws) and a Thin Body Acoustic Custom guitar (no visible attachment).
Courtesy of Bill Ingalls Jr.

remaining inventory. Alan's Kern Guitar World came away from the sale with a lot of instruments. "We had about a hundred of them," Lipco averred. "We had every color, every body. We bought almost all of the leftover inventory when the factory closed—three-tone sunburst, red, black, fuchsia pink, white."

As noted earlier, Bill Gruggett recalled buying parts at the Standel auction to use on some of his Stradette model guitars. Standel later briefly marketed a higher-end series of acoustic and semiacoustic guitars made by the Harptone company of New Jersey. It's ironic that the third and final Bakersfield manufacturer of Standel-branded instruments produced the most guitars and basses bearing that moniker and logo, but its brief chronicle remains nebulous.

Coda

To their credit, the Ventures would continue to autograph Mosrite instruments in spite of their decades-long "divorce," thus validating Bob Bogle's 1996 rumination about a perpetual stereotype between the band and the brand. Mel Taylor died in August 1996, Bogle died in June 2009, Nokie Edwards died in March 2018, and Gerry McGee (who had first replaced Nokie in 1968) died in October 2019. As of this writing, founding Ventures guitarist Don Wilson is retired, and the touring band consists of Bob Spalding, Leon Taylor (Mel's son), Luke Griffin, and Ian Spalding (Bob's son).

The Ventures were inducted into the Rock & Roll Hall of Fame in 2008. The Ramones were inducted into the Rock & Roll Hall of Fame in 2002, their first year of eligibility. John Cummings's (Johnny Ramone) white mongrel Mosrite guitar is now on display at that facility in Cleveland, Ohio.

Cummings succumbed to prostate cancer in September 2004. An eight-foot statute of the guitarist (playing a Mosrite Ventures II guitar) was erected in the Hollywood Forever Cemetery and dedicated in 2005.

In January 2015, one of Cummings's Mosrite guitars, a red modified Ventures Model Mark I, sold at auction for over $71,000. It had been autographed by the guitarist in 1990.

The front cover of Glen Campbell's 2008 album *Meet Glen Campbell* included a posterized photo of the legendary singer-guitarist

John "Johnny Ramone" Cummings's Mongrel Mosrite Ventures II.
Photo by Sam Howzit / Wikimedia Commons

Ventures Mark V signed by Don Wilson, Gerry McGee, Leon Taylor, and Bob Bogle. Its Pearl White finish has yellowed over the decades.
Willie G. Moseley

Photo by Donmike10 / Wikimedia Commons

playing what appeared to be a Mosrite Ventures Model Mark I. Campbell passed away in 2018 after an extended public battle with Alzheimer's disease.

Marshall Crenshaw has continued to stay active as a touring and recording artist. Releases in 2020 included a new two-CD live set, as well as a reissue of a 1996 album titled *Miracle of Science*, with new artwork and bonus tracks. Crenshaw was also producing a documentary about legendary record producer Tom Wilson, and was gigging on occasion with a legendary New Jersey rock band.

"I'm doing shows as a 'guest vocalist' with the Smithereens," he said. "They were recently inducted into the New Jersey Hall of Fame. As far as Mosrites go, right now I have a Dave Alexander–style Ventures bass in black, and a blue Ventures twelve-string, which is my official 'Smithereens guitar,' at least up to now."

Courtesy of Bob Shade

Marshall Crenshaw wields his Mosrite Mark XII in concert.
Courtesy of Gayle Miller

The Hunger reunion concert, 2018.
Courtesy of John Morton

Ted Smith demos a Mosrite-made Melobar.
Courtesy of Ted Smith

The Hunger band reunited for a fiftieth anniversary show in May 2018. Guitarist John Morton played a new Hallmark Swept-Wing model in a silver sparkle finish.

In 2018, Ted Smith recorded a demo video for YouTube explaining how to convert a Mosrite-made Melobar from a ten-string version to a six-string. He also recounted a bit of the history of Mosrite and Melobar. The instrument still looked and sounded unique. "I get a lot of e-mails about how to use the ten-string tuning," Smith said, "and I do believe the six-string is the only way to string it up for a standard guitar pickup, or if the spacing is too tight."

Jorma Kaukonen no longer owns his Melobars. "Sad to say, the instruments were casualties of many moves and an ex-marriage," the guitarist reflected, over a half-century after the "Summer of Love." "I do wish I still had a Melobar. Today I would know what to do with it. It was a great invention." Kaukonen turned eighty on December 23, 2020, and was still an active musician as of this writing.

The MC5's Fred "Sonic" Smith died in 1994, when his son Jackson was twelve years old. "I used the 'Sonic Smith' silver Mosrite live," Jackson recalled, "in louder bands when I was younger. It was a bit unruly at high volumes." A documentary titled *MC5: A True Testimonial* was released in 2002, but its distribution was limited, due to legal entanglements. A placard/ad for the movie featured a photo of Fred Smith playing his iconic white Mosrite guitar.

"It's a fantastic movie," said Jackson. "I wish more people had gotten to see it."

Interestingly, the younger Smith has been more active in the twenty-first century as a musician in the country and western genre.

A 2016 film titled *Gimme Danger*, directed by Jim Jarmusch, chronicled the saga of Michigan's proto-punk band the Stooges. The promotional material included several posters, including solo layouts of each original member and later guitarist James Williamson. Dave Alexander's poster showed a closeup view of the bassist playing his Mosrite instrument. Alexander is deceased, having joined rock music's notorious "27 club" in 1975.

In 2012, a large full-color, three-section mural was erected in downtown Bakersfield to salute the city's guitar-building history. It depicts a plethora of instruments of numerous brands that were made in the Bakersfield area—even Raindrop examples are seen. The display, created by Sebastian Muralles and Al

Fred Smith and his Mosrite guitar appeared in promotional material for *MC5: A True Testimonial*.
Courtesy of Leni Sinclair

Dave Alexander

The award-winning guitar tri-mural, seen in downtown Bakersfield.
Courtesy of artists Sebastian Muralles and Al Mendez

Mendez, includes images of Mosrite, Hallmark, Gruggett, and Standel instruments. The artwork won a "Beautiful Bakersfield" award in 2014.

In his Maryland shop, luthier Bob Shade has retained a multilaminate guitar body made by Joe Hall as well as a neck made by Bill Gruggett. Shade wasn't predicting when he would get around to building an instrument utilizing those items.

Willie G. Moseley

Veteran Bakersfield drummer Jim Phillips ended up with a decades-long alternate career in nearby Tehachapi as a barber. Among the regular customers in his shop was retired astronaut Vance Brand, a veteran of 1975's Apollo-Soyuz mission and three space shuttle flights.

Fuzz guitarist Davie Allan would continue to be associated with a doubleneck Mosrite guitar for decades (as exemplified by the cover of a 1994 album, *Loud, Loose and Savage*), even though he had sold his own doubleneck in the 1970s.

Roger Fritz continues to be influenced by the legacy of Semie Moseley in his own luthiery. "I would have to say [it's] the feel of the necks and the capability of having low, clear action," said Fritz. "I have also used the German carve—which is done by hand—on a model called the 'Rat Bastard.' My patented stainless steel nut gets the same result as the Mosrite zero fret and metal string guide. Their finishes were also inspiringly beautiful.'

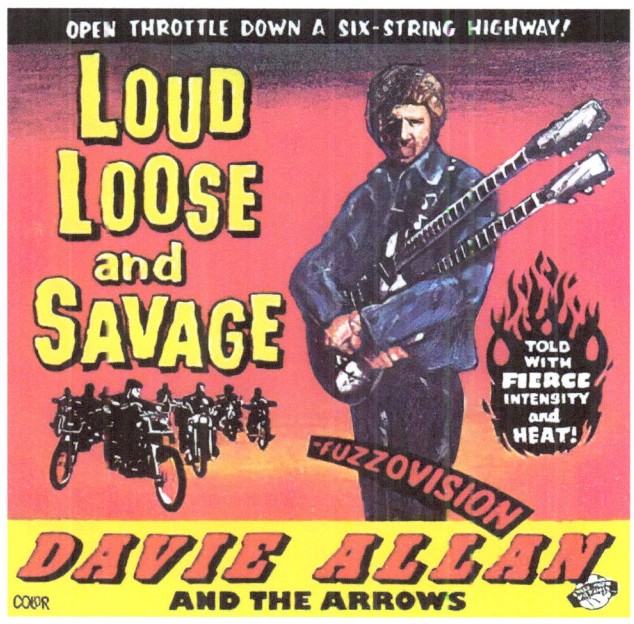

Andy Moseley died in 2013. So did Sugarfoot Bonner. George Barris died in November 2015. Lorrie Collins and Ed King died in August 2018.

Over a half-century after the glory days of the Bakersfield Sound and the parallel golden age of Bakersfield guitar builders, the twang of a Fender Telecaster is still the predominant and desired guitar tone in the local music scene, as purveyed at Buck Owens's Crystal Palace and elsewhere.

Bakersfield still beckons to music fans like Tony Brown, a retired firefighter and paramedic from Texas who relocated to Bakersfield in 2016 and is now a luthier himself. Brown offered a succinct summary of Bakersfield's guitar history:

> My observation is that Bakersfield guitars elicit an emotional response—a love/hate effect, if you will—pertaining to pickers in this town. Some have a reverence for them, treating them with the utmost care and respect, while others seem to have an almost contemptible attitude towards them.
>
> The former appreciate and identify with the historical significance, or perhaps their own personal affinity towards their first guitar and the personal journey it initiated. The latter seem to have a desire to unbridle the restraints of the past and move forward, thus distancing themselves from their predecessors and securing their own identity.
>
> The Fender Telecaster is undeniably a giant element of the Bakersfield Sound. I'd even go so far as to say that the Bakersfield Sound put the Telecaster on the musical map, and perhaps vice versa. It was a marriage made in heaven. That's not to take anything away from guitars produced in Bakersfield. In fact, many artists and bands were playing Mosrites at one time or another. Perhaps Fender had a larger marketing budget and was able to reach more artists as a result. But that is merely speculation.

Brown also noted that the legacy of Bill Gruggett—whom Brown never met—can be inspirational to aspiring modern-day luthiers like himself: "Bill created some of the most interesting designs I've ever seen. He wasn't afraid to experiment with shape. That resonates with me. I think we shared a desire to move beyond the status quo and expand the art of guitar building."

An odd doubleneck instrument that apparently has Bakersfield roots—or, at least, many of its parts do—has been seen from time to time on websites that cater to fans of certain music genres or particular guitar brands. It sports a "Buck-O-Roo" moniker on its headstocks, and the name on the fretboards, Dee Corby, is that of a player and deejay who was reportedly active in middle and southern California in the 1960s and 1970s (he was quoted in a December 19, 1960, issue of *Billboard* magazine while working for KVEC in San Luis Obispo in central California).

And the advent of the internet has generated inquiries into the history and authenticity of the instrument. One website posted the text of a note that was allegedly from Corby. It stated that the instrument was made for him by a former Mosrite employee when Corby was a deejay in Santa Maria, California, a coastal town about eighty-five miles from Bakersfield.

The guitar is a curious microcosm of Bakersfield's guitar history, even if it wasn't made or assembled there. Its features include:

- A solid body that seems to have Gruggett Stradette influences (but Stradettes were semihollow)
- A fourteen-string neck that appears to be a Mosrite product (one extra string each for the middle two courses, D and G)
- A six-string neck that appears to be a (short-lived) Epcor item
- A vibrato plate sporting the Standel "snake" logo
- Pickguard and arm rest stylings that reference Semie Moseley's earliest creations from the 1950s—and those instruments weren't made in Bakersfield, either.

Bibliography and References

In addition to dozens of interviews conducted by the author specifically for this project, the following information sources were also used:

Extensive catalog and memorabilia research was done via the Bob Shade collection, www.vintaxe.com and other sources.

PERIODICAL AND ONLINE ARTICLES AND IMAGES
"Andy Moseley," National Association of Music Merchandisers, www.namm.org/library/oral-history/andy-moseley.
Carlton, Jim. "Mary Osborne—Charlie's Angel." *Vintage Guitar Magazine*, February 2011.
Carter, Walter. "Rockabilly Flash—Lorrie Collins' Martin D-28." *Vintage Guitar Magazine*, October 2018.
Dickerson, Deke, and Bob Shade. "California Weird Factor—Doublenecks and Triplenecks." *Vintage Guitar Magazine*, April 2005.
Dickerson, Deke. "The Kids' Instruments through the Years." *Vintage Guitar Magazine*, February 2013.
Guitar Nerd, www.guitarnerd.com.au.
Hallmark Guitars, www.hallmarkguitars.com.
Heritage Auctions, www.ha.com.
Hilmar, Jim. "Larry Collins—Talking MosRite, Country and Rockabilly Music." *Vintage Guitar Magazine*, November 1992.
Kienzle, Rich. "Buck Owens and the Buckaroos—A Bunch of Twangy Guitars." *Vintage Guitar Magazine*, May 2007.
Mayer, Steve. "Bakersfield's Master Guitar Maker Dies at 75." *The Bakersfield Californian*, October 10, 2012.
———. "Murals Multiply across Bakersfield's Cityscape." *The Bakersfield Californian*, August 3, 2018.
Meeker, Ward. "The Story of Nudie's Mosrite Mandolin." *Vintage Guitar Magazine*, September 2006.
Melobar Ted, http://melobarted.blogspot.com/.
Moseley, Willie G. "Basses from Bakersfield." *Vintage Guitar Magazine*, July 2012.
———. "Bill Gruggett—Still Buildin' 'Em In Bakersfield." *Vintage Guitar Magazine*, February 1997.
———. "Ca. 1961 Standel-by-Mosrite—Primeval Bakersfield Instrument." *Vintage Guitar Magazine*, April 2010.
———. "Ed Sanner—Fuzz Redux." *Vintage Guitar Magazine*, March 2014.
———. "Gospel Guitars—Semie Moseley's Venerated Brand." *Vintage Guitar Magazine*, November 2018.
———. "Hallmark Guitars—Then and Now." *Vintage Guitar Magazine*, June 2004.
———. "Mosrite Basses: The Golden Age—Ventures and Beyond." July 2013.
———. "Mosrite Joe Maphis." *Vintage Guitar Magazine*, November 2006.
———. "Requiem For 'Uncle Semie.'" *Vintage Guitar Magazine*, September 1992.
———. "Retro-Inspired Basses." *Vintage Guitar Magazine*, August 2008.
———. "Semie Moseley, Guitar Builder (1935-1992)—A 1992 Interview." *Vintage Guitar Magazine*, September 1992.
———. "The Bass Space: Hallmark Swept-Wing Semi-Hollow." *Vintage Guitar Magazine*, August 2009.
———. "The Bass Space: Mosrite Ventures Model 'TV' Bass." *Vintage Guitar Magazine*, July 2004.
———. "The Encor El Toro—Swept-Wing Precursor." *Vintage Guitar Magazine*, January 2020.
———. "Tim Bogert—Still Bottoming Out after All These Years." *Vintage Guitar Magazine*, June 1993.
———. "Unified Sound Association, Inc.—Keeping The Mosrite Legacy Alive." *Vintage Guitar Magazine*, March 1993.
———. "Venture of the Month—Bob Bogle." *Vintage Guitar Magazine*, May 1997.
———. "Venture of the Month—Don Wilson." *Vintage Guitar Magazine*, March 1997.
Nickell, Jeff. "History of the Bakersfield Sound." *Historic Kern*, Spring 2002.
Nokie Edwards, National Association of Music Merchandisers, https://www.namm.org/library/oral-history/nokie-edwards.
Normington, Mick. "Legends Live on in Logan County." *Democrat-Gazette* (Booneville, Arkansas), August 28, 1992.
Popovich, Fred, and Jim Hilmar. "A Look at the Earliest Days of MosRite." *Vintage Guitar Magazine*, November 1992.
Price, Robert. "To Know This Sound You Must First Know This Town." *The Bakersfield Californian*, February 10, 2006.

Ronnie Foster, www.ronniefoster.com.
Sachs, Bill. "Folk Talent and Tunes." *Billboard*, December 19, 1960.
Saunders, Mae. "Mosrite Brand: Rags to Riches." *The Bakersfield Californian*, October 2, 1965.
Soest, Steve. "The Mosrite 'Surfrite.'" "Collector's Farm" column, *Guitar Magazine* (Japan), August 1990.
———. "The Beginnings of the Mosrite Ventures Model." "Collector's Farm" column, *Guitar Magazine* (Japan), June 1991.
"Vox Guitars, Mosrite Announce Merger." *Billboard*, October 26, 1968.
Wheeler, Tom. "Encore." *Guitar Player Magazine*, November 1997.
Wright, Michael. "Acoustic Black Widow." *Vintage Guitar Magazine*, July 1998.
———. "Mosrite Stereo 350." *Vintage Guitar Magazine*, January 2008.
———. "Semie Moseley—The Lost Interview" (Parts I, II and III). *Vintage Guitar Magazine*, January–March 2007 (three-part transcription of 1981 audio interview by William Smart and interpretive commentary).

BOOKS

Bacon, Tony. *The History of the American Guitar*. New York: Backbeat Books, 2011.
Bechtoldt, Paul. *Guitars from Neptune*. Peckville, PA: Backporch Publications, 1995
Carson, Bill (with Willie G. Moseley). *Bill Carson: My Life and Times with Fender Musical Instruments*. Bismarck, ND: Vintage Guitar Books, 1998.
Creem: America's Only Rock 'N' Roll Magazine, Robert Matheu and Brian J. Bowe, editors. New York: Collins, 2007.
Dalley, Robert J. *Surfin' Guitars: Instrumental Surf Bands of the Sixties*, 2nd edition. Ann Arbor, MI: Popular Culture, 1996.
Goudy, Rob. *Electric Guitars*. Atglen, PA: Schiffer, 1999.
Gruhn, George, and Walter Carter. *Electric Guitars and Basses: A Photographic History*. San Francisco, CA: Miller Freeman Books, 1994.
———. *Gruhn's Guide to Vintage Guitars*, third edition. Milwaukee, WI: Backbeat, 2010.
Halterman, Del (with Josie Wilson, Don Wilson, and Bob Bogle). *Walk Don't Run: The Story of the Ventures*. Self-published, 2008.
Moseley, Willie G. *The Bass Space: Profiles of Classic Electric Basses*. Atglen, PA: Schiffer, 2018.
———. *Vintage Electric Guitars: In Praise of Fretted Americana*. Atglen, PA: Schiffer, 2001.
Moust, Hans. *The Guild Guitar Book: The Company and the Instruments, 1952–1977*. LN Breda, the Netherlands: Guitarchives, 1995.
Nickell, Jeff, and Sarah Woodman. *Hard Drivin' Country: The Honky Tonks, Musicians, and Legends of the Bakersfield Sound*. Self-published, 2009.
Price, Robert E. *The Bakersfield Sound: How a Generation of Displaced Okies Revolutionized American Music*. Bloomington, IN: iUniverse, 2015.
Roberts, Jim. *American Basses: An Illustrated History and Player's Guide to the Bass Guitar*. San Francisco, CA: 2003.
Shaw, Robert. *Great Guitars*. Fairfield, CT: Hugh Lauter Levin Associates, 1997.
Tober, Adam. *Fine Musical Instruments and Memorabilia featuring the Collection of Little Jimmy Dickens*. Boston, MA: Skinner, 2016.
Wheeler, Tom. *American Guitars: An Illustrated History*, revised and updated edition. New York: HarperCollins, 1992.